Jobs for Travel Lovers ✈

By Ron and Caryl Krannich

CAREER AND BUSINESS BOOKS AND SOFTWARE
101 Secrets of Highly Effective Speakers
201 Dynamite Job Search Letters
America's Top 100 Jobs for People Without a Four-Year Degree
America's Top Jobs for People Re-Entering the Workforce
America's Top Internet Job Sites
Best Jobs for the 21st Century
Change Your Job, Change Your Life
The Complete Guide to Public Employment
The Directory of Federal Jobs and Employers
Discover the Best Jobs for You!
Dynamite Salary Negotiations
Dynamite Tele-Search
The Educator's Guide to Alternative Jobs and Careers
The Ex-Offender's Job Hunting Guide
Find a Federal Job Fast!
From Air Force Blue to Corporate Gray
From Army Green to Corporate Gray
From Navy Blue to Corporate Gray
Get a Raise in 7 Days
High Impact Resumes and Letters
I Want to Do Something Else, But I'm Not Sure What It Is
Interview for Success
The Job Hunting Guide: Transitioning From College to Career
Job Hunting Tips for People With Hot and Not-So-Hot Backgrounds
Job Interview Tips for People With Not-So-Hot Backgrounds
Job-Power Source and Ultimate Job Source (software)
Jobs and Careers With Nonprofit Organizations
Military Transition to Civilian Success
Military Resumes and Cover Letters
Moving Out of Education
Moving Out of Government
Nail the Cover Letter!
Nail the Job Interview!
Nail the Resume!
No One Will Hire Me!
Re-Careering in Turbulent Times
Savvy Interviewing
The Savvy Networker
The Savvy Resume Writer

TRAVEL AND INTERNATIONAL BOOKS
Best Resumes and CVs for International Jobs
The Complete Guide to International Jobs and Careers
The Directory of Websites for International Jobs
International Jobs Directory
Jobs for Travel Lovers
Mayors and Managers in Thailand
Politics of Family Planning Policy in Thailand
Shopping and Traveling in Exotic Asia
Shopping in Exotic Places
Shopping the Exotic South Pacific
Travel Planning On the Internet
Treasures and Pleasures of Australia
Treasures and Pleasures of Bermuda
Treasures and Pleasures of China
Treasures and Pleasures of Egypt
Treasures and Pleasures of Hong Kong
Treasures and Pleasures of India
Treasures and Pleasures of Indonesia
Treasures and Pleasures of Italy
Treasures and Pleasures of Mexico
Treasures and Pleasures of Paris
Treasures and Pleasures of Rio and São Paulo
Treasures and Pleasures of Santa Fe, Taos, and Albuquerque
Treasures and Pleasures of Singapore and Bali
Treasures and Pleasures of Singapore
Treasures and Pleasures of South America
Treasures and Pleasures of Southern Africa
Treasures and Pleasures of Thailand and Myanmar
Treasures and Pleasures of Turkey
Treasures and Pleasures of Vietnam and Cambodia

JOBS
for TRAVEL
LOVERS

Opportunities at
Home and Abroad

5th Edition

Ron and Caryl Krannich, Ph.Ds

Impact Publications | Manassas, VA

Jobs for Travel Lovers

Library of Congress Cataloging-in-Publication Data

Krannich, Ronald L.
    Jobs for travel lovers: opportunities at home and abroad / Ronald L. Krannich and Caryl Rae Krannich. – 5th ed.
       p.   cm.
    Includes bibliographical references and index.
    ISBN 1-57023-252-0 (alk. paper)
    1. Vocational guidance. 2. Travel. 3. Employment in foreign countries. I. Krannich, Caryl Rae. II. Title
HF5381.K688   2006
331.7'02—dc21   2006922493

Publisher: For information on Impact Publications, including current and forthcoming publications, authors, press kits, online bookstore, and submission requirements, visit our website: www.impactpublications.com

Publicity/Rights: For information on publicity, author interviews, and subsidiary rights, contact the Media Relations Department: Tel. 703-361-7300, Fax 703-335-9486, or email: query@impactpublications.com

Sales/Distribution: All bookstore sales are handled through Impact's trade distributor: National Book Network, 15200 NBN Way, Blue Ridge Summit, PA 17214, Tel. 1-800-462-6420. All other sales and distribution inquiries should be directed to the publisher: Sales Department, IMPACT PUBLICA-TIONS, 9104 Manassas Drive, Suite N, Manassas Park, VA 20111-5211, Tel. 703-361-7300, Fax 703-335-9486, or email: query@impactpublications.com

Contents

v

Jobs for Travel Lovers ✈

1

✈

The Exciting World of Travel-Work

WE LOVE TRAVELING. So do millions of other people. Whether for work, study, or pleasure, travel is rewarding in so many ways. It educates, liberates, exhilarates, and heals. Despite a dramatically changed post-9/11 environment that has made travel increasingly burdensome – more difficult, expensive, insecure, and security conscious – many people would still love to have a job that enabled them to travel to exciting places. Indeed, in 2006 nearly 4.5 million Americans lived overseas (4 million civilian and 500,000 military). Approximately 190,000 U.S. students study abroad each year and thousands of other students are interested in working abroad both before and after graduation (30,000 actually do). Each year voluntourism and purpose-driven (responsible) travel involving short-term work experiences are attracting a growing number of travel lovers who want to make a difference in the lives of others as they travel the globe.

Some people already have their dream job – one that takes them to wonderful destinations they once only dreamed of visiting. Best of all, many of them have a well paying job that allows them to pursue one of life's great passions – travel. They visit interesting places where they work

1

on challenging assignments, meet fascinating people, and enjoy a delight-ful, and sometimes decadent, local lifestyle. Instead of traveling to work, they work to travel. Indeed, work becomes a form of travel-play.

For the Love of Travel

Just how interested are you in pursuing a travel-related job? Let's start by responding to the following questions:

1. Is travel one of your passions?

2. Are you bored with what you're doing and the people you're working with?

3. Do you have an entrepreneurial streak that's not being satisfied in your current work?

4. Do you know what really motivates you to be happy? Does it relate to travel?

5. Would you love to have a job that allows you to travel to interesting and exciting places?

6. Do you prefer doing things that involve travel and working with people who share your travel interests?

7. Do you often daydream about the next trip you would like to take, but you're not sure if you'll have enough money and vacation time to go?

8. Do you often spend time visiting international- and travel-related websites or gravitating to the travel sections of book-stores and libraries?

9. Are there places you would like to go and things you would like to do that seem beyond your reach because of your present job and/or your finances?

10. Are some of your fondest memories related to times you traveled or studied abroad or worked in a job that involved travel?

11. Would you love to take a year off and work in another country?

12. Have you thought of taking a short-term volunteer vacation that would take you to some exotic location where you would have an opportunity to improve the lives of others?

If you answer "yes" to any of these questions, you're ready to join an interesting group of people who have managed to combine work and play. They have the travel bug, an often frustrating addiction they are unwilling to abandon. It's hard to shake or even explain to others. It's a common affliction or obsession one either overcomes or soon succumbs to. If you decide to succumb, which is the focus of this book, you'll join many other people who stopped procrastinating and dreaming what seemed to be the impossible dream.

> *Join a growing club of travel-workers who want more out of life than just another job – combine work and travel into a wonderful worklife!*

They raised the perfect questions and focused on answering them right: If I love to travel, why not find a wonderful job that also allows me to pursue my passion for travel? Why not get paid to do what I really love to do?

You love to travel. But unlike most people, you would like to travel and earn a decent living at the same time. You've come to the right place. You're ready to explore some job and career options that would allow you to pursue your passion for travel. That's what this book is all about – finding jobs that enable you to travel to your heart's content.

Like you, we have a passion for travel. It permeates both our worklife and lifestyle. Like many others who have been bitten by the travel bug, we've managed to combine our work with travel to some of the world's most exciting and exotic places. Indeed, our most recent five-week "work adventure" took us to Australia and Indonesia where we once again worked hard and played hard, from experiencing fine hotels, restaurants, and shopping to visiting gorgeous beaches, climbing the Sydney Harbour Bridge, flying into pristine islands, and surveying local markets. Prior to that trip we spent several months doing similar "work" in Paris, Singapore, Argentina, Bolivia, Ecuador, Peru, Bermuda, Thailand, Burma, Mexico, Mexico, Namibia, Botswana, Zimbabwe, South Africa, and Turkey. And we're planning our next adventures to China, Hong Kong, India, Ethiopia, UAE, Oman, and Italy. While we often work 14-hour days, we love every minute of it. We can hardly wait to get back on the road again visiting these and many other great destinations that beg to be discovered in our line of work. Yes, we have a hopeless work-travel addiction that we find very satisfying and rewarding!

Join an Exclusive Club

Welcome to the fascinating and rewarding world of work-travel or travel-work – whichever order fits you best. You're joining a growing club of passionate travel-workers who want more out of life than just another job. While many jobs enable you to take a trip or two each year, other jobs offer more frequent and exciting travel. Like many others, you're probably afflicted with that inexplicable urge to travel – see new places, meet new people, experience new environments, or just be in motion, going from one place to another. You may even be a travel junky, requiring a "travel fix" every two months or so!

Life As Work and Play

Unlike most people, you have a lifestyle preference that combines work and travel. Put another way, you want to work and play at the same time – the ultimate worklife. You would like to travel on a regular basis rather than just during your annual vacation. If you could create your ideal job, you would probably design one that avoids a regular 9-to-5, Monday through Friday, office routine. You would probably be working in your favorite country, traveling to and from your favorite cities, or just roaming a country or the globe in pursuit of meaningful work and play. You might even start your own business, one which would permit you to frequently travel.

Some critical observers might say you have an attitudinal or a motivational problem; you're a daydreamer. Others would say you have the ideal job in mind! You might say you have a bad case of wanderlust that needs to be satisfied in some type of meaningful travel-work setting. Whatever the case, you would like to turn your dreams into new realities!

You and millions of others share a common bond – an urge to travel and keep traveling on a regular basis. For some people, the love of travel is one of those important seasons of life – they did it when they were young, perhaps as a student or when they were single, but they have since resigned themselves to a more stationary lifestyle. For others, the continuing urge to travel is part of their basic motivational pattern for work – they need to travel and constantly change their environments in order to remain motivated, enthusiastic, and productive.

If you could create your ideal job, you would probably design one that avoids a regular 9-to-5 office routine.

Rather than confine travel to a particular season of life, you recognize that travel is an important part of your life; you have a need to place it at center stage in your worklife. Better still, you should find jobs that incorporate the type of travel you find both personally and professionally rewarding. They unleash your entrepreneurial spirit. Such jobs take you to new places where you meet fascinating people and do exciting work. In other words, you're someone who needs to find a worklife that is synonymous with a lifestyle.

Take the Right Action

Fortunately for you and millions of other individuals, numerous jobs do combine work and travel. These jobs enable you to pursue a particular lifestyle that is both professionally and personally rewarding.

If you really want to land one of these jobs, you'll have to do five things:

- Identify what jobs are most compatible with your desired work-travel lifestyle.

- Develop a clear travel-work objective that keeps you focused on what you really want to do.

- Know where these jobs can be found and whom to contact for vacancy information.

- Acquire the necessary job search skills for landing a job, from conducting research and writing a resume to networking and interviewing for the job.

- Take repeated action, follow through, and persist in pursuing your objective despite disappointments and rejections.

Our task in the following pages is to guide you in acquiring sufficient information and knowledge to make your worklife dreams come true. Like us, you probably would love a job – perhaps even pursue a career – that permits you to regularly engage in travel.

Welcome to the club. You'll be joining millions of other individuals who seek jobs that enable them to pursue their passion for travel. Let's have some fun putting together a job portfolio that may indeed combine work and play into an exciting worklife/lifestyle.

Where Are They Going, What Are They Doing?

Stroll through any airport or visit a railway or bus station and you'll observe hundreds of people on their way to somewhere. Some are in the pursuit of pleasure; others are fulfilling family and friendship obligations; and still others operate these major transportation hubs for the benefit of all types of travelers. But the majority are working – going to and from work sites that define their occupations. Many look happy; others look anxious to complete this transportation process; and some look tired, probably hoping to be going somewhere else soon where they can escape long lines and the indignities of security checks.

We've always wondered what all those other people on our plane or train do for a living. As soon as our plane lands or our train stops, many fellow passengers pull out their cell phones or head for the row of pay phones to begin conducting business. Lugging fat briefcases, lightweight computers, PDAs, iPods, and other electronic devices, most of these travelers are probably salespeople making their first connections to what hopefully will become a successful deal to justify their trips.

For years we have traveled both at home and abroad for pleasure and business. Our fat passports testify to our ambitious work and lifestyles. They have become so full of immigration stamps that we now have difficulty locating evidence of our last stop. Like others, we carry a laptop computer wherever we go – the ultimate office-on-the-go. Be it San Francisco, Chicago, Boston, New York, London, Amsterdam, Paris, Rome, Florence, Venice, Prague, Casablanca, Marrakesh, Moscow, Bombay, New Delhi, Beijing, Tokyo, Hong Kong, Bangkok, Yangon, Kuala Lumpur, Singapore, Jakarta, Bali, Manila, Melbourne, Sydney, Christ Church, Auckland, Papeete, Port Moresby, Honolulu, Cape Town, Johannesburg, Durban, Windhoek, Mexico City, Oaxaca, Rio, São Paulo, La Paz, Quito, Buenos Aires, or Lima, we're never really away from our Virginia-based business. And we love what we do – traveling and working at the same time. Indeed, if it weren't for our work, we might not enjoy travel!

> *We love what we do – traveling and working at the same time. Indeed, if it weren't for our work, we might not enjoy travel!*

From Addiction to Habit to an Exciting Career

We simply love to travel. At one time, like many other people, we dreamed of finding enough free time and money to indulge our travel fantasies. A job was something we did most of the year; travel was something we did in our free time. Our first taste of travel came early in life – the ubiquitous annual family vacation and summer camps. Next came college and those wonderful semester breaks, foreign language classes, study-abroad programs, a round-the-world college choir tour, Peace Corps, and graduate research abroad. High school and later college teaching jobs enabled us to use our two- to three-month summer breaks for pursuing interesting work and play abroad as well as enjoying travel adventures at home.

We were, and still are, discriminating worker-travelers. We had a bias for working in exotic places, knowing some day soon these developing areas would graduate to the status of not-so-exotic destinations. One year it was Tokyo and Beirut, another year Hawaii and Thailand, and the next year Mexico and the Caribbean – all part of study and work. Travel

seemed to easily merge with education and work. It was enjoyable, en-
lightening, and profitable.

After being teachers, freelance researchers/writers, and development
workers/consultants abroad, we eventually turned our travel addiction
into the ultimate work/travel combination – the inauguration of a new
travel guide series on shopping in exotic places. Making three to four trips
abroad each year, we're now into our twenty-third travel volume. We
have plans to further expand our travel research and writing activities in
the decade ahead which may also include an emphasis on voluntourism.

We have an unabashed addiction to travel which we can't shake even
if we tried. Returning exhausted from our latest travel/work adventure –
and vowing not to travel again for another year – within two months we
get that unexplained urge to hit the road again.

Ours is a hopeless addiction we share with thousands of other people,
perhaps including yourself. Admitting, and finally succumbing to, our
addiction, we decided to turn it into a strength that also became a financially rewarding habit and career.

We love to combine travel with our work. Indeed, many of our earlier
career choices were conscious decisions to marry what we loved to do
professionally with interesting travel experiences. And we are not alone.
We've met numerous people who have a similar addiction to travel. Using
their two to four weeks of vacation each year to satisfy their travel needs,
many people would love to turn their vacation experiences into some type
of full-time avocation. Others have been able to fashion careers that
enable them to work and travel at the same time. Some have even been
fortunate enough to turn their yearly vacations into long-term careers that
enable them to work, live, and travel in exciting places.

A Love/Hate Relationship

Travel is not for everyone. Nor is it something you may love all of the
time or for all seasons of your life. In fact, many people have a love/hate
relationship with travel. They love the fond memories surrounding the
positives of travel, but they frequently forget the negatives associated with
many travel problems. They may love arriving at and experiencing a new
and unfamiliar destination, but they often hate the transportation process
involved in getting there. Long waiting lines at airline counters, security
check points, and taxi queues, traffic jams, delayed schedules, crowded

planes and trains, and bad food, accommodations, and service quickly take the excitement out of travel.

For others, how you travel and work may change with the seasons of life. At one time – especially when you are young and single – you may enjoy living and traveling abroad or being on the road two or three days a week. Perhaps you took the crowded road of backpackers and budget travelers who all seemed to congregate at the same places recommended by the popular *Lonely Planet* or *Rough Guides* travel guidebooks. But at other times, age, marriage, children, and family preferences modified your free-wheeling travel lifestyle. You started to upgrade your style of travel and discovered another exciting world of travel associated with the finer things in life.

A new scenario might go something like this: After living and working abroad for several years, your spouse lands a great job he or she really loves, one involving little or no travel; your children attend good schools, which they and your spouse prefer they attend until graduation; or you've become a comfort creature – preferring to frequent five-star hotels and restaurants, gladly living without another uncomfortable Third World experience. You now prefer a more settled life at home with an occasional trip abroad for short periods of time. Perhaps you've joined the new upscale voluntourism crowd: you travel to India for three weeks where you will spend two weeks working in an orphanage in Kolkatta (Calcutta) and a final week luxuriating in a five-star spa near Jaipur! You still love to travel, but it no longer consumes your lifestyle and negatively affects your personal life. Your new season in life puts travel and work in a much different perspective. But you're still a travel bug.

Pursue Your Passion

Whatever your present season in life, you should at least explore job and career options that best appeal to your lifestyle values, interests, skills, and abilities. Get ready to join thousands of other individuals who pursue their career passions by landing jobs that are both professionally and personally rewarding.

During the past two decades we have spoken with many people who simply love to travel but feel stuck in jobs that offer little or no opportunities for travel. We're often reminded of the divorce lawyer who had attended a summer-abroad program in Europe and majored in international studies as an undergraduate. For years he had dreamed of working abroad, especially in Italy or France. Instead, he went on to law school and became a successful divorce lawyer – his insistent parents both pushed and approved of this respectable and potentially lucrative career choice. While he made lots of money, he disliked his work, especially the people he worked with and the ethics surrounding divorce cases. His interests and values no longer were conducive to a healthy career in divorce law. What he really wanted to do was to find a more personally rewarding job that involved international work, especially travel. It was his undergraduate study-abroad experience, rather than his successful legal practice, that had actually given him personal and professional satisfaction.

> *Try to find the perfect career marriage – a job that incorporates your occupational interests, skills, abilities, and values with your love of travel.*

We're also reminded of the highly paid, over-stressed physician who had a successful practice working 14 hours a day with little time for enjoying vacations. She really wanted to work in rural Africa providing basic health care services. Even though she expected a dramatic reduction in income and very basic living conditions, she preferred this global lifestyle to what was considered by her peers as a model of success for a physician.

And we know many people who are seeking greater purpose in their lives. Some want to join the Peace Corps or a similar development-oriented international organization. Others want to help the world's poor and ill or those afflicted by natural disasters. They simply want to do something more meaningful with their lives.

Our divorce lawyer, physician, and others are by no means atypical. We've encountered numerous lawyers, physicians, nurses, teachers, salespeople, secretaries, engineers, architects, entrepreneurs, and retirees who are anxious to find jobs that would incorporate their love for travel. For them, travel is the missing link in what is ostensibly a successful career. Some of these people have been able to find jobs within their present career that enable them to travel more. Others have changed careers in order to pursue what has been a lifelong passion – travel.

Whatever you are doing or planning to do with your life, you should at least explore job and career options for people who love travel. See if you can find the perfect career marriage – a job that incorporates your occupational interests, skills, abilities, and values with your love of travel. You need not pursue jobs in the travel industry nor ones that require living abroad for long periods of time. Thousands of jobs involve different types of travel, and some of those may be the perfect fit for you.

The following chapters explore numerous job options for people who love travel. They include descriptions of jobs as well as information – names, address, phone/fax numbers, and websites – for contacting potential employers. The book concludes with a listing of additional resources which should prove useful for pursuing your passion.

Where Do You Go From Here?

We wish you the best as you pursue your career and travel interests. While we are primarily concerned with outlining job and career options for people with a passion for travel, we also recognize the need to examine other important concerns central to conducting an effective job search. Indeed, knowing your job and career interests and options will only take you so far toward landing the job you want. You must also possess **capabilities** to land a job. This involves using effective job search skills and strategies for opening the doors of employers.

We examine the most important job search skills required for landing jobs in today's job market in several other books: *The Job Hunting Guide, High Impact Resumes and Letters, 201 Dynamite Job Search Letters, Nail the Job Interview, Nail the Resume, Nail the Cover Letter, Interview for Success, America's Top Internet Job Sites, I Want to Do Something Else But I'm Not Sure What It Is, The Savvy Networker, Dynamite Salary Negotiations, No One Will Hire Me,* and *Change Your Job, Change Your Life.* We also address particular job and career fields and job search skills for individuals interested in international-related jobs: *The Directory of Websites for International Jobs* and *Best Resumes and CVs for International Jobs.* Many of these resources are available in your local library and major bookstores, or they can be ordered from Impact Publications (see the "Career and Travel Resources" section on pages 303-309). Most of these resources, along with hundreds of others, are available through the publisher's website: www.impactpublications.com. Impact's site also includes job search tips, downloadable catalogs and flyers, and job search tips for keeping you in touch with the latest in career information and resources. Their international catalog, *Global Work, Travel, and Study*, should be of special interest to you. This catalog includes over 300 books on international work, travel, and study. The catalog can be downloaded from the front page of Impact's website: www.impactpublications.com (go to the "Downloadable Catalogs and Flyers" section on the right side of the site). You also can download eight "Travel/International" flyers from this section of the website and request a free paper copy of the "Jobs for Travel Lovers" flyer by sending a self-addressed stamped envelope to:

IMPACT PUBLICATIONS
ATTN: Jobs for Travel Lovers
9104-N Manassas Drive
Manassas Park, VA 20111-5211

Many of the major titles found in this catalog and specialty flyers as well as recommended throughout this book are included in the order form on pages 303-309.

Discover What You Really Love to Do

The following pages are designed to assist you in pursuing one of your work and lifestyle passions – travel at home or abroad. Once you identify jobs most appropriate for your interests and skills, be sure to follow through with a well organized job search campaign designed to put you in contact with potential employers. This will involve conducting further research, writing resumes and letters, networking for information and advice, and conducting informational and job interviews. If you do this, you too can find a job involving the type of travel you love!

2

✈

What's Your LTQ and ICQ?

J   UST HOW PREPARED ARE YOU for finding and doing jobs that
     involve travel? While many people may be high on desire and moti-
     vation to find travel-related jobs, these same people may lack the
     necessary knowledge and skills for landing such jobs.
     Let's examine how you orient yourself to jobs involving travel as well
as probe your level of knowledge and skills for landing the perfect job.
Just how realistic, motivated, and prepared are you for finding a job
involving travel? What exactly are your qualifications? What about your
educational level, training, and experience? What job search and travel
skills do you possess? If you are interested in international travel and
relocation abroad, are you prepared to travel abroad for an interview as
well as quickly move abroad if necessary?

Your LTQ

While the chapters that follow will help you answer many questions
about the "what" and "where" of jobs involving both domestic and
international travel, here we want to examine your motivation and ability

13

to find and do those jobs. The following exercise identifies your "Love to Travel Quotient" (LTQ). Respond to each statement according to the instructions and then compile your composite LTQ score at the end.

INSTRUCTIONS: Respond to each statement by circling which number at the right best represents your level of knowledge, skill, attitude, experience, or behavior.

SCALE: 5 = strongly agree   2 = disagree
               4 = agree   1 = strongly disagree
               3 = maybe, uncertain

1. I love to travel and do so often.   5 **(4)** 3   2   1

2. When traveling for pleasure, I often think about having a job that would enable me to make the same or similar trip.   **(5)** 4   3   2   1

3. Each year I take ____ trips for at least three days each (circle the number of trips).   5   4   3 **(2)** 1

4. After returning from a trip, within three months I'm usually ready for another road adventure.   5 **(4)** 3   2   1

5. I prefer a job that enables me to spend at least 20% of my work time traveling.   5 **(4)** 3   2   1

6. I have a resume designed for a job involving travel.   5   4   3 **(2)** 1

7. I have skills that are highly sought after for travel-related jobs.   5   4 **(3)** 2   1

8. I know how to locate companies and employers that have travel-related jobs.   5   4   3   2   1

9. I know how to get potential employers interested to contact me for a job interview.   5   4   3   2   1

10. I know at least five people who have jobs involving travel and who are willing to give me job leads.   5   4   3   2   1

11. I have set aside at least 20 hours per week to conduct my job search.   5   4   3   2   1

12. I'm good at networking for information, advice, and job referrals. 5 4 3 2 1

13. I know how to best use the Internet in my job search. 5 4 3 2 1

14. I'm prepared to move to a new job location within 30 to 60 days. 5 4 3 2 1

15. I have a particular city, region, or country in mind where I would like to work. 5 4 3 2 1

16. I have a clear idea of what type of organization and employer I want to work with. 5 4 3 2 1

17. I have a clear idea of what I want to do and have stated this at the beginning of my resume. 5 4 3 2 1

18. I know how to conduct a long distance job search campaign. 5 4 3 2 1

19. I am a flexible person who can easily adapt to different situations and changing circumstances. 5 4 3 2 1

20. I'm usually successful at what I do. 5 4 3 2 1

21. I welcome and thrive on adventure, challenges, and changing and unique situations. 5 4 3 2 1

22. I'm not like most other people I meet back home in terms of my motivations, goals, and career pattern. 5 4 3 2 1

23. I'm generally a very happy and contented person. 5 4 3 2 1

24. While money is important to me, it's not the driving force behind my desire to seek a job involving travel. 5 4 3 2 1

25. I have a sense of commitment and responsibility to what I do. 5 4 3 2 1

26. I usually make a favorable impression on employers. 5 4 3 2 1

27. I try to keep my knowledge and skills
    as current as possible in my profession.   5   4   3   2   1

28. I'm strongly motivated to work hard at
    finding the right job involving travel.   5   4   3   2   1

29. I'm generally a very patient person.   5   4   3   2   1

30. I'm also a very persistent and tenacious
    person.   5   4   3   2   1

31. I have a good sense of humor.   5   4   3   2   1

32. I don't take myself too seriously.   5   4   3   2   1

33. I'm interested in learning more about others.   5   4   3   2   1

34. I believe I'm a realistic person – I do my
    research, analyze situations in terms of
    pros and cons, and arrive at sensible and
    successful decisions.   5   4   3   2   1

35. I know how to get my first job interview
    within four weeks and the first job offer
    within 60 days.   5   4   3   2   1

36. I know how to negotiate salary and benefits.   5   4   3   2   1

TOTAL

If your total score is above 145, you may well be on your way to quickly finding a job involving travel. If your score is between 115 and 144, you need to work on those items on which you scored between 1 and 3. If your score is below 115, you need to get yourself well organized for the job market by following this and several other job search books.

Your ICQ

While most of the above 36 statements relate to jobs involving travel, as well as the job search in general, several others specifically relate to finding an international job. Indeed, the knowledge and skills required for finding an international job differ in many ways from finding jobs in general. If you are interested in international jobs, respond to the following statements. Add your score to your previous score to get your ICQ – "International Career Quotient":

37. I've traveled to 1, 2, 3, 4, or 5 countries within the last three years (circle the corresponding number to the right).   5   4   3   2   1

38. I know whom to contact abroad for information on international jobs.   5   4   3   2   1

39. I'm familiar with several websites that have useful international job information.   5   4   3   2   1

40. I'm willing to wait 6 to 18 months before landing an international job.   5   4   3   2   1

41. I can read, write, and speak fluently at least one foreign language.   5   4   3   2   1

42. I've taken 0, 1, 2, 3, 4, or 5+ college level courses in international business, finance, marketing, and economics (circle number to right).   5   4   3   2   1

43. I have a high school diploma (1), B.A. (2), M.A. (3), Ph.D. (4), or Post-Doctorate (5) (circle number to right representing your highest education).   5   4   3   2   1

44. I've lived abroad for 1, 2, 3, 4, or 5+ years (circle number to right).   5   4   3   2   1

45. I already have held international jobs for 1, 2, 3, 4, or 5+ years (circle number to right).   5   4   3   2   1

46. I know what I should and should not do when looking for an international job.   5   4   3   2   1

47. I know what is the best educational background for landing an international job.   5   4   3   2   1

48. I know what international skills employers are looking for in today's international job market.   5   4   3   2   1

49. Many of my friends and acquaintances are from other countries.   5   4   3   2   1

50. I keep abreast of international developments
    and thus consider myself knowledgeable
    about the international arena.   5   4   3   2   1

51. I know how the international hiring
    process works in most organizations.   5   4   3   2   1

52. I'm willing to travel abroad at my own
    expense to interview for a job.   5   4   3   2   1

53. I'm generally tolerant of others and
    their ways of life.   5   4   3   2   1

54. I'm a good listener who empathizes
    with others.   5   4   3   2   1

55. I tend to get along well with people
    from other societies and cultures
    without going "native."   5   4   3   2   1

56. Ambiguities don't bother me much.   5   4   3   2   1

57. Within 30 minutes I can get three
    international job leads by phone.   5   4   3   2   1

58. I love living and traveling abroad.   5   4   3   2   1

TOTAL

If your total score for all 56 items is above 235, you may well be on your way to quickly finding an international job. If your score is between 180 and 234, you need to work on those items on which you scored between 1 and 3. If your score is below 180, you need to get yourself well organized for the international job market by following this and several other books on finding an international job.

Improving Your Score and Skills

Now review each of the above items on which you scored below 3. Make notes as to what you need to do to move your score on these items into the 4 and 5 columns. Some of the following chapters will assist you. You may also want to consult our *The Job Hunting Guide, No One Will Hire Me!*, or *Change Your Job, Change Your Life*, which may help you avoid job search errors as well as develop specific job search skills. Other items may require additional education, experience, skills, and patterns of behavior as well as effective job search skills – things that are beyond the scope of this book but within your control.

Once you finish this book as well as work on your job search skills, complete these exercises again. You should increase your score by 20 percent. If you put what you learn from this book into practice over the coming weeks by spending 20 hours each week on your job search, you should improve your score by another 20 percent. Better still, you should eventually land the travel-related job you want!

3

✈

Motivations, Myths, and Methods

I F YOU LOVE TO TRAVEL, you'll probably love a job that lets you travel on a regular basis to places you really enjoy visiting. But travel is not for everyone. Nor do most people seek jobs involving travel.

You're different. Only certain types of people seek jobs involving travel. These individuals have a particular **motivational pattern** that affects how they relate to the world of work. Some pursue predictable career paths with a single company or industry. They may move into a job involving travel or promoted to an international position within their company. Others engage in a great deal of job hopping as they pursue their passion for travel. And others, unwilling to take the necessary actions to change jobs or careers, only dream about finding a travel-related job – perhaps after they retire from their relatively secure job.

For those who do love travel, the positives of travel tend to outweigh the negatives. At the same time, many people are very particular about where they want to travel. Some prefer jobs that take them away from the office for several hours a day or a few days each week or month. Others enjoy living abroad for lengthy periods of time or traveling abroad several weeks or months each year. Most are restless; many are driven.

Heading for the Last Frontier

Whatever your travel preferences, be sure you understand where you are coming from in terms of your motivations. Indeed, individuals seeking jobs that incorporate their love for travel exhibit motivational patterns that are different from other job seekers. Few are able to clearly separate their personal and professional lives. Many wish to pursue a **lifestyle** which merges both lives into one. Rather than seek just any job, they want jobs that enable them to pursue a unique and enjoyable lifestyle in which travel plays a central role.

In many respects, the international employment arena is the last great frontier for striking out on one's own. It's filled with myths, martyrs, misfits, and missionaries – a particular breed of job seeker who is simultaneously fascinating, frustrated, and focused. Indeed, we can think of few other employment arenas – other than perhaps the film culture of Hollywood – that generate so many unrealistic job seekers who are high on fantasies and motivation but low on information and skills. Individuals pursuing jobs in this arena defy most career counseling advice on how to best find a job.

> *The international employment arena is the last great frontier for striking out on one's own.*

It's Okay to Be Unrealistic

But being unrealistic is not necessarily negative for people who love to travel, and especially for international job seekers. Ironically, it is the dreams, fantasies, illusions, and unrealistic expectations – coupled with an unending drive, persistence, and entrepreneurial spirit – that successfully lead many individuals into the international job market. They often confound career counselors with their restlessness, sense of mission, and commitment to "go international" despite all odds and their general lack of goals, skills, and information. Setting goals based upon dreams and passions, rather than on an established pattern of motivations, skills, and experience, these people tend to defy standard career planning and job search methods.

We Did It Our Way

Travel plays a central role in motivating international job seekers. Indeed, for over 35 years we've pursued our own international jobs and careers. We've worked for others as well as for ourselves. We've lived and worked abroad, counseled others on how to find international and travel jobs, served as the first online Work Abroad Advisor for Monster.com, assisted international workers in re-entering the U.S. domestic job market, and created our own international travel guidebook series that regularly takes us abroad to exciting destinations.

We've fashioned an exciting career and lifestyle that enable us to regularly work abroad while maintaining our career base in the U.S. Indeed, we spend from two to five months each year working and traveling abroad.

We've met our share of interesting and intelligent international entrepreneurs, social dropouts, those possessed with a cause, individuals obsessed with becoming culturally neutral and linguistically competent, and a wide range of expatriates, short-termers, tourists, and travelers who are all doing something interesting in the international arena. From hotel managers, public relations specialists, professional photographers, and tour operators to business consultants, factory managers, relief workers, trainers, shopkeepers, doctors, lawyers, architects, and sales associates, these tend to be passionate people pursuing career and lifestyle goals.

We've served as employees to others' organizations as well as freelanced and engaged in our own form of entrepreneurship.

We've frequently wondered how others ever got involved with international jobs, and what continues to drive them in such careers.

And we regularly hear from numerous individuals who seek to break into the international job market after having been struck by the travel bug, a case of wanderlust, a sense of mission, or a yearning to do something different, challenging, unique, or exotic. Travel seems to give special meaning to their lives.

Career Risk-Takers Pursuing a Lifestyle

In contrast to most job seekers we encounter, international job seekers are very different types of individuals in terms of motivation, goals, skills, and lifestyles. While the typical job seeker is usually motivated by money, career advancement, and "success" within some organizational structure, more often than not, the international job seeker is motivated by a certain degree of restlessness to do something different; a need to travel and change work environments; a commitment to pursue an important cause or idea; or a desire to speak another language and experience a different culture, society, and lifestyle. Most are special types of entrepreneurs.

International job seekers are the ultimate career risk-takers who are seldom obsessed with their careers. Many reject the conventional model of the "successful job seeker" that assumes you must have clear-cut goals and accumulate marketable skills that lead to career advancement and career success. Instead, such job seekers often take any job they can get, if it involves travel, and willingly compromise their career goals and skills to the requirements of particular jobs. They are always on the lookout for

> *The desire for an international lifestyle is often the driving force for seeking a job.*

new job opportunities that may well become their next job hop within a highly unstable and unpredictable international job market.

While many international job seekers are looking for jobs and careers that allow them to frequently travel, they also seek to fashion a particular

lifestyle that takes priority over any particular job or career. Indeed, the desire for an international lifestyle is often the driving force for seeking a job – any type of job – in order to "stay" abroad. Many are hopelessly addicted to international life and travel.

As a result, many international job seekers are less concerned with formulating clear job and career objectives and developing marketable skills than with finding a job in their favorite part of the world, be it Europe, Australia, Africa, Asia, Latin America, or the Middle East. Many have a passion or obsession for returning to their favorite regions, countries, or cities. Their self-indulgent dream is to live and work in Europe, Asia, Africa, the Middle East, or the Americas – or London, Paris, Rome, Madrid, Casablanca, Bangkok, Singapore, Hanoi, Hong Kong, Shanghai, Sydney, Tokyo, Rio, or São Paulo – and they act accordingly by seeking jobs that will put them into their desired places. They are impatient with such basic career planning questions as *"What do you really want to do?,"* because they've already answered this question with a lifestyle answer: *"Get out of my present confining job and go work in*

France or, more specifically, in Paris. " Rather than deal with the fundamentals of career planning and the job search process – developing an
objective, identifying skills, conducting research, writing resumes; networking for job leads, and interviewing for jobs – many of these people
are preoccupied with locating job vacancies which they hope they can
"fit" themselves into. They are more concerned with finding out *"where
the jobs are"* than with *"what the jobs are"* and *"how to go about finding
a job."* They are especially interested in acquiring names, addresses,
telephone and fax numbers, e-mails, and websites of potential international employers so they can contact them directly for a job.

Advice From the Experts?

Not surprising, international job seekers pose a basic dilemma for career
counselors: What kind of career advice do you give someone whose
primary concern is to find a job that will support an international lifestyle
or a passion for travel rather than to find a job they do well and enjoy
doing and which leads to career advancement? How does one deal with
the fundamentals of motivation and goal setting when such individuals
do not fit into the conventional pattern of successful career planning?

The very nature of the international job market challenges many
conventional career planning and job search methods. Career planning
approaches, for example, requiring job seekers to first assess their skills,
abilities, and work values and then formulate a career objective that
guides their job search toward satisfying long-term careers and progressive
career advancement do not work well for people who just want a job so
they can continue to pursue their travel passion.

The international employment arena simply is not structured to permit
the success of such models and methods. Rather, this is a highly fragmented and segmented job market; access is often difficult if not impossible for many types of jobs; employment is frequently short-term – with
a three-year contract considered an excellent job opportunity; job-hopping
among many disjointed jobs requiring different mixes of skills is a
common pattern for those intent upon continuing employment abroad;
and geographic location and cultural settings of employment blur the
more traditional skill requirements for job performance. This structure
forces international job seekers into a particular pattern for finding and
maintaining jobs. While they increasingly use the Internet to locate

employers and job vacancies, they quickly learn the art of networking for developing professional relationships as well as for accessing job vacancy information. In short, those seeking international jobs must be prepared to address both the lifestyle and career questions simultaneously.

Other job seekers with a passion for travel, but not necessarily for living and working abroad, pose a similar dilemma for career counselors. They are often more concerned with satisfying their obsession with travel than with pursuing a successful career. What they most need is an ideal job that permits them to simultaneously engage in on-the-job travel while pursuing a successful career.

You're Different From Others

Over the years we have met and worked with hundreds of individuals who love travel. Many pursued international jobs and careers. We've encountered our share of journalists, corporate executives, bankers, missionaries, educators, researchers, lawyers, artists, writers, development workers, medical personnel, government bureaucrats, politicians, tour operators, military personnel, soldiers of fortune, volunteers, contractors, consultants, and entrepreneurs to write a separate book on interesting international personalities! We regularly hear from hundreds of other individuals who are interested in breaking into the international job market, re-entering it after a lengthy absence, or changing international jobs and careers. We also have conducted job search seminars abroad for those interested in re-entering the U.S. job market or finding other international employment.

We've always been fascinated with the international arena and the many interesting people who work abroad. We wonder how and why they got involved with international work rather than stay home to follow traditional careers or pursue a standard American lifestyle complete with a home mortgage and stable community life.

What we've learned over the years is that these people are different from the people we know back home in terms of motivations, personalities, and lifestyles. While some go international for the money, most are simply restless, curious, or stricken with that unexplained addiction to travel and a desire to pursue an idea, cause, or lifestyle that cannot be satisfied in a job back home. Some are international junkies who thrive overseas. Others literally dropped out of their own societies and work-driven lifestyles back home for more easygoing and personally rewarding lives abroad. Some are social misfits, criminals, or ex-offenders who attempt to build new identities in other cultures. For many of these people, getting ahead and achieving career success means moving on to another interesting, challenging, and satisfying international job. Someday they may have to return home to "settle down" and pursue legitimate work, but in the meantime many believe they are having the time of their lives; they want to continue this lifestyle indefinitely – as long as they can remain employed abroad in some type of job. Many work in jobs that are not particularly glamorous nor interesting, but their jobs enable them to do what they most enjoy – living abroad. Most are successful in changing jobs to continue their international lifestyles.

Motivation and Reality

What concerns us most are the motivations and job search behavior exhibited by individuals who have never worked abroad but who want to "break into" the field. Many of these people are students who have some foreign language competency, have traveled or studied abroad, or pursued an international course of study. Others are ex-military personnel who have lived abroad but now want to become international consultants or literally "make big bucks" abroad to compensate them for their many lean years working for Uncle Sam. Many are ex-Peace Corps volunteers and medical personnel who have worked in health care and rural development for a few years and now want to find another interesting and personally rewarding international job. Some are frustrated State Department and USAID employees who work in organizations most recently noted for low morale and blocked career advancement opportunities. And others are construction workers – heavy equipment operators, electricians, carpenters – who have never worked abroad but who "heard" they can make big money in a hurry working overseas. We also hear from numerous entrepreneurs who seek our advice on developing contacts for importing products from the Asian and Pacific regions – unexpected contacts with individuals who have used our travel guides.

What motivates these people to pursue international jobs and careers or strike out on their own into an unfamiliar employment frontier? What is it they really want to do? How do they differ from the ordinary job seeker? The career and motivation patterns for experienced international workers are fairly evident. Many, for example, got started by accident rather than by design. They lived abroad as children of international workers or were military brats. Some signed up for the military or Peace Corps and received interesting assignments that convinced them that they should pursue an international career. Many began as students who took a course, joined a study program abroad, or just traveled abroad during their summer break. They found the international experience and lifestyle interesting, so much so that they wanted to do it full-time. Many journalists, corporate executives, and business people also got involved accidentally; many were transferred abroad as part of the corporate promotion process. Missionaries, Peace Corps Volunteers, development workers, and many government personnel seem to initially pursue international jobs and careers by design.

We also see patterns among those who are interested in "breaking into" the international job market. Many have totally unrealistic expectations and questionable motivations. Like common perceptions of Hollywood, they see international jobs as being glamorous and high profile jobs that are well paid and result in major changes in people's lives and relations between nations. And as in Hollywood, there are a few such international jobs, but they are few and far between the many other types of less glamorous, low profile, and low to average paying jobs most commonly found abroad.

Let's take a look at some of the most common myths that motivate individuals to pursue jobs involving travel. Many of these same myths prevent individuals from achieving job search success. Several of the myths relate to the international job market and various steps in the job search process. By examining these myths and corresponding realities, you should get a clearer picture of your motivations and how to best organize yourself for finding a job involving travel.

Myths and Realities

Jobs involving travel have a certain lure and mysticism which was once reserved for itinerant missionaries, anthropologists, and soldiers of fortune of decades ago. Indeed, there are probably more myths about such jobs than any other type of work.

Most job seekers are unprepared and naive in approaching the job market; some might be best termed "job dumb." They play around the periphery of this job market with little success in penetrating it success-fully. They muddle through the job market with questionable perceptions of how it works. Combining facts, stereotypes, myths, and folklore – gained from a mixture of logic, experience, movies, nightly news reports, and advice from well-meaning friends and relatives – these perceptions lead job seekers down several unproductive paths. They are often respon-sible for the self-fulfilling prophecy and lament of the unsuccessful job seeker: *"There are no jobs available for me."*

Travel-Related Jobs

Some of the more important myths preventing individuals from finding jobs involving travel include:

MYTH 1:   **Jobs involving travel generally pay well.**

REALITY: It depends on the job. For example, many jobs in the travel industry, especially travel agents, are relatively low-paying jobs. Even owners of a typical travel agency have relatively low earnings. But individuals in these jobs often receive numerous travel perks, such as free or deeply discounted trips and special rates on transporta-tion and accommodations, to compensate for their low earnings. On the other hand, many sales positions involving travel pay well, depending on the sales perfor-mance of the individual.

MYTH 2:   **Jobs involving travel normally go to individuals with a great deal of work experience and nu-merous skills.**

REALITY: Again, it depends on the particular job. Many jobs involving travel are entry-level sales or marketing positions – new employees are required to travel in order to familiarize themselves with a regional, national, or international organization, clientele, and territory. Other jobs will be reserved for experienced personnel. This is particularly true in organizations with interna-tional offices. Generally, only the most experienced personnel receive overseas assignments. Some of the easiest international jobs to land, which require little experience and limited training, involve teaching English abroad.

MYTH 3: **Jobs involving travel are usually more exciting and challenging than non-travel jobs.**

REALITY: This may be true for some jobs, but the excitement and challenge of jobs largely depends on the individual. Many jobs involving travel are boring – involve lots of airports, taxis, and hotels that all look the same after a few trips. After a while, many people in these so-called glamorous jobs yearn for a job involving little or no travel!

MYTH 4: **Most jobs involving travel are either in sales or international business.**

REALITY: The range of jobs involving travel is extremely large. Almost every occupation, be it teaching, accounting, engineering, health care, or information technology, has jobs involving different degrees of travel – both domestic and international.

MYTH 5: **Jobs involving travel are more difficult to find than jobs involving little or no travel.**

REALITY: You'll discover thousands of jobs involving travel. Indeed, at least one in three jobs involves some degree of travel. If you develop a well organized job search focused around your major interests, skills, and abilities, you'll likely find the right travel-related job for you.

MYTH 6: **Individuals with extensive travel experience are more likely to get travel-related jobs than those with little or no travel experience.**

REALITY: Not necessarily so. Those who get these jobs generally have other important job-related skills. Travel is merely

one of many means by which they are expected to
perform their job, or it becomes a job perk associated
with certain types of positions.

MYTH 7:   **Most jobs involving travel relate to international
work and require traveling abroad.**

REALITY: The large majority of jobs involving travel are found at
home rather than abroad. While many of these jobs
may not seem as exotic or exciting as those involving
international travel, they nonetheless provide numerous
on-the-job travel opportunities.

International Jobs

Several other myths and realities relevant to jobs involving travel specifically focus on international jobs:

MYTH 8:   **International employment pays extremely well
compared to salaries back home.**

REALITY: The financial rewards of international employment vary
greatly. Some jobs – especially international consulting
– can pay very well. Jobs with many nonprofit organizations and schools often pay poorly. For those living
abroad, special financial benefits are often offset by
additional expenses incurred in trying to maintain a certain lifestyle as well as lost opportunities for supple-
menting income, such as appreciation on property in
the States or job opportunities for one's spouse.

MYTH 9:   **International jobs are very challenging and interesting.**

REALITY: Some international jobs are exciting, but many are dull
and boring. The excitement tends to come from the
lifestyle which involves traveling and learning about
other cultures, eating different foods, meeting new and
different people, and encountering unique events.
Foreign Service officers often end up stamping travel

documents in some dreadful, hot, and dirty capital city where the most exciting things to happen are to receive a letter from home, take a trip outside the country, acquire a new video, or check into a first-class hotel which has hot water and air conditioning. These are the events that make working and living abroad interesting for many people. They are often the subjects of people's "war stories" about *"how it was when we lived and worked abroad."*

MYTH 10:   **International work often involves exciting and exotic travel.**

REALITY: Travel is definitely a benefit for many individuals who have international jobs. However, the excitement of travel often wears off after age 40; after children reach high school age; after the third move in five years; after the tenth flight in a single year; and after the third lost suitcase and another terrifying taxicab ride from another chaotic airport. On the other hand, young, single people tend to disproportionately enjoy the novelty of international travel. Like all novelties, this one can wear off after a while.

MYTH 11:   **International development work is personally rewarding because of the positive changes one is able to make in the lives of others.**

REALITY: International development work is personally rewarding for individuals who can make a difference in the lives of others. But development work also is one of the most frustrating areas of international work. Few changes actually take place; the process tends to be very political, and development work fails more often than it succeeds. Individuals working for the USAID missions in Third World countries, for example, are more likely to be preoccupied with obligating funds and putting out brush fires on problematic USAID projects than in making progress in development. For many people, development work becomes more of a personal ego trip than one of concrete long-term accomplishments. Satisfaction comes more from "mingling with the locals" – speaking the local language, eating the local foods, laughing at the local jokes, and receiving the exaggerated status accorded to well-educated foreign development workers.

MYTH 12: **International lifestyles are better than back home.**

REALITY: International lifestyles vary considerably, depending on your situation. Living abroad can mean a large and comfortable home with servants and a good international school for one's children. But such comforts are often offset by daily inconveniences of local transportation, housing, and communication, by poor health and recreation facilities, by cultures which are better remembered rather than lived, and by the unemployed spouse situation. In many countries one spends a great deal of time on the basics of living, such as shopping for food and getting from point A to point B. Local health facilities may be rudimentary or downright dangerous. And one's spouse is likely to be unemployed – a recurring and serious problem for two-career couples who have chosen to live abroad and then find international living a tremendous strain on their marriage, often ending in divorce. Local cultures may place constraints on women. Consequently, adverse living conditions may result in a low level of work output and little professional development. For families with teenage children, the international lifestyle often becomes a serious liability because excellent international high schools are only found in a few countries. At this point in life, many people are anxious to return home or be transferred to a country which has a good international school. Others get tired of international living. Added to these adverse conditions are safety considerations attendant with the continuing rise of international terrorism and anti-Americanism. Consequently, the international life-style is not for everyone, nor is it for some people at particular stages in their lives.

MYTH 13: **It's easier to find an international job while traveling or living abroad than by networking or applying from the U.S.**

REALITY: From where one should best look for an international job depends on several factors. Expatriates living in-country often have an advantage in landing short-term contract jobs because of their location. Many companies prefer hiring someone already in the field for small jobs that may only involve $10,000 to $30,000 in labor expenses. It's cheaper to recruit such people than to transport someone from abroad to do these jobs. Consequently, expatriates will be in a good posi-

> *The Internet has quickly become the international job hunter's best friend. Be sure to include the Internet in your job search.*

tion to find many of these short-term jobs. On the other hand, many government agencies and companies prefer hiring their long-term field personnel from the States because they find a larger pool of qualified candidates based there. They have a bias for hiring individuals who are one step removed from the local situation. Such individuals are more involved in the professional mainstream which is based back home rather than in some isolated location abroad. Most important of all, recruitment and hiring decisions tend to be centralized with headquarters staff. They publicize vacancies, interview candidates, and select the finalists. Living and working abroad tends to place one outside this centralized recruitment process. Ironically, expatriates living abroad are well advised to make regular trips back home in order to better position themselves in the international job market. At the same time, the Internet is transforming the way employers recruit people with international expertise and the way individuals network and find international jobs. Many of the major Internet employment sites, such as Monster Board (www.monster.com), include hundreds of international jobs on their sites. Monster Board also has an online international career center complete with Q&A. You can now conduct an international job search 24 hours a day anywhere in the world. Using the Internet, you can search sites for job vacancies, research employers, join chat groups, enter your resume online, transmit letters and resumes by e-mail, and conduct online interviews. The Internet has become the international job hunter's best friend. Whatever you do, make sure you incorporate the Internet in your job search. For starters, you might want to explore these useful sites:

> www.escapeartist.com/jobs/overseas.htm
> www.overseasjobs.com
> www.jobsDB.com
> www.transitionsabroad.com
> www.iagora.com
> http://workabroad.monster.com

MYTH 14:   **One must have a great deal of international experience to get an international job.**

REALITY: It depends on the situation and the job. Many jobs require little or no international experience – only a specific or exotic skill that is difficult to find. If, for example, you were skilled in solving Y2K computer problems in 1999, you were in an excellent position to find international jobs, regardless of your international experience. Like many IT (information technology) workers, you had a marketable skill that was highly sought after in most countries throughout the world. *"Have skill, will travel"* is often more important in today's global economy than international experience.

MYTH 15:   **Travel experience and foreign language competency are essential to finding an international
job.**

REALITY: This is one of the great myths of finding an international job. Anyone who tells you this is probably
marketing their services for specific types of international educational services. While travel experience
and foreign languages may help you relate better to
the international arena, they are not necessarily prerequisites for entering the international job market,
which requires a lot more than good intentions and
understanding. Indeed, many people break into this
job market without such backgrounds. They possess
other more important skills which are in demand. In
many countries, English is the working language of
international jobs. Knowing a foreign language may be
crucial to one's job in some countries, such as Japan,
China, Indonesia, and France, but not so for many
jobs in other countries, such as Hong Kong, Singapore,
the Philippines, India, Australia, or New Zealand.

MYTH 16:   **An international-related educational background
is essential for finding an international job.**

REALITY: An international education may be helpful in better
understanding the international arena, but it is no
guarantee of gaining entrance to the job market. At
best, such an education will help motivate and focus
you to seek an international job as well as provide
numerous opportunities to network with others who
have international jobs. If you have a strong background in accounting, marketing, management, computers, and information technology, you have very
marketable skills both at home and abroad. History,
art, culture, sociology, education, interdisciplinary
Third World courses, and even international business
may be interesting to take and will definitely enrich
your stay abroad. But few such courses will directly

help you find an international job since they have
little skill content other than teaching the same courses to others either at home or abroad. At the same
time, education in general is important for many
international jobs, especially in cultures where "qualifications" are equated with higher educational degrees
– regardless of the particular field of study. Education
and qualifications have different meanings in different
cultures. Thus, the higher one's educational level –
measured as the possession of a B.A., M.A., or Ph.D.
– the better your chances of landing an international
job. In fact, international jobs are more sensitive to
educational credentials and how they translate into
status in other countries than to specific performance
skills. All things being nearly equal, a candidate with
an M.A. is more likely to be hired than someone with
only a B.A. Therefore, the more educational credentials you can accumulate, the better positioned you
should be in the international job market. Even a B.A.
degree does not mean a great deal abroad these days.

MYTH 17: **Living and working abroad is dangerous.**

REALITY: It can be dangerous, but it seldom is. Living and working abroad may actually increase your safety quotient.
It's much safer to work abroad than in many places in
the U.S. where your chances of being in an accident,
mugged, or killed are among the highest in the world.
However, some countries in the Middle East, Latin
America, Africa, and Eastern Europe have reputations
for being dangerous places for foreigners, especially for
Americans. If you work in one of these countries, you
should take sensible precautions to ensure your safety,
such as hiring guards and a driver, locking your doors,
changing your daily routines, avoiding places where
foreigners congregate, and never walking alone at
night. Check out the U.S. Department of State's travel
warnings (http://travel.state.gov/travel/cis_pa_tw/ tw/
tw_1764.html) and acquire a copy of Robert Young

Pelton's book, *The World's Most Dangerous Places*, and heed its advice (see the Career Resources section at the end of this book).

MYTH 18: **There are few international jobs available today.**

REALITY: There are numerous international jobs available today for those who have the right skills, who know where the jobs are located, and who understand how to find them. In fact, we expect to see the number of international job opportunities to increase steadily over the next decade as the world economy becomes even more interdependent, national boundaries become more open, and populations move more easily between countries. The basic problem is breaking into what often appears to be a relatively closed job market. If you shed many of your preconceptions of the international job market, examine your motivations, develop an intelligent plan of action, clearly communicate your marketable skills, and simply persist with a well organized and focused international job search, you should be able to join millions of others who work in this fascinating employment arena.

MYTH 19: **It's best to use an international job placement service to get an international job.**

REALITY: You should be able to do just as well in finding an international job on your own than by hiring someone to help you. In fact, many of these so-called placement firms have bad reputations for exploiting clients and engaging in fraudulent practices; be especially cautious of any firms that operate from Florida or Canada. Some misrepresent their services by convincing vulnerable job seekers that they have special access to international job vacancies and employers. Many require up-front fees for the promise of helping you find a job. Few do much more than mail your resume to different organizations that have overseas operations. This you can easily do on your own by spending a few hours in your local library surveying international directories and with the same results – few if any invitations for interviews. The most reliable firms are the headhunters and executive search firms that are paid by employers to hire specific types of individuals. If you follow the advice of this book, you should have no problem penetrating the international job market and finding the job that best fits your interests, skills, and motivations. You will do much better than many firms that try to get you to buy into their questionable placement services. In the meantime, if you decide to use such a firm, be sure you carefully examine their performance record before you accept their promises of performance. Paying up-front fees is a likely sign you are buying promises rather than paying for performance. But do yourself a favor. Check out the resources we recommend in this book. Spend a few hours exploring relevant sites on the Internet. You'll quickly discover you can conduct an international job search on your own and thus avoid the costs and disappointments associated with firms that claim they can do this work for you.

MYTH 20: **One has to have "connections" in order to break into the international job market. Whom you know is more important than what you can do.**

REALITY: While "connections" and knowing people are important to finding any job, and especially important when seeking an international job where information on job vacancies and opportunities is difficult to access, they are by no means essential. Your most important asset will be your marketable skills in a job market that places high value on unique job skills. How well you communicate your skills, experience, and motivations to employers – be it through resumes, letters, application forms, word-of-mouth, headhunters, executive search firms, classified ads, the Internet, or contacts and "connections" – will largely determine your success in getting the job. You should use contacts and "connections" not because they are **the** way to get an international job, but as some of the most efficient and effective ways of communicating your availability and qualifications in a job market noted for being highly decentralized, fragmented, and chaotic. The system, or lack thereof, is not organized well for efficiently and effectively communicating job vacancy information nor linking qualified candidates with job vacancies. Therefore, your job is to organize your own system for best communicating your qualifications to potential international employers. Contacts, "connections," and networking strategies should become a few of your many methods in this unique job market.

MYTH 21: **Most international jobs involve a great deal of travel. An international job will enable me to see and experience the world.**

REALITY: Many international jobs involve very little travel. The most traveling you may ever do is when you move from your home base to the job site abroad, and then return for a home visit once or twice in a two- to three-year period. Some international jobs involve working in one location, sometimes isolated, for one to two years at a time. If you are looking for an international job because you particularly like to travel, you may be better off looking for a job that involves a great deal of travel. These jobs are most likely found with headquarters staff, in international sales, or in the travel industry. This is one of the major mistakes some individuals make when choosing to "go international" with their career. Their major motivation for wanting an international job is travel. They assume that international jobs involve a great deal of travel to many interesting places or such a job will give them an opportunity to do more travel. They quickly learn they may have greater opportunities for international travel if they stayed home and found a good paying job with generous vacation time or one that involved periodic travel abroad. In fact, many international jobs involve visa, work permit, and local tax requirements that limit one's ability to travel beyond the borders of a host country. Whatever you do, don't assume an international job will give you more opportunities to travel. It may or may not. If you really want to travel abroad to many places, make international travel your career or start your own international business. An international job may result in getting stuck in some undesirable location that neither gives you the income nor time to do the travel you dreamed of doing while living and working abroad. Always start by examining your motivations for seeking an international job.

MYTH 22: **Most international jobs require moving and living abroad.**

REALITY: Many do but many others don't. Many international jobs are based in the United States and involve periodic travel to work sites abroad. International consultants and contractors, for example, may spend one to two months at a time on projects abroad, but their work base is back home. Educators, researchers, foundation employees, and business people often spend only a few weeks a year working abroad. Even employees of the State Department and USAID will spend much of their career in Washington, DC. City and state government employees involved in promoting tourism and trade are based in their home communities from where they conduct international business. In fact, many people enjoy their international jobs, careers, and lifestyles precisely because they have the best of both worlds – based at home and regularly travel and work abroad. They can still remain a part of their own society and communities while maintaining an exciting international career. In so doing, they avoid many of the hassles involved in full-time living and working abroad. Ironically, some of these people might change careers if their international jobs required lengthy residence abroad!

MYTH 23: **If one wants to work in the international arena, it's best to work for government or a multinational corporation.**

REALITY: Government agencies and multinational corporations do offer numerous international job opportunities, but they are only a few of the many players in the international job market. In fact, you may find some of the most interesting and rewarding jobs are found with nonprofit organizations or nongovernmental organizations (NGOs) and small or medium-size businesses in the travel and hospitality industries. On the other hand, you may discover being an international entrepreneur – either as some type of freelancer, independent consultant, or importer-exporter – to be much more interesting than working for others who will largely determine your work agenda and your future in the international arena. Indeed, the most rewarding international and travel job may be the one you create for yourself in today's global economy.

MYTH 24: **The best international jobs are found within the U.S. State Department, USAID, or the United Nations.**

REALITY: These may be great jobs for some people, but they aren't for others, including many present employees who are looking for other more rewarding alternatives. While these high-profile organizations appear to offer many glamorous international jobs, in reality competition is keen for these jobs; in fact, many are often disappointing and boring jobs. In recent years, morale has greatly declined in the U.S. State Department and USAID because of downsizings, the rise of international terrorism, and recurring changes in the personnel systems that may or may not reward individuals with international or area expertise and experience. Recent proposed personnel changes centered around the concept of "transformational diplomacy" will reward Foreign Service officers who are assigned to remote and insecure locations and who are area and language specialists. Once an innovative and proud organization noted for its exceptional international talent, today USAID is a shadow of its former self – significantly downsized and stripped of its traditional development roles. Benefits continue to erode as these agencies cut back on traditional perks. Furthermore, many of the jobs primarily involve the procurement process – from obligating funds to monitoring contracts. Individuals who go into these organizations with the expectation of doing important international work often are disappointed to discover they are primarily pushing paper, stamping passports, monitoring problematic projects, and financing contractors. The "hands on" exciting international work is often contracted out to consultants, contractors, nonprofit organizations, and universities. However, this situation is changing with new roles thrust on USAID to help reconstruct Afghanistan and Iraq. United Nations work, while well paid, is often boring and very political. Competition for jobs and promotions tends to follow nationalistic lines since a certain percentage of jobs are reserved for specific nationals. Many jobs are simply boring – involve little work content, numerous unproductive meetings, and a great deal of bureaucratic routines. If you are interested in getting things done, seeing the results of your international labors, and productivity

> *Today USAID is a shadow of its former self – significantly downsized and stripped of its traditional development roles.*

and responsiveness, these organizations may not be appropriate for you. Indeed, many employees with these organizations often wonder whatever happened to the really interesting international jobs and exciting lifestyles they expected when joining the organizations. Few recommend their jobs to their friends or relatives. Needless to say, there are many other more interesting and rewarding international jobs than those found with these high-profile organizations. A real bright spot in government is the U.S. Peace Corps, which is undergoing a major expansion of Volunteers and staff positions.

MYTH 25: **The international hiring process seems to take forever. It takes a longer time to find an international job than to land a job back home.**

REALITY: This also depends on the situation. Some organizations, especially government and the United Nations, may take an extraordinary amount of time to fill a vacancy because of the large number of candidates applying for a position, numerous decision-making levels, and the need for security clearances. Other organizations may take a long time because they are looking for someone with a highly specialized or technical skill that is difficult to find even with the hiring of an executive search firm. But other organizations may do just the opposite – hire in a very short period of time. Since many of the organizations have few legal restrictions on their hiring practices – especially time-consuming affirmative action and equal opportunity requirements – they have a great deal of flexibility in determining how they will hire. Many also use the Internet for quickly recruiting candidates. In short, they will do what they want and need to do. As soon

> *More and more employers use the Internet to recruit candidates.*

as an impending vacancy becomes apparent, for example, hiring officials will often "spread the word" within their old boy/girl networks to identify candidates who have the proper mix of skills, experience, and motivation for the job. This network may be very efficient in identifying the three top candidates within a matter of hours without having to hire a firm to recruit someone or list the vacancy in some publication or job bank. If you make yourself known by plugging into these networks, you may discover finding an international job takes less time than landing a domestic job. Therefore, it's extremely important that you learn how to effectively network for international job information, advice, and referrals – an essential skill for continuing international job and career success.

MYTH 26: **It's difficult to start one's own international business in today's economy.**

REALITY: Depending on what you want to do as well as your entrepreneurial skills, it's relatively easy to get started and operational within a short period of time. You need a marketable product or service, some basic information, a business plan, contacts, and the resources to finance the

> *Starting your own business may be an ideal solution to the "international career" question.*

initial stages of your venture. Start-up costs are minimal for many virtual businesses. In fact, the coming decade should be an unparalleled period for international entrepreneurship as "development" of countries increasingly becomes defined in terms of encouraging greater foreign investment, joint ventures, and import-export arrangements. Government agencies are becoming increasingly oriented toward encouraging and promoting private business involvement abroad, from large multinationals to small businesses and individual entrepreneurs. Since the technologies to start a business are relatively inexpensive, the costs of getting into many types of businesses can be minimum. Numerous resources also are available to assist would-be entrepreneurs (see Chapter 10). If you love to travel, starting your own business may be an ideal solution to the "international career" question.

MYTH 27: **The job search techniques that work for finding a domestic job also work well for finding an international job.**

REALITY: Some do, but many don't because they are based upon a culturally biased model of achieving career success in the American job market. They assume that job applicants are primarily motivated to get jobs they do well and enjoy doing and then make job moves that demonstrate career growth and advancement. Such skilled and motivated people are supposed to be oriented toward career success. However, many international job applicants could care less about such career success. Many of them are primarily oriented toward experiencing adventure and unique experiences as well as pursuing ideas, causes, challenges, and lifestyles. If an international career somehow develops from these experiences and pursuits, so be it. But success measured in terms of positions, money, and advancement up someone's organizational hierarchy is a cultural bias implicit in the standard career planning and job search models used by most career counselors.

MYTH 28: **It's best to learn about other cultures and adjust one's behavior to meet the local expectations. The more I act like the locals, the easier it will be for me and my job.**

REALITY: Yes, you should understand and be sensitive to other cultures. But it's not necessary to go to extremes by always behaving like the locals. Indeed, many people become overly sensitive to other cultures and engage in silly behaviors that are even embarrassing to the locals, who aren't sure who such foreigners think they are! Other cultures have expectations for both foreigners and expatriates which are not the same as for the locals. You are permitted to be different as long as you are not offensive. If you try to "go bush," you may not be respected as much as when you maintain your own identity. In addition, today's "global village" is changing rapidly and thus it's difficult to know exactly what the local expectations are for foreigners and expatriates. Furthermore, the international business, government, and development cultures have increasingly become Americanized. Except for a few local cultural peculiarities, you should be able to adjust well to an international employment culture without having to "go native." Your identity should always be an asset when functioning in the international job market. Just don't become obnoxious and offensive.

The Job Search

Several other myths and realities directly relate to the job finding process. Taken together, they comprise a set of principles for conducting an effective job search. These myths illustrate important points for organizing and implementing your job search. These principles are outlined in several popular books on job finding strategies and techniques. The following 25 myths and realities should help you launch a successful search for a job involving travel:

MYTH 29:   **Anyone can find a job; all you need to know is how to find a job.**

REALITY: This classic "form versus substance" myth is often associated with popular career planning exhortations that stress the importance of having positive attitudes and self-esteem, setting goals, dressing for success, and using interpersonal strategies for finding jobs. While such approaches may work well in an industrial society with low unemployment, they constitute myths in a post-industrial, high-tech society which requires employees to demonstrate both **intelligence** and **concrete work skills** as well as a **willingness to relocate** to new communities offering greater job opportunities. For example, many of today's unemployed are highly skilled in the old technology of the industrial society, but they live and own homes in communities that offer few rewarding job and career opportunities. These people lack the necessary **skills and mobility** required for getting jobs in high-tech, growth communities. Knowing job search skills alone will not help these people. Indeed, such advice and knowledge will most likely frustrate such highly motivated and immobile individuals who possess skills of the old technology.

MYTH 30: **The best way to find a job is to respond to classified ads, use employment agencies, and apply to human resources offices.**

REALITY: Except for certain types of organizations, such as government, these formal application procedures are not the most effective ways of finding jobs. Such an approach assume the presence of an organized, coherent, and centralized job market – but no such thing exists. The job market is highly decentralized, fragmented, and chaotic. Classified ads, employment agencies, and personnel offices tend to list low-paying yet highly competitive jobs or high-paying, highly skilled positions that are hard to fill. Most jobs are neither listed nor advertised; they are most likely found through word-of-mouth. Your most fruitful strategy will be to conduct

> _Despite attempts to organize it electronically, the job market remains highly decentralized, fragmented, and chaotic._

research and informational interviews on what career counselors call the "hidden job market."

MYTH 31: **Few jobs are available for me in today's job market.**

REALITY: This may be true if you lack marketable skills and insist on applying for jobs listed in newspapers, employment agencies, and personnel offices or posted online. Competition in the advertised job market usually is high, especially for jobs requiring few skills. Numerous jobs with little competition are available on the hidden job market. Jobs requiring advanced technical skills often go begging. Little competition may occur during periods of high unemployment, because many people quit job hunting after a few disappointing weeks of concentrating job search efforts on working the advertised job market.

MYTH 32: **I know how to find a job, but there are no opportunities for me.**

REALITY: Even during periods of high unemployment, numerous opportunities are available for job-savvy individuals. But most people don't know the best way to find a job, or they lack marketable job skills. They continue to use ineffective job search methods, such as only responding to classified ads and online job postings with resumes and cover letters. Opportunities are readily available for individuals who understand the structure and operation of the job market, have appropriate work-content skills, and use job search methods designed for the hidden job market. They must learn to develop an effective networking and informational interviewing campaign for uncovering promising job leads. And they must persist in prospecting for new job leads as well as learn to handle rejections. As we note in *No One Will Hire Me! Avoid 15 Mistakes and Win the Job* (Impact

Publications), most job seekers make numerous mistakes which often turn this myth into a self-fulfilling prophesy.

MYTH 33:   **I'm over-qualified in the eyes of many employers. They don't want to hire over-qualified individuals.**

REALITY: Yes, if you're seeking a $40,000 a year job, but you have experience and qualifications for an $80,000 a year job! Why would you even want to consider such a job? Who wants to hire someone who is over-qualified and thus likely to leave for greener pastures once they get their wake-up call that they are underemployed and under-compensated? This is the classic self-fulfilling prophecy of many career changers who don't know how to best communicate their qualifications to prospective employers. You're never over-qualified if you seek jobs for your level of skills and experience. Employers who view you as over-qualified are the wrong employers to whom to apply. They do you a favor by not giving you a job. Thank them for being so discriminating. They serve as your wake-up call. You need to get a better sense of where you fit into the job market. Stop under-selling yourself and thus contributing to this over-qualification myth. You need some job market smarts before you approach any more employers.

MYTH 34:   **Employers are in the driver's seat; they have the upper hand with applicants.**

REALITY: Most often no one is in the driver's seat since both the employer and the job seeker have a problem to solve. Not knowing what they want, many employers make poor hiring decisions. They frequently let applicants define their hiring needs. If you can define employers' needs as your skills, you might end up in the driver's seat!

MYTH 35:   **Employers hire the best qualified candidates. Without a great deal of experience and qualifications, I don't have a chance.**

REALITY: Employers hire people for all kinds of reasons. Most rank experience and qualifications third or fourth in their pecking order of hiring criteria. Employers seldom hire the best qualified candidate, because "qualifications" are difficult to define and measure. Employers normally seek people with the following characteristics: competent, intelligent, honest, enthusiastic, and likable. "Likability" tends to be an overall concern of employers – will you fit in and get along well with your superiors, co-workers, and clients? Employers want **value** for their money. Therefore, you must communicate to employers that you are such a person. You must overcome employers' objections to any lack of experience or qualifications. But never volunteer your weaknesses. The best qualified person is the one who knows how to get the job – convinces employers that he is the **most** desirable for the job.

MYTH 36:   **It is best to go into a growing field where jobs are plentiful.**

REALITY: Be careful in following the masses to the "in" fields. First, many so-called growth fields can quickly become no-growth fields, such as aerospace engineering, nuclear energy, telecommunications, and dot com jobs. Second, by the time you acquire the necessary skills, you may experience the "disappearing job" phenomenon: too many people did the same thing you did and consequently glutted the job market. Third, since many people leave no-growth fields, new opportunities may arise for you. Fourth, if

> *If you go after a growth field, you will try to fit into a job rather than find a job fit for you.*

you go after a growth field, you will try to fit into a job rather than find a job fit for you. If you know what you do well and enjoy doing, and what additional training you may need, you should look for a job or career conducive to your particular mix of skills, interests, and motivations. In the long run you will be much happier and more productive finding a job fit for you. If you find a job you really love, you will be better compensated emotionally than if you only focused on finding a job that pays a high salary.

MYTH 37: **People over 40 have difficulty finding a good job; employers prefer hiring younger and less expensive workers.**

REALITY: Yes, if they apply for youth jobs. Age should be an insignificant barrier to employment if you conduct a well organized job search and are prepared to handle this potential negative with employers. Age should be a positive and must be communicated as such. After all, employers want experience, maturity, and stability. People over 40 generally possess these qualities. As the population ages and birth rates decline, older individuals will be able to change jobs and careers with ease.

MYTH 38: **It's best to use an employment firm to find a job.**

REALITY: It depends on the firm and the nature of employment you are seeking. Employment firms that specialize in your skill area may be well worth contacting. For example, many law firms use employment firms to hire paralegals rather than directly recruit such personnel themselves. Many employers now use temporary employment firms to recruit both temporary and full-time employees at several different levels, from clerical to professional. Indeed, many temporary employment firms have temp-to-perm programs that link qualified candidates to employers who are looking for full-time employees. But make sure you are working with a legitimate employment firm. Such firms get paid by employers or they collect placement fees from applicants only **after** the applicant has accepted a position. Beware of firms that want up-front fees for promised job placement assistance.

MYTH 39:   **I must be aggressive in order to find a job.**

REALITY: Aggressive people tend to be offensive and obnoxious individuals who quickly wear on other people. They also make pests of themselves. Try being purposeful, persistent, and pleasant in all job search activities. Such behavior is well received by potential employers!

MYTH 40:   **Hiring a professional to help you find a job is a waste of time and money.**

REALITY: It depends on the professional. Hiring a career professional to help you with your job search can save you a great deal of time and wasted effort. A career professional should serve as a coach in helping you through a job search process. Many people can benefit from the structure, discipline, and direction provided by such a professional. If you're interested in contacting a career professional, visit the following websites, which are linked to associations of career professionals: www.nbcc.org, www.ncda.org, www.certifiedcareer coaches.com, and www.careernetwork.org.

MYTH 41:   **I should not change jobs and careers more than once or twice. Job-changers are discriminated against in hiring.**

REALITY: While this may have been generally true 30 years ago, it is no longer true today. America is a skills-based society: individuals market their skills to organizations in exchange for money and position. Furthermore, since most organizations are small businesses with limited advancement opportunities, careers quickly plateau for most people. For them, the only way up is to get out and into another organization. Therefore, the best way to advance careers in a society of small businesses is to change jobs frequently. Job-changing is okay as long as such changes demonstrate career advancement and one isn't changing jobs every few months. Most individuals entering the job market today will undergo several career and job changes regardless of their initial desire for a one-job, one-career life plan.

MYTH 42:   **People get ahead by working hard and putting in long hours.**

REALITY: Success patterns differ. Many people who are honest, work hard, and put in long hours also get fired, have ulcers, and die young. Some people get ahead even though they are dishonest and lazy. Others simply have good luck or a helpful patron. Moderation in both work and play will probably get you just as far as the extremes. There are other ways, as outlined near the end of this chapter, to become successful in addition to hard work and long hours.

MYTH 43:   **I should not try to use "connections" to get a job. I should apply through the front door like everyone else. If I'm the best qualified, I'll get the job.**

REALITY: While you may wish to stand in line for tickets, bank deposits, and loans – because you have no clout – standing in line for a job is not the best approach. Every employer has a front door as well as a back door. Try using the back door if you can. It works in many cases. Our separate book, _The Savvy Networker_ (Impact Publications), shows how you can develop your contacts, use connections, and enter **both** the front and back doors.

MYTH 44:   **I need to get more education and training to qualify for today's jobs.**

REALITY: You may or may not need more education and train-ing, depending on your present skill levels and the needs of employers. Most employers want to recruit individuals who are intelligent, communicate well, take initiative, and are trainable. Since they train their employees to respond to the needs of their organiza-tion, they want people who can quickly learn new skills. You first need to know what skills you already possess and if they appear appropriate for the types of jobs you are seeking. Also, be sure to communicate to employers that you enjoy learning and are trainable.

MYTH 45:   Once I apply for a job, it's best to wait to hear from an employer.

REALITY: Waiting is not a good job search strategy. If you want action from employers, you must first take action. The key to getting a job interview and offer is follow-up, follow-up, follow-up. You do this by making follow-up telephone calls as well as writing follow-up and thank you letters to employers.

MYTH 46:   I don't need a resume. I can get a job based solely on my network contacts.

REALITY: While networking is one of the most effective methods for finding employment, it does not erase the need for a resume. The resume is your calling card; it provides a prospective employer with a snapshot of your background and skills. Employers often want to first see you on a computer screen or on paper (resume) before meeting you in person (interview). Whether you like it or not, chances are you'll need a resume very early in your job search, especially when a contact asks you to *"send me a copy of your resume."*

MYTH 47:   A good resume is the key to getting a job.

REALITY: While resumes play an important role in the job search process, they are often overrated. The purpose of a resume is to communicate your qualifications to employers who, in turn, invite you to job interviews. The key to getting a job is the job interview. No job interview, no job offer.

MYTH 48:   **I should include my salary expectations on my resume or in my cover letter.**

REALITY: You should **never** include your salary expectations on your resume or in a cover letter, unless specifically requested to do so. Salary should be the very last thing you discuss with a prospective employer. You do so only after you have had a chance to assess the **worth** of the position and communicate your **value** to the employer. This usually comes at the end of your final job interview, just before or after being offered the job. If you prematurely raise the salary issue, you may devalue your worth.

MYTH 49:   **My resume should emphasize my work history.**

REALITY: Employers are interested in hiring your future rather than your past. Therefore, your resume should emphasize the skills and abilities you will bring to the job as well as your interests and goals. Let employers know what

> *Employers are interested in hiring your future rather than your past.*

you are likely to do for them **in the future**. When you present your work history, do so in terms of your major skills and accomplishments.

MYTH 50:   **It's not necessary to write letters to employers – just send them a resume or complete an application.**

REALITY: You should be prepared to write several types of job search letters – cover, approach, resume, thank you, follow-up, and acceptance. In addition to communicating your level of literacy, these job search letters enable you to express important values sought after by employers – your tactfulness, thoughtfulness, enthusiasm, likability, and follow-up ability. Sending a resume without a cover letter devalues both your resume and your application.

MYTH 51: **You need an electronic resume to land a job.**

REALITY: Electronic resumes are increasingly important for job seekers and employers alike. These resumes come in two major forms: e-mail resumes and scannable resumes. More and more employers request that resumes be sent to them by e-mail. Therefore, you need to create an e-mail version of your resume. Large employers also use the latest resume scanning technology to quickly screen hundreds of resumes. Therefore, it's also in your interest to write a "computer friendly" resume based on the principles of electronic resumes. These are very different resumes compared to conventional resumes. Structured around keywords or nouns which stress capabilities, electronic resumes are ideally suited for scanners. Keep in mind that electronic resumes are primarily written for electronic scanners and high-tech distribution systems rather than for human beings. Since human beings interview and hire, you should first create a resume that follows the principles of human communication and intelligence. Three good sources for developing electronic resumes are Joyce Lain Kennedy's *Resumes for Dummies* (John Wiley and Sons), Susan Britton Whitcomb's and Pat Kendall's *e-Resumes* (McGraw-Hill), and Pat Criscito's *e-Resumes* (Barron's Educational Series).

MYTH 52: **Individuals who post their resumes online to resume databases, such as <u>Monster.com</u>, <u>Hot Jobs.Yahoo.com</u>, and <u>CareerBuilder.com</u>, are more likely to get high paying jobs than those who don't.**

REALITY: Don't get carried away in your job search with all the bells, whistles, and hype of the many Internet employment sites that offer resume databases and thousands of job postings. Basically operated for their paying customers – employers – these are largely high-tech classified ad operations that also enable employers to search thousands of online resumes by keywords. There is no evidence that individuals who conduct an online job search find better jobs than those who do not. In fact, the Internet is a big disappointment for many job seekers who spend a disproportionate amount of time submitting resumes to databases and applying for jobs online. Recent surveys indicate that fewer than 20 percent of candidates get jobs through such online job search efforts. While individuals are well advised to include an Internet component in their job search, they also are well advised to spend most of their time engaged in job search activities that have real payoffs, such as networking for information, advice, and referrals and contacting employers by telephone and in person. The Internet is especially useful for conducting research on jobs, employers, and communities and for communicating with individuals by e-mail. It's a wonderful tool for international job seekers who need to research companies around the globe and quickly communicate with potential employers overseas.

MYTH 53:   **Salaries are pre-determined by employers.**

REALITY: Most salaries are negotiable within certain ranges and limits. Before you ever apply or interview for a position, you should know what the salary range is for the type of position you seek. When you finally discuss the salary question – preferably at the end of the final job interview – do so with this range in mind. Assuming you have adequately demonstrated your value to the employer, try to negotiate the highest possible salary within the range.

MYTH 54: **It's best to concentrate on negotiating a gross salary figure rather than focus on benefits and perks.**

REALITY: It depends on the employer and situation. Benefits and perks can translate into a significant amount of compensation. In fact, the U.S. Department of Labor reports that on average 43 percent of total compensation is in the form of benefits. Benefits such as stock options, profit sharing, disability insurance, and child care can add up to a significant amount of compensation. Make sure you look at the total compensation package rather than just the gross salary figure. For example, a $50,000 base salary with Employer X may actually be worth $80,000 with benefits, whereas a $60,000 base salary with Employer Y may only be worth $70,000 with benefits.

MYTH 55: **It's best to move to a booming community.**

REALITY: Similar to the "disappearing job" phenomenon for college majors, today's economically booming communities may be tomorrow's busts. It's best to select a community that is conducive to your lifestyle preferences as well as has a sufficiently diversified economy to weather boom-and-bust economic cycles.

MYTH 56: **It's best to broadcast or "shotgun" my resume to as many employers as possible.**

REALITY: Broadcasting your resume to employers is a game of chance in which you usually waste your time and money. It's always better to target your resume on those employers who have vacancies or who might have openings. Your single best approach for uncovering job leads will be the process called networking.

MYTH 57: **Electronic resumes are the wave of the future. You must write and distribute them in order to get a good job.**

REALITY: During the past 15 years electronic resumes (scannable, e-mailable, HTML, video, and multimedia) have played important roles in the job search and recruitment processes. Since large employers increasingly used Optical Character Recognition (OCR) software to scan resumes as well as requested applicants to e-mail their resumes, job seekers were well advised to write both scannable and ASCII versions of their resumes in response to the technological requirement of such employers.

However, numerous changes have taken place during the past few years due to rapid advances in resume screening and processing technology. For example, scannable resumes have become obsolete, as have resumes sent in ASCII format. Software advances now allow employers to

> *Develop separate resumes designed for the different applicant screening requirements of employers.*

receive resumes in other forms. Ugly duckling ASCII resumes are disappearing as employers increasingly receive resumes via the Internet with all the "dress for success" elements that usually come with nicely crafted paper resumes. Many employers now require applicants to complete an online form that produces a "profile" in lieu of a regular resume.

Therefore, given this transition period in resume technology, it is in your interests to understand the particular resume requirements of individual employers by asking what type of resume they prefer receiving, especially their technology requirements. At present no single electronic resume fits all employers. If you are still writing only paper resumes, you should educate yourself on writing "computer friendly" and e-mail versions of your resume based on the principles of electronic resumes. These principles, along with examples, are outlined in several resume books: Fred Jandt and Mary Nemnich, *Cyberspace Resume Kit,* Rebecca Smith, *Electronic Resumes and Online Networking,* Pat Criscito's *e-Resumes,* and Susan Britton Whitcomb and Pat Kendall, *e-Resumes.* However, some of these books may be obsolete given recent changes in electronic resumes and online applicant systems. Rebecca Smith also provides useful advice on electronic resumes through her website: www.eresumes.com.

Electronic resumes differ from conventional resumes. Most are structured around keywords or nouns which stress capabilities. While such resumes may be excellent candidates for searchable resume databases and online application systems, they may be weak documents for human readers. Keep in mind that electronic resumes are primarily written for high-tech distribution systems (employment databases) rather than for human beings. Since human beings interview and hire, you should first create a high impact resume that follows the principles of human communication. For now, we also recommend developing a separate resume designed for e-mail transmission. We're less enthusiastic about HTML, video, and multimedia resumes.

For the most recent update on the changing technology of employers for receiving, screening, and processing resumes, see Joyce Lain Kennedy's latest edition of *Resumes for Dummies* (John Wiley & Sons), where she focuses on the return of the "beautiful resume" with the new technology.

At the same time, keep in mind that the resume requirements of employers differ, given the size of the company. A company with 50,000 employees and an over-worked HR department will more likely be on the technological cutting edge for receiving, screening, and processing resumes than a company with only 25 employees. A large company must automate many aspects of the initial application process, whereas a small company can still handle applicants the old-fashioned way – paper and telephone. Your job is to understand the needs of different employers and craft different versions of your resume that respond to different technological requirements.

Today, many job seekers are interested in creating an online portfolio as an alternative to the traditional paper and electronic resume. For information on how to develop these portfolios, along with examples of such work, see Susan Amirian and Eleanor Flanigan, *Create Your Digital Portfolio* (JIST Publishing), and Wendy S. Enelow and Louise M. Kursmark, *Executive Job Search for $100,000 to $1 Million+ Jobs* (Impact Publications).

MYTH 58: **Individuals who include their resumes in resume banks or post them online in resume databases are more likely to get high-paying jobs than those who don't.**

REALITY: During the past 15 years most electronic resume banks have become victims of the "free" Internet. They have either gone out of business or have transformed their operations by becoming resume databases on the Internet. While some resume banks and databases still charge users monthly or yearly membership fees, most are now supported by employers who advertise on the sites and/or pay fees to access resumes online through particular Internet employment sites. Essentially a high-tech approach for broadcasting resumes, inclusion of your resume in these resume banks and databases means your resume literally works 24 hours a day. Major employers increasingly use these resume banks and databases for locating qualified candidates, especially for screening individuals with technical skills. And we know some individuals who join these resume banks do get jobs. However, there is no evidence that most people belonging to these groups ever get interviews or jobs through such membership. Nor is there any evidence that membership results in higher paying jobs than nonmembership. The real advantage of such groups is this: they open new channels for contacting employers whom you might not otherwise come into contact with. Indeed, some employers only use these databases for locating certain types of candidates rather than use more traditional channels, such as newspapers and employment offices, for advertising positions and recruiting candidates. Employers find the Internet to be a much cheaper way of recruiting personnel than through the more traditional approach of purchasing classified ads or hiring employment firms or headhunters.

MYTH 59: **The video resume is the wave of the future. You need to develop a video resume and send it to prospective employers.**

REALITY: The video resume is a novel approach to the employment process. However, since it is video-based, it's really a misnomer to call these videos a form of "resume." The so-called video resume functions more as a screening interview than a resume. Remember, the purpose of a resume is to get an interview. A video includes key elements that are best presented in a face-to-face interview – verbal and nonverbal communication. Unless requested by an employer in lieu of a traditional resume, we recommend avoiding the use of the video resume. However, if you are applying for a position that requires good presentation skills best demonstrated in the video format, such as in sales, broadcasting, entertainment, or modeling, the video resume may be the perfect approach to employers. But make sure you do a first-class job in developing the video. Avoid amateur productions that will probably reflect badly on your skills.

MYTH 60: **You should develop your own home page and direct employers to your website.**

REALITY: Do this only if you are a real professional and can customize your site to particular employers. Like the video resume, home pages can be double-edged swords. Some employers may like them, but others may dislike them. Your particular site may reflect poorly on your qualifications, especially if it is not designed like a resume, i.e., stresses your accomplishments and goals. Furthermore, since most employers are too busy trying to get through paper resumes and letters and handling resumes submitted online, few have the time or desire to spend time accessing personal websites –

> *Like the video resume, home pages can be double-edged swords. Some employers may like them, but others don't.*

unless your paper or e-mailed resume sufficiently motivates them to do so. Like viewing videos, accessing sites on the Internet takes time. Remember, employers can still screen a paper resume and letter within 30 seconds! Why would they want to spend 15 minutes trying to access and review your site when they could be dispensing with another 30 resumes and letters during that time? If you decide to go this route, you'll need to give employers a good reason why they should invest such time looking for you on the Internet!

You also should be aware of several other realities which will affect your job search or which you might find helpful in developing your plan of action for finding a job or changing a career:

- **You will find less competition for high-level jobs than for middle and low-level jobs.** If you aim high yet are realistic, you may be pleasantly surprised with the results.

- **Human resources or personnel offices seldom hire.** They primarily screen candidates for employment within operating units of organizations. Knowing this, you should focus your job search efforts on those who do the actual hiring – the hiring managers within the operating units.

- **Employment firms and personnel agencies may not help you.** Most work for employers and themselves rather than for applicants. Few have your best interests at heart. Use them only after you have investigated their effectiveness. Avoid firms that require up-front money for vague promises of performance.

- **It is best to narrow or "rifle" your job search on particular organizations and individuals rather than broaden or "shotgun"** it to many alternatives. If you remain focused, you will be better able to accomplish your goals.

- **Most people can make satisfying job and career changes.** They should minimize efforts in the advertised job market and concentrate instead on planning and implementing a well organized job search tailored to the realities of the hidden job market.

- **Jobs and careers tend to be fluid and changing.** Knowing this, you should acquire and market skills, talents, and abilities which can be transferred from one job to another.

- **Millions of job vacancies are available every day** because new jobs are created, and people resign, retire, get fired, or die.

- **Most people, regardless of their position or status, love to talk about their work and give advice** to both friends and strangers. You can learn the most about job opportunities and alternative careers by talking to such people.

- **Politics are both ubiquitous and dangerous in many organizations.** If you think you are above politics, you may quickly become one of its victims. Unfortunately, you only learn about "local politics" **after** you accept a position and begin relating to players in the organization.

As you conduct your job search, you will encounter many of these and other myths and realities about how you should relate to the job market. Several people will give you advice. While much of this advice will be useful, a great deal of it will be useless and misleading. You should be skeptical of well-meaning individuals who most likely will reiterate the same job and career myths. You should be particularly leery of those who try to **sell** you their advice. Always remember you are entering a relatively disorganized and chaotic job market where you can find numerous job opportunities. Your task is to organize the chaos around your skills and interests. You must convince prospective employers that they will like you more than other "qualified" candidates.

> *You should be particularly leery of those who try to sell you their advice.*

Advantages and Disadvantages of Travel Jobs

The preceding myths and realities provide a glimpse into some of the perceived advantages and disadvantages that motivate individuals to pursue jobs involving travel. They may raise important questions about your own motivations and desire to pursue such jobs. The major motivations most job seekers exhibit appear to be:

1. **Money:** Everybody wants it but only a few people really make big money in jobs and careers involving travel. The biggest money is usually made by people who manage other people's money – the investors, bankers, and venture capitalists who operate on percentages and at high risk levels. Many international jobs pay excellent salaries which may also be exempt from federal, state, and local taxes back home (the first $80,000 is exempt from federal taxes if one lives abroad for at least 11 consecutive months). This tax break applies to private sector employees living and working abroad. Federal government employees working abroad are not exempt from federal taxes, and many private sector employees must pay taxes to their countries of residence. But given additional housing and living adjustment benefits, as well as lower costs of living in many countries, many individuals working abroad do well financially.

Comparable jobs back home may pay less and offer fewer benefits.

2. **Adventure:** Especially for young, restless, inexperienced, and single individuals, jobs involving travel can be very exciting, especially travel abroad. Working in Latin America, Africa, Europe, the Middle East, or Asia is for some people the last great frontier. New places and different cultures become extremely life-enriching experiences.

3. **Curiosity:** Jobs involving travel are objects of curiosity for many people who always thought about having jobs involving a great deal of mobility. They may feel it is now time to do something different in their lives, so they decide to try a job involving travel to see what it's all about.

4. **Pursue a cause:** Several public causes can be pursued through international employment. Many individuals want to promote U.S. foreign policy, international peace, population planning, environmental control, health care, or rural development. You'll find numerous government agencies, private development organizations, religious groups, and nonprofit organizations that are organized to pursue such causes.

5. **New challenges:** International work does offer new and unusual challenges, from basic living to getting a job done. Individuals often find such work challenges their basic assumptions about people as well as work itself.

6. **Lifestyle:** Many individuals are motivated to acquire jobs involving travel because of the seemingly attractive lifestyle. The work itself may bring them into contact with new and interesting cultures; the work may change constantly; and they are given an extraordinary amount of status and authority – the "big fish in a small pond" phenomenon – not commonly found with many jobs in the United States. Indeed, exaggerated status and bloated egos are widespread among many international workers.

7. **Travel:** Many people are hopelessly addicted to travel. Like clockwork, every three, six, or twelve months they have a burning desire to take to the road to discover new and exciting places. Many of these people believe it may be best to incorporate their travel addiction into a job or career that involves frequent travel.

8. **Escape and revitalization:** Some people wish to escape from their present jobs which may be boring, dead end, and unrewarding. Some are dissatisfied with the state of their country's politics and economics. Some are unemployed individuals seeking new opportunities. Others may have just experienced a divorce. They believe a travel-related job will revitalize their careers and lead to renewed career success and happiness.

Those who work long term in jobs involving travel often find the advantages outweigh the disadvantages in defining their motivations to continue pursuing such types of jobs and careers. In addition, many long-term international workers don't know what else they could or would do if they left this employment arena. Therefore, they see no other alternatives to their career and lifestyle.

Becoming Successful Abroad

Jobs involving travel abroad are not for everyone. Most organizations working in this arena identify a particular type of individual who is best suited for international work. The most effective international workers tend to have the following characteristics:

1. **Adaptability and flexibility:** Willing to adapt to changing circumstances and adjust to the norms of the situation.

2. **Tolerance and empathy:** Listen to others, understand their behavior, accept different behaviors as legitimate, tolerate ambiguities, be open-minded, and respect others' beliefs.

3. **Sensitivity to cultural differences:** Adjust to cultural differences without going "native"; maintain one's own identity.

4. **Patience and perseverance:** Balance the American work ethics of punctuality, productivity, and getting things done now with work cultures that place higher value on maintaining and expanding power, developing harmonious interpersonal relations, avoiding face-to-face confrontations, and solving problems through consensus rather than through other rational decision-making techniques.

5. **Humor:** Maintain a sense of humor, especially in situations which are sometimes frustrating; don't take oneself too seriously. Many cultures respond well to people who always wear a friendly smile and an attitude of fun and humor.

6. **Curiosity:** Be open to new experiences, willing to learn, and accepting of new and unfamiliar patterns.

7. **Self-confidence and initiative:** Be willing to take initiative without being offensive or threatening the power of others. Entrepreneurs who are also sensitive to local decision-making practices are highly valued in the international arena.

8. **Facility in foreign languages:** Especially for individuals living and working in countries where the local language is important to day-to-day business, they should have some ability to learn a second or third language.

While the above "success" characteristics are common among many individuals who work in the international arena, there is also a negative side to them. Indeed, there is a fine line between being tolerant, sensitive, and patient, and being useless on the job. Some individuals adjust **too** well and thus accomplish little or nothing other than "enjoy" their international lifestyles. For many career-oriented professionals, international employment can take a serious toll on their professional development.

Several excellent books focus on how to best live, work, and travel abroad with special emphasis on cross-cultural communication. We highly recommend the *Culture Shock! Series* (Times Books), which now includes separate books on over 60 countries. We also recommend the following books, most of which are available through Impact Publications:

The Art of Crossing Cultures, Craig Storti (Nicholas Brealey, 2001)

Breaking Through Culture Shock, Elisabeth Marx (Nicholas Brealey, 2001)

Do's and Taboos Around the World, Roger A. Axtell (John Wiley & Sons, 1993)

Do's and Taboos of Humor Around the World, Roger A. Axtell (John Wiley & Sons, 1999)

Gestures: Do's and Taboos of Body Language Around the World, Roger A. Axtell (John Wiley & Sons, 1997)

Global Etiquette Guide to Africa and the Middle East, Dean Foster (John Wiley & Sons, 2002)

Global Etiquette Guide to Asia, Dean Foster (John Wiley & Sons, 2000)

Global Etiquette Guide to Europe, Dean Foster (John Wiley & Sons, 2000)

Global Etiquette Guide to Mexico and Latin America, Dean Foster (John Wiley & Sons, 2002)

Global Smarts: The Art of Communicating and Deal Making Anywhere in the World, Richard Lewis (John Wiley & Sons, 2000)

Kiss, Bow, or Shake Hands, Terri Morrison, Wayne A. Conaway, and George A. Borden (Adams Media, 1995)

Mind Your Manners: Managing Business Cultures in Europe, John Mole (Nicholas Brealey, 1996)

Multicultural Manners, Norine Dresser (John Wiley & Sons, 1996)

Survival Kit for Overseas Living, L. Robert Kohls (Nicholas Brealey, 2001)

The Ugly American, Eugene Burdick and William J. Lederer (W.W. Norton & Company, 1999)

Prerequisites for Success

How successful you will be in landing a job involving travel as well as continuing in such employment depends on several factors that relate to you as an individual as well as the organizations offering job opportunities. Like any job, jobs involving travel have advantages and disadvantages, positives and negatives, ups and downs. Some people are fortunate enough to find jobs they really love. Many become obsessed with their work to the exclusion of all other interests and pursuits. Most people, however, find jobs that are okay but nothing particularly special or exciting. They are not unhappy with their jobs, nor are they particularly happy with them. To many, a job is a job is a job; its advantages outweigh possible disadvantages of not having the job at all.

However, we do know what leads to job search success both at home and abroad. Success is determined by more than just a good plan getting implemented. It is not predetermined, nor is it primarily achieved by intelligence, thinking big, time management, or luck. Based upon experience, research, and common sense, we believe you will achieve career planning success by following many of these 22 principles:

1. **You should work hard at finding a job:** Make this a daily endeavor and involve others. Expect to spend 40 to 80 hours a week conducting an effective job search. Focus on routinizing high-payoff job search activities, such as networking.

2. **You should not be discouraged by setbacks:** You are playing the odds, so expect disappointments and handle them in stride. You will have many *"no's"* before uncovering the one *"yes"* that's right for you.

3. **You should be patient and persevere:** Expect three months of hard work before you connect with the job that's right for you. Keep focused and active throughout this period.

4. **You should be honest with yourself and others – but not stupid:** Honesty is always the best policy. But don't confuse honesty with frankness and the confessional. Indeed, many people say the stupidest things about themselves in the name of honesty. Naive job seekers often volunteer their negatives and shortcomings to potential employers. They present an unfortunate image of someone who lacks street smarts and who potentially will say the darnest things to clients and customers even about the inner workings of the business!

5. **You should develop a positive attitude toward yourself:** Nobody wants to employ guilt-ridden people with inferiority complexes and low self-esteem. Focus on your positives with enthusiasm. Sell your positive self – those things you do well and enjoy doing.

6. **You should associate with positive and successful people:** Finding a job largely depends on how well you relate to others. Avoid associating with negative and depressing people who complain and have a "you-can't-do-it" attitude. Run with winners who have a positive "can-do" outlook on life.

7. **You should set goals:** You should have a clear idea of what you want and where you're going. Without these, you will present a confusing and indecisive image to others. Clear goals help direct your job search into productive channels. Setting high goals will help you work hard in getting what you want.

8. **You should plan and implement for success:** Convert your goals into realistic action steps that are organized as short-, intermediate-, and long-range plans. Then put these plans into action by taking the necessary steps that should lead to success. Unfortunately, many people are good at planning their job search but fail to implement properly. Planning without implementation is a waste of time.

9. **You should manage your time and get organized:** Translate your plans into activities, targets, names, addresses, telephone numbers, and materials. Develop an efficient and effective filing system and use a large calendar for setting time targets and recording appointments and useful information.

10. **You should be a good communicator:** Take stock of your oral, written, and nonverbal skills. How well do you communicate? Since most aspects of your job search involve communicating with others, and communication skills are one of the most sought-after skills, always present yourself well both verbally and nonverbally.

11. **You should be energetic and enthusiastic:** Employers are attracted to positive people who appear to be energetic and demonstrate that magical quality called **drive**. They don't like negative and depressing people who toil at their work. Generate enthusiasm both verbally and nonverbally. Check on your telephone voice – it may be less enthusiastic than your voice in face-to-face situations. After all, your first interview is likely to take place over the telephone.

12. **You should ask questions:** Your best information comes from asking questions. Asking questions also communicates interest and intelligence. Learn to develop questions that are non-aggressive, probing, polite, and interesting to others. But don't ask too many questions and thereby dominate conversations and become an annoying inquisitor.

13. **You should be a good listener:** Being a good listener is often more important than being a good questioner and talker. Learn to improve your face-to-face listening behavior (nonverbal cues) as well as remember and use information gained from others. Make others feel they enjoyed talking with you, i.e., you are one of the few people who actually **listens** to what they say.

14. **You should be polite, courteous, and thoughtful:** Treat gatekeepers, especially receptionists, like human beings. Avoid being aggressive or too assertive. Try to be polite, courteous, and gracious. Your social graces are being observed. Remember to send thank-you letters – a very thoughtful thing to do in a job search. Even if rejected, thank employers for the "opportunity" given to you. After all, they may later have additional opportunities, and your letter will help them remember you. In the end, employers want to hire people they like.

15. **You should be inclusive, give credit to others, and help others look good:** Avoid the egocentrism of taking credit for everything by constantly referring to "I." Give credit to others by referring to "we" when discussing your accomplishments, and "us" or the "company" when speculating about your future role. Employers love to work with competent employees who make them look good even though the credit belongs to others.

16. **You should be tactful:** Watch what you say to others about other people as well as yourself. Be very careful how you talk about previous employers and co-workers, especially anything negative about your relationships and others' competence. Don't be a gossip, back-stabber, or confessor.

17. **You should demonstrate your intelligence and competence:** Present yourself as someone who gets things done and achieves results – a **producer**. Talk about your accomplishments by including examples of what you did and with what consequences. Employers want to see proof of performance. They generally seek people who are bright, hard-working, responsible, energetic, have drive, can communicate well, have positive personalities, maintain good interpersonal relations, are likable, observe dress and social codes, take initiative, are talented, possess expertise in particular areas, use good judgment, are cooperative, trustworthy, and loyal, generate confidence and credibility, and are conventional. In other words, they like people who can score in the "excellent" to "outstanding" categories of a performance evaluation.

18. **You should maintain a professional stance:** Be neat in what you do and wear, and speak with the confidence, authority, and maturity of a professional.

19. **You should not overdo your job search:** Don't engage in overkill and bore everyone with your "job search" stories. Achieve balance in everything you do. Occasionally take a few days off to do nothing related to your job search. Develop a system of incentives and rewards – such as two non-job search days a week if you accomplish targets A, B, C, and D.

20. **You should be open-minded and keep an eye open for "luck":** Too much planning can blind you to unexpected and fruitful opportunities. You should welcome serendipity. Learn to re-evaluate your goals and strategies. Seize new opportunities if appropriate.

21. **You should evaluate your progress and adjust:** Take two hours once every two weeks and evaluate your accomplishments. If necessary, tinker with your plans and reorganize your activities and priorities. Don't become too routinized and thereby kill creativity and innovation.

22. **You should focus on what's really important in conducting a successful job search:** If you spend most of your job search time sending your resume in response to job ads or submitting your resume in response to online job listings, you're not conducting a smart job search. Instead, focus most of your job search activities on research, networking, and making direct contacts with employers. Above all, use the Internet wisely for acquiring information and advice rather than only for responding to job listings.

These principles should provide you with an initial orientation for starting your travel-related job search. As you become more experienced, you will develop your own set of operating principles that should work for you in particular employment situations.

Take Time to Sail

Let's assume you have the necessary skills to open the doors to employers for the job you want. Your next step is to organize an effective job search. Organization, however, does not mean a detailed plan, blueprint, or road map for taking action. If you strictly adhere to such a plan, you will most likely be disappointed with the outcomes. Instead, your job search should approximate the art of sailing – you know where you want to go and the general direction for getting there. But the specific path, as well as the time of reaching your destination, will be determined by your environment, situation, and skills. Like the sailor dependent upon his or her sailing skills and environmental conditions, you tack back and forth, progressing within what is considered to be an acceptable time period for successful completion of the task.

Too much planning can blind you to unexpected occurrences and opportunities, or that wonderful experience called serendipity.

While we recommend planning your job search, we hope you will avoid the excesses of too much planning. The plan should not become the **end** – it should be a flexible **means** for achieving your stated job and career goals. Planning makes sense, because it requires you to set goals and develop strategies for achieving the goals. However, too much planning can blind you to unexpected occurrences and opportunities, or that wonderful experience called **serendipity**.

We outline on page 76 a hypothetical plan for conducting an effective job search. This plan incorporates seven distinct but interrelated job search activities over a six-month period. If you phase in the first four job search steps during the initial three to four weeks, and continue the final four steps in subsequent weeks and months, you should begin receiving job offers within two to three months after initiating your job search. Interviews and job offers can come at any time – often unexpectedly – during your job search. An average time is three months, but it can occur within a week or take as long as several months. Recessions can easily add two to three months to a job search.

While three months may seem a long time, you can shorten your job search time by increasing the frequency of each job search activity. If you

Organization of Job Search Activities

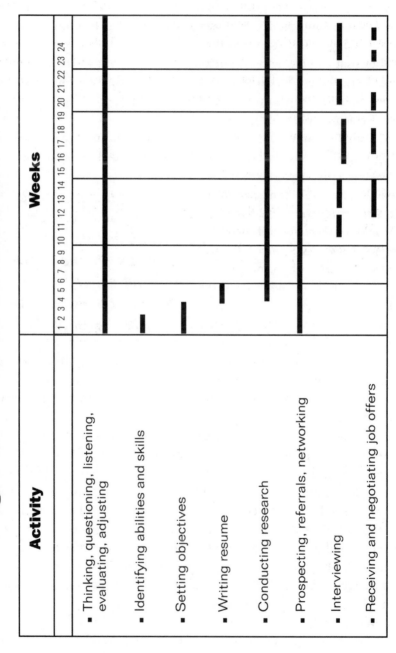

Activity	Weeks
	1 2 3 4 5 6 7 8 9 10 11 12 13 14 15 16 17 18 19 20 21 22 23 24
▪ Thinking, questioning, listening, evaluating, adjusting	
▪ Identifying abilities and skills	
▪ Setting objectives	
▪ Writing resume	
▪ Conducting research	
▪ Prospecting, referrals, networking	
▪ Interviewing	
▪ Receiving and negotiating job offers	

are job hunting on a full-time basis, you may be able to cut your job search time in half. But don't expect to get a professional level job quickly. It requires time, hard work, and persistence.

This hypothetical time frame is generally applicable to most domestic jobs. The time frame for international jobs, however, may be longer given the logistics of recruiting and hiring. In some cases, the selection process will take a long time because the organization will need to narrow a large number of candidates in order to interview only a few in the field location abroad. Other jobs may require lengthy security clearances. And in still other cases the time between when a vacancy is announced and filled may be very short, because an organization relies heavily on the informal word-of-mouth networking process for recruiting candidates.

For more detailed information about these and other job search principles and techniques that are beyond the scope of this book, you may want to consult several of the resources outlined at the end of the book. We especially recommend Ron Krannich's latest edition (9th) of *Change Your Job, Change Your Life* (Impact Publications, 2005).

4

✈

The Travel and Hospitality Industry

IF YOU WANT A JOB involving travel, consider exploring job opportunities in the travel industry. After all, many travel professionals do exactly what you want to do – engage in a lot of travel. And you'll often travel free or receive major discounts on transportation to and accommodations at your favorite destinations. Envious friends and acquaintances will most likely think you have a "really tough job" – probably the best around. Indeed, they probably believe you either receive some great job perks or you have a job that gives you terrific tax write-offs. Many would like to do what you're doing!

While many myths characterize jobs in the travel and hospitality industry, you will also discover some exciting realities that will both push and pull you into this industry. If you join this industry, you'll most likely become part of a group of very satisfied professionals who belong to an extremely interesting work culture. Travel is simply a great adventure.

International Job Seekers and Travel

Many individuals seek international jobs with business, government, international organizations, and nonprofit groups because they have had interesting and enjoyable international travel experiences. They now want to turn their pleasures into a full-time job or career involving international travel or residence abroad.

But working abroad is not the same as traveling abroad. Many successful international job seekers soon discover they would be much happier if they sought a job that enabled them to frequently travel rather than live abroad. Better still, they might really enjoy working in an industry that enables them to pursue their real passion – travel to exciting and exotic locations.

Domestic U.S. Travel Industry

According to the Travel Industry Association of America, in 2005 travel was a $1.3 trillion industry within the United States – up from $570.5 billion in 2000. Directly employing 7.3 million people, it's the country's second largest employer. In 28 states and the District of Columbia, travel is the first, second, or third largest industry, which generates a tremendous amount of employment and tax revenue. Altogether, the U.S. travel industry annually generates more than $100 billion in tax revenue.

Despite once rosy growth projections, all has not been well in the travel industry since September 11, 2001. Many of the high-flying players in this industry have scrambled to survive in a new economy often characterized by stagnant to declining travel and new bright spots centered on adventure travel and voluntourism. While normally a growth industry, increasing at nearly 3 percent annually during the 1990s, the travel industry took major economic hits in 2001 and 2002 with the double whammy of a global recession and the chilling events of 9/11. In 2003 the industry experienced a triple whammy as the war with Iraq further discouraged both business and leisure travel and put the travel industry into an even deeper recession. Indeed, a survey of travel agents by *Travel Weekly* (February 17, 2003) indicated that only 38 percent of travel agents reported a profit in their business; 28 percent were showing losses and 34 percent were breaking even.

Since 2004, the U.S. domestic travel industry has rebounded, nearly doubling in terms of revenue generated from travel and tourism. Much of this growth is due to increases in leisure travel within the U.S. – a major beneficiary of post-9/11 realignment of American travel preferences – and sharp increases in the cruise industry. International tourism has steadily increased among non-U.S. travelers, with travel to Europe and Asia showing major gains despite terrorism and a series of major international natural disasters (tsunamis, hurricanes, earthquakes, floods) and health alerts (avian flu).

However, employment levels in the travel industry have remained relatively stagnant. In addition, several major airlines have declared bankruptcy and some have gone out of business in the wake of rising fuel, labor, legacy, security, and operations costs and the inability to reorganize their companies in the face of intense competition. In 2005 Merrill Lynch estimated U.S. airline revenue shortfalls to be as follows:

- AMR Corp. (American Airlines) $600 million
- Continental Airlines Inc. $250 million
- Delta Air Lines Inc. $600 million
- Northwest Airlines Co. $400 million
- UAL Corp. (United Airlines) $500 million
- US Airways Group Inc. $200 million

Overall, the travel industry has entered a period of increased uncertainty and volatility. While more and more people want to travel and many people want to work in this attractive industry, a combination of unique events and rising costs has resulted in slow employment growth. Many travelers and travel-related companies continue to take a wait-and-see attitude toward all types of travel, a characteristic of this industry that was especially prevalent in the immediate aftermath of 9/11.

> *The travel industry will undergo major changes in the decade ahead.*

Troubled Industry, Uncertain Future

During the past decade the travel and hospitality industry had been one of the largest and fastest growing industries in the world. As business and leisure travel grew in the boom economy of the 1990s, so did airlines, cruise lines, hotels, tour operators, and car rentals, and other travel and hospitality providers. The industry appeared to be on an inevitable growth trend with numerous job opportunities available throughout the industry. During this period the travel and hospitality industry also underwent major restructuring due to its dynamic growth, the role of the Internet, and increased competition among airlines, hotels, and tour operators. The industry was expected to grow even bigger in the decade ahead, out-performing most other industries.

The rosy assumption, based on nearly eight years of unprecedented economic growth, was that as economies improved, businesses expanded, an affluent population aged, and more and more people traveled, the travel and hospitality industry would undergo major expansion in the years ahead. It would offer some of the most exciting job and career opportunities for people who love travel. If you were interested in the travel and hospitality industry, now was the time to get into what was expected to be an extremely rewarding long-term career.

How times have changed and clouded what was assumed to be a dynamic, optimistic, and expansive industry. In the end, the industry's future always hedged on economic growth and security. A faltering global economy coupled by a U.S. bubble economy and security threats of international and domestic terrorism hit the travel and hospitality industry hard in the early 2000s. As business and leisure travel declined, so did various segments of a highly over-invested industry.

> *Despite a recent boom-and-bust cycle, millions of people still travel and economies do change for the better.*

Several airlines, cruise lines, tour operators, car rental companies, and hotels either went bankrupt, merged, or experienced major financial problems as they laid off thousands of employees. Trying to survive in the troubled world of travel became imperative for many people in this industry. By the year 2002, finding a job in this wonderful industry, especially among airlines, had became increasingly difficult because of the general economic downturn and the fact that this industry was rapidly shedding jobs. The industry probably experienced greater difficulties due to the twin shocks of terrorism and a continuing global economic slump. More and more individuals postponed business and leisure travel or made last-minute travel decisions in response to attractive travel specials. At the same time, by 2003 the travel industry was aggressively attempting to "revitalize the industry" as well as "reduce its high distribution costs" – code words for cutting personnel, eliminating middlemen, and downgrading services. Not surprisingly, such changes did not bode well for anyone attempting to launch a career as a commercial pilot, flight attendant, cruise director, or travel agent!

Nonetheless, millions of people still travel and economies do change for the better. Indeed, this industry frequently experiences booms and busts in response to economic and security changes. In fact, worldwide tourism since 2002 has been growing annually by more than three percent despite global economic difficulties and threats of war and terrorism. According to the World Tourism Organization (WTO), international tourist arrivals increased from 693 million in 2001 to 715 million in 2003. While tourist arrivals in the United States were down and fewer Americans traveled abroad, tourism in Europe, Asia, and the South Pacific increased by nearly 5 percent, with Spain, Italy, Greece, the United Kingdom, and Australia doing very well.

The travel industry remains very large and vibrant, although it is undergoing major restructuring in the United States, especially consolidation, because of difficult economic times and the continuing application of technology to travel planning. For example, some observers believe only two major U.S. air carriers will survive in the decade ahead. Several cruise lines may merge because of over-capacity. Online travel services are likely to further erode the traditional role of the commission-based travel agent.

Most important of all for job seekers, the travel and hospitality industry remains one of the most exciting and satisfying of any industry. During tough economic times, competition will be keen for many jobs which only a few years ago appeared plentiful. For dedicated and passionate travel professionals, many of whom have weathered previous economic cycles, this industry will continue to reward them in many ways. For some people, this may be the perfect time to break into an uncertain industry, especially if they have the right set of skills and motivations to contribute to an employer's bottom line or are entrepreneurial enough to launch their own travel business.

The Industry and Its Many Players

The travel industry is much more than the stereotypical travel agent arranging tickets, tours, and hotels for tour groups and anxious tourists. This is a highly segmented industry consisting of a network of mutually dependent players – airlines, hotels, resorts, cruise lines, restaurants, wholesalers, incentive groups, retail tour agents, car rental companies, catering firms, meeting planners, corporate travel divisions, educators, journalists, and travel writers. These as well as a host of related organizations, individuals, and jobs are focused on the business of moving and managing people from one location to another.

The travel industry is a challenging, exciting, and highly entrepreneurial industry. Its many players report a high degree of job satisfaction. Indeed, many claim to have found *"the best job in the world"* – and with all the perks to prove it! Public relations directors in major hotels, for example, often meet and entertain celebrities, work closely with the local business community, and participate in numerous community activities – a worklife many still can't believe they "fell into" in the travel industry.

> *Individuals working in this industry manage to advance their careers by moving from one player to another with relative ease.*

While many of these travel businesses, such as major airlines and hotel chains, are huge corporations, most travel-related businesses appear big but are actually small and highly entrepreneurial. They appear large because they are connected to one another through efficient communication and marketing systems which place everyone within a mutually interdependent network of business transactions. It's the type of business where there is a high degree of competition as well as mutual dependence and cooperation. Individuals working in this industry manage to advance their careers by moving from one player to another with relative ease.

Motivation and Skills

If your major motivation for seeking a job is your desire to travel and see and experience new places, and if you seek challenges, like to do different things, and have a sense of entrepreneurship, you should seriously investigate the variety of job and career opportunities available in the travel industry. If you are especially interested in an international job, this may be the perfect industry for you. In contrast to many other international jobs that require a great deal of education, foreign language expertise, and international experience, the international travel business favors those who demonstrate entrepreneurship and job performance skills relevant to the particular industry. In other words, it's much easier to break into this field than into many other international fields. Many individuals with only a high school education and little initial experience are able to pursue successful careers in the travel industry.

Positives and Negatives

Like any other industry, the travel industry has its positives and negatives. Depending on which segment of the industry you enter, you will find few high-paying jobs. In fact, individuals in these sectors make about 20 to 30 percent less than people in other industries, including government. However, they do get special travel benefits and perks not available elsewhere, and employees in this industry report a high degree of job satisfaction. Many people in the industry do not travel as much as they originally thought they would, or they travel too much to the point where travel is no longer as exciting as it once was.

This is a truly global industry with a great deal of movement of employees among countries and segments of the industry.

At the same time, given the highly segmented and interdependent nature of the industry, careers in travel may involve working for several segments within the industry. For example, you may start out working on a cruise line, then later work for a hotel or resort chain, and finally move into the incentive travel business or the airlines. This mobility among segments within the industry leads to interesting and challenging career changes and work environments. It enables individuals to advance their careers with many different employers.

A Highly Segmented Industry

The travel industry is the ultimate example of a highly segmented yet integrated industry where entrepreneurship plays a key role in the continuing vitality and expansion of the industry as well as the career mobility of individuals within the industry. Within the United States, it's an industry that moves over $1.3 trillion in travel spending each year. It employs nearly 8 million people in over 500,000 businesses, from small mom-and-pop travel agencies to large corporate hotels and airlines. Huge franchised travel agencies such as Carlson Wagonlit (www.carlsontravel.com) and American Express Travel Services (www.americanexpress.com/travel), incentive travel groups such as Carlson (www.carlsonconnected.com) and Maritz (www.maritztravel.com), and the military/government-focused SatoTravel (www.satotravel.com) offer thousands of job opportunities. When linked to travel industries in other countries – including airlines, hotels, tour companies, ground operators, and incentive groups – this is a truly global industry characterized by a great deal of movement of employees among countries and segments of the industry.

The major segments or sub-industries and players within the travel industry include operators, suppliers, promoters, and supporters:

- travel agencies and operators
- corporate travel managers
- tour operators
- incentive travel companies
- accommodations and lodging industry
- convention and meeting planners
- airlines
- cruise lines
- rail services
- car rentals
- bus lines
- advertising agencies
- research and marketing groups
- publishing and journalism
- travel clubs
- resorts and spas
- theme parks
- tourist sites and attractions
- restaurants
- airport and aviation management groups
- government tourist promotion offices
- travel insurance
- tour guiding
- travel writers and photographers
- culture and arts promotion groups

- travel education and training
- advertising
- public relations
- sales and marketing
- computer support services
- travel websites (e-travel)

Not surprisingly, the travel industry employs numerous types of workers from accountants, computer specialists, and lawyers to market researchers, artists, and doctors. Many people also are able to freelance in this industry as wholesalers, travel agents, writers, photographers, trainers, and consultants.

You don't need a great deal of education and training to make it in this industry.

While many people in this industry do little travel, others may do a great deal of travel as part of their day-to-day work. Onboard cruise personnel, tour operators, guides, travel agents, travel writers, and photographers are frequently "on assignment" covering a variety of destinations. They are the well-heeled travelers of the cruise industry. On the other hand, individuals working in hotels, resorts, spas, restaurants, and e-travel and those involved with such support services as public relations, advertising, education, research, and law may do very little travel. However, if they work abroad, they may be involved in exciting international work environments that enable them to engage in the type of travel they most desire.

Breaking In

There are no hard and fast rules on how to break into the travel industry. The bad news is that it is a highly competitive industry given its glamorous reputation and the numerous job seekers who want to break in. The good news is that it is a multi-faceted growth industry that offers many opportunities for individuals with the right combination of motivation, skills, abilities, interests, and drive. The good news also is that for many jobs you don't need a great deal of initial education and training to make it in this industry. The necessary skills are specific to each segment within the industry, and they are best acquired on the job.

Therefore, what you most need are an entry-level job, an ability to learn, and entrepreneurial drive. With these you can acquire skills and contacts that will help you to later move within this dynamic industry.

While hundreds of trade schools, colleges, and universities offer travel programs and several travel schools offer courses of study that ostensibly lead to travel careers, the industry has yet to recognize such formal educational mechanisms as necessary prerequisites for entry into and advancement within the industry. Nonetheless, many of these programs and schools can assist you in specialized areas within the industry. They also can assist you in finding jobs through their network of contacts within the industry.

If you are interested in attending a travel school, many of which offer six-month to one-year full-time courses of study, some of the best known and respected ones include: Bay Path College, Wilma Boyd Career Schools, Colorado School of Travel, Echols International Travel and Hotel School, Intensive Trainers, International Aviation and Travel Academy, International Travel Institute, International Travel Training Courses, Mundus Institute of Travel, The New York School of Travel, Southeastern Academy, Omega Travel School, Travel Career School of Minnesota, Travel Education Center, and Travel Trade School.

Numerous community colleges and distance learning institutions also offer travel programs. Many of these schools can be found through the "Travel School Directory" attached to the "How to Become a Travel Agent" document provided by the American Society of Travel Agents (www.astanet.com/join/tsc.asp). Also, check out the travel, hospitality, and culinary schools sections of these websites:

- **Directory of Schools**   www.directoryofschools.com
- **Education Online Search**   www.education-online-search.com
- **The Education Portal**   http://education-portal.com
- **Trade-Schools.net**   www.trade-schools.net
- **W³Education.org**   www.w3education.org

If you are interested in the hotel industry, Cornell University's School of Hotel Administration has a fine reputation. Other universities offering special degree programs in travel include: Adelphi University, Clemson University, Florida International University, George Washington University, Metropolitan State College (Denver), Michigan State University,

National College (Rapid City), New School for Social Research, Parks College of St. Louis University, Quinsigamond Community College, Rochester Institute of Technology, Santa Ana College, University of Hawaii, University of Nevada, University of New Haven, University of New Orleans, and University of Notre Dame.

An excellent resource for identifying appropriate education and training programs related to hospitality and tourism is CHRIE's *A Guide to College Programs in Hospitality, Tourism, and Culinary Arts.* It's available in CD-ROM and downloadable formats. This is a rich resource for locating programs that best relate to your interests. Information on this publication, as well as this professional organization, can be found by visiting its website: www.chrie.org.

You will also find several internship opportunities available with businesses in the travel industry. An internship can be an important way to acquire specialized experience and develop contacts within the industry. For information on internships, including extensive coverage on international internships, see the latest edition of the annual internship book *Internships* (Peterson's) and/or visit these websites:

- InternJobs.com   www.internjobs.com
- Internsearch.com   www.internsearch.com
- InternshipPrograms.com   http://internships.wetfeet.com
- Internships.com   www.internships.com
- Rising Star Internships   www.rsinternships.com

For information on international internships, visit the internship section of the University of California, Irvine, Center for International Education's website: www.cie.uci.edu/iop/internsh.html.

While many of the formal education and training programs do have placement programs for graduates, your best strategy for breaking into the travel industry will be to **network** among individuals within the various segments of this industry. Join travel-related associations, attend conferences, make contacts, conduct informational interviews, and locate job vacancies that best fit your interests, skills, and abilities. Most entry-level positions will be based in the U.S. and hopefully provide opportunities to travel and work abroad.

Travel Agencies and Operators

Travel agencies and operators primarily provide travel services for individuals, businesses, and government. Operating as the critical link between travel suppliers and the public, travel agencies and operators arrange airline tickets, cruises, hotels, and car rentals; offer packaged tours; and provide advice on the latest travel itineraries and costs.

The World of Agencies and Operators

The world of travel agencies and operators consists of nearly 80,000 firms, from small mom-and-pop travel agencies to a few large mega-firms such as American Express and Carlson Wagonlit, which have hundreds of offices nationwide and abroad. The trend within the industry is toward consolidation with larger firms offering a wide variety of travel services. Indeed, the 2003 merger of Rosenbluth International with American Express was one of the largest such mergers in the history of the travel industry.

The travel agent is the most common position operating within this industry. Approximately 120,000 travel agents were working nationwide in 2006. By the year 2012 employment of travel agents is expected to decline due to numerous changes within the industry that have reduced the need for travel agents. More than 80 percent of travel agents work for travel agencies. Nearly 50 percent of travel agencies are located in suburban areas; 40 percent are found in large cities; and the remainder operate in small towns and rural areas. Many travel agents are self-employed and increasingly use the Internet to do their work.

Since the late 1990s, travel agents have experienced numerous challenges to their future career development. Indeed, the travel agent has become an endangered occupation given three recent trends in the travel industry: airlines capping or eliminating commissions to travel agencies; the ability of individuals to make direct reservations via the Internet through e-travel companies; and ticketless airline reservations. Caps on and elimination of agency commissions have forced many travel agencies to cut back on personnel who normally handle ticketing arrangements. Thousands of travel agencies have gone out of business during the past five years because of this change in commission structure. The rapid development of Internet booking services has allowed over 70 percent of all travelers in 2006 to make their own reservations directly with airlines or on travel websites and thereby bypass travel agents who now charge service fees for arranging airline tickets. Since most airlines have gone to a ticketless reservation system (e-tickets), the need for travel agencies to make reservations and issue tickets has significantly declined. We expect the number of travel agents to continue to decline in the face of such ongoing restructuring. Others will become more specialized by focusing on cruises, hotels, tours, car rentals, and international travel, from which they continue to receive a 7-10 percent commission.

The number and variety of job opportunities will vary depending upon the size of an agency. Small mom-and-pop agencies, with annual sales of $1-2 million a year, primarily have two or three travel agents whose main job is to make travel reservations for individuals and corporations. Linked to travel suppliers through computerized reservation systems, the ostensibly glamorous job of travel agent is often anything but glamorous. Travel agents often operate in a pressure cooker atmosphere; they are constantly on the telephone and computer terminal arranging travel itineraries for clients.

Larger agencies – those with annual sales of $25 million or more – offer numerous other travel services as well as additional job opportunities for customer service representatives, account executives, human resources specialists, trainers, accountants, meeting planners, product development managers, fare negotiators, public relations professionals, marketing managers, cruise specialists, and inventory control coordinators. The largest agencies tend to specialize in corporate travel rather than individual travelers. Many of the mega-agencies have more than 75 percent of their business tied to the lucrative corporate travel market. The larger agencies tend to be disproportionately found in major metropolitan areas. Some large agencies, such as Omega World Travel (www.owt.net), also operate their own travel schools.

Salaries, Benefits, and Opportunities

Salaries and career opportunities with large agencies are much better than among small travel agencies. The median annual earnings of travel agents in 2004 was $27,640. The lowest 10 percent earned less than $17,180 per year. The highest 10 percent earned more than $44,090 per year.

For many individuals, the real benefit of working for travel agencies lies with the travel perks available for travel professionals. Travel suppliers, such as airlines, cruises, car rentals, hotels, and tour operators, routinely give travel agents discounts on their services. These discounts range from as little as 25% to as much as 50% or more. In some cases, travel agents receive free or greatly discounted services, especially when familiarization or "fam" trips are offered to travel agencies in exchange for promoting new tour packages. In practice, however, only a few travel agents have the time or money to take advantage of such travel perks. In fact, many travel agents confine their "travel experience" to arranging itineraries and reservations for their clients and hearing about everyone else's travel experiences! Nonetheless, travel benefits can be substantial for travel professionals who take advantage of the many opportunities available for discounted travel.

Breaking In

There are no hard and fast rules for breaking into travel agencies. Many people with high school educations and little work experience readily find entry-level jobs with small travel agencies. Those with good telephone and organizational skills, computer competence, ability to work under pressure, and a knowledge of geography tend to do well in these jobs. However, the trend among travel agencies is toward recruiting individuals with more specialized training. This hiring preference reflects the fact that few agencies are willing to give on-the-job training.

Many individuals now gain entry into travel agencies by first attending vocational schools, travel schools, or specialized training programs to acquire basic travel agency skills. Indeed, travel agencies more and more turn to these schools for recruiting trained personnel.

More than 1,200 travel schools operate a variety of programs for individuals interested in breaking into this field. These programs can vary widely in quality as well as breadth and depth of skills training. Many vocational schools offer 3- to 12-week full-time programs as well as evening and weekend programs. Many adult education programs, business schools, community colleges, and four-year colleges offer travel courses. A few colleges and universities offer bachelor's and master's degrees in travel and tourism.

If you are interested in surveying training opportunities, contact the following groups for copies of their directories of travel schools:

American Society of Travel Agents (ASTA)
1101 King Street, Suite 200
Alexandria, VA 22314
Website: www.astanet.com
Tel. 703-739-2782

ASTA provides numerous services to aspiring travel professionals, including membership in a Future Travel Professionals Club, job fairs, job listings (job board), and scholarships. They also offer home-study courses and online education programs.

Tourism Cares for Tomorrow
585 Washington Street
Canton, MA 02021
Website: www.ntfonline.org
Tel. 781-821-5990
info@tourismcares.org

Created in 2003 by combining the National Tourism Foundation and the Travelers Conservation Foundation, this organization supports the travel and tourism industry by investing and distributing millions of dollars in scholarships, internships, and grants. It also maintains an online database of more than 600 schools (see its "What We Do – Students – Find a School" section) that offer credentials in tourism programs, from certificates to Ph.Ds. Also includes internships, job fairs, job openings, scholarships, networking opportunities (links to practitioners), and a calendar of events.

The Travel Institute
www.thetravelinstitute.com

Maintains a database of Licensed Schools that offer education and training programs for different types of certifications: Certified Travel Associate (CTA), Certified Travel Counselor (CTC), Destination Specialist (DS), or Lifestyle Specialist (LS).

Other professional travel and hospitality organizations with information on education opportunities include:

International Society of Travel and Tourism Educators
23220 Edgewater
St. Clair Shores, MI 48082
Website: www.istte.org
Tel./Fax 586-294-0208

**International Council on Hotel, Restaurant, and
Institutional Education**
2613 North Parham Road, 2nd Floor
Richmond, VA 23294
Website: www.chrie.org
Tel. 804-346-4800

**Educational Institute of the American Hotel
and Lodging Association**
800 N. Magnolia Avenue, Suite 1800
Orlando, FL 32803
Website: www.ei-ahma.org
Tel. 407-999-8100

National Restaurant Association Educational Foundation
175 West Jackson Boulevard, Suite 1500
Chicago, IL 60604-2814
Website: www.nraef.org
Tel. 800-765-2122

Some of the larger mega-agencies, such as American Express Travel Services and Carlson Wagonlit Travel, operate their own schools and training programs from which they recruit their own personnel. The following companies offer Internet-based distance learning programs on tourism:

Travel Education Center
Bay Path College
Website: www.traveleducation.com
Tel. 800-782-7284

TravelCampus
Education Systems
11038 Longdale Circle
Sandy, UT 84092
Tel. 800-288-3987
Website: www.travelcampus.com

One of the most widely recognized and respected educational programs in the industry is offered by The Travel Institute (previously known as the Institute of Certified Travel Agents – ICTA). Individuals completing their programs become a Certified Travel Counselor (CTC), Certified Travel Associate (CTA), or Certified Travel Industry Executive (CTIE). The programs are designed for self-study, and many are offered at Licensed Schools throughout the U.S. For information on these programs, contact:

The Travel Institute
148 Linden Street, Suite 305
Wellesley, MA 02482
Website: www.icta.com
Tel. 800-542-4282 or fax 781-237-3860

Travel agencies and operators are truly entrepreneurial operations. While these are very competitive businesses whose fortunes tend to fluctuate with general economic conditions and the overall state of the travel industry, the good news is that the travel industry will continue to grow in the coming decade despite recent downturns. Expect more and more job opportunities in most segments of this industry, and especially among the large and mega-agencies which continue to develop new and highly specialized service capabilities. The jobs increasingly require higher levels of education, training, and experience. Expect more and more agencies to turn to specialized training programs for meeting their recruitment and training needs.

For many people, this end of the travel business gets into their blood; they simply love the customer contacts and the organizational challenges – with or without the accompanying travel perks. While much of their work will be confined to the office, telephone, and computer terminal, they can travel – and travel well – if they choose to do so. Indeed, taking an occasional trip and working with satisfied customers who share their travel experiences contribute a great deal to high levels of job satisfaction.

Resources

The following books should provide useful for finding a job or starting a business in this segment of the travel and hospitality industry:

Careers in Travel, Tourism, and Hospitality, Marjorie Eberts, et. al (McGraw-Hill, 2005)

Heads in Beds: Hospitality and Tourism Marketing, Ivo Raza (Prentice Hall, 2004)

Home-Based Travel Agent, 5th Edition, Kelly Monaghan (Intrepid Traveler, 2006)

How to Organize Group Travel for Fun and Profit, Carl Meadows (ETC Publishing, 2002)

Inside Secrets to Finding a Career in Travel, Karen Rubin (JIST Publishing, 2001)

Start Your Own Specialty Travel & Tour Business (Entrepreneur Press, 2004)

Tourism: The Business of Travel, 3rd Edition, Roy A. Cook, Laura J. Yale, and Joseph J. Marqua (Prentice Hall, 2005)

The Travel Agent's Complete Desk Reference, 4th Edition, Kelly Monaghan (The Intrepid Traveler, 2006)

Useful Websites

The following websites are of special interest to travel agents. These high-traffic websites will quickly introduce you to the professional world of travel agents. Some websites provide access to thousands of travel agents – great resources for networking with individuals in the profession.

- American Society of
  Travel Agents   www.astanet.com
- Business Travel News   www.btnmag.com
- Hotel and Travel Index   www.htihotelink.com
- The Travel Institute   www.icta.com
- International Air
  Transport Association   www.iata.org
- Mail Pound   www.mailpound.com
- Modern Agent   www.modernagent.com
- TAedge   www.taedge.com
- Travel Trade   www.traveltrade.com
- Travel Weekly   www.travelweekly.com

Other useful websites relevant to travel agents, as well as individuals interested in breaking into this industry include:

- Airlines Reporting Corp.   www.arccorp.com
- American Express
  Travel Services   www.americanexpress.com
- Association of Retail
  Travel Agents   www.artaonline.com
- Carlson Wagonlit   www.carlsontravel.com
- Incentive Travel   www.carlsontravelexperience.com
- Intelliguide   www.intelliguide.com
- International Airlines
  Travel Agent Network   www.iatan.org
- Maritz   www.maritztravel.com
- National Association of
  Commissioned Travel Agents   www.nacta.com
- Travel Agent Central   www.travelagentcentral.com
- Vacation.com   www.vacation.com

Anyone interested in developing their own e-travel agency, or adding an e-commerce component to their travel-related website, should check out the affiliate programs offered by these major online travel companies and well as become associated with the major e-travel organizations:

E-Travel Affiliate Programs:

- Expedia   www.expedia.com
- Orbitz   www.orbitz.com
- Priceline   www.priceline.com
- Travelocity   www.travelocity.com
- World Choice Travel   www.worldchoicetravel.com

Major E-Travel Players (including e-travel affiliates):

- Amadeus   www.amadeus.com
- American Express   www.americanexpress.com
- Cendant   www.cendant.com
- CheapTickets   www.cheaptickets.com
- Hotwire   www.hotwire.com
- OneTravel.com   www.onetravel.com
- Orbitz   www.orbitz.com
- Priceline.com   www.priceline.com
- Trip.com   www.trip.com
- World Choice Travel   www.worldchoicetravel.com

e-Travel Organizations:

- E-Travel   www.e-travel.com
- Interactive Travel
  Services Association   www.interactivetravel.org
- PhoCusWright   www.phocuswright.com

In fact, you can have your own travel website instantly developed by using the travel website development services of travel agency-related TAedge: www.taedge.com/infotcsb. Plug into one of the travel affiliate programs and you can be off and running with your own online travel agency as well as reap the travel benefits extended to professional travel agents! WorldChoiceTravel (www.worldchoicetravel.com) also offers its affiliates ready-to-use travel websites. Our own travel website – www.travel-smarter.com – is a good example of a website developed through such affiliate relationships.

Airline Industry

Here's one of the most interesting and rewarding industries in the travel business. Despite an 11-percent drop in employment during 2001 – from 732,000 to 653,000 jobs – everyone seems to love this high-flying feast-and-famine industry. For airline employees, jet fuel seems to get in their blood! For airport security personnel, the airline industry appears to be a growth industry as thousands of new positions were created in 2002 to ensure greater airport and airline security.

A highly volatile industry, due to a combination of airline deregulation since 1978, occasional recessions, and major mergers and restructuring, the airline industry nonetheless offers excellent opportunities for individuals interested in travel. Today, over 130 carriers operate within the United States. Three major carriers – United, American, and Delta – control over 60 percent of the airline market as well as monopolize air travel in and out of their major hubs (Chicago, Atlanta, Dallas/Ft. Worth).

Today over 500,000 individuals work for the airline industry. In 2002 U.S. airlines with the largest number of employees included:

Airlines	Employees (January 2002) (Full time and part time)
Alaska	10,515
American Airlines	91,076
American Eagle	9,038
American Trans Air	6,967
American West	12,181
Continental Airlines	39,461
Delta Airlines	74,103
DHL	10,634
Federal Express	141,028
Northwest Airlines	45,701
Southwest Airlines	32,674
United Airlines	84,113
USAir	37,095

Other national and regional airlines, such as Air Wisconsin, Aloha, Atlantic Southeast, Frontier, Hawaiian, Horizon, JetBlue, Midway Express, and Spirit employed between 2,000 and 4,000 each.

However, the airline industry has been in a major economic crisis since 2002 due to a combination of rising fuel costs, increased competition, declining business travel, high personnel costs, and crippling legacy costs. Nearly 40 percent of airline costs relate to personnel – one of the highest of any industry. As a result, several airlines have declared bankruptcy, merged with other troubled airlines, significantly cut back employee wages and benefits, and eliminated personnel and passenger services. Indeed, between 2002 and 2006, the major airlines shed over nearly 150,000 jobs. While this was not a good time to seek employment with U.S. airlines, nonetheless, many job opportunities still exist with airlines.

Like any big business, the airlines seek individuals with a variety of business and technical skills – accountants, salespeople, clerical workers, word processors, computer programmers and technicians, managers, marketers, engineers, mechanics, security personnel, public relations specialists – as well as individuals with skills more specific to the industry – pilots, flight attendants, and ticketing and reservation clerks.

Future Growth and Hiring

The U.S. airline industry transports nearly 700 million passengers a year. A highly competitive industry which often experiences cutthroat competition, periodic shake-outs, consolidation, and major financial losses, the airlines are expected to face several challenges in the next few years. Indeed, expect U.S. airlines to further consolidate as two or more major airlines go out of business and others merge.

On the other hand, hiring does not necessarily follow general growth and decline patterns. Airline personnel, generally, are the highest paid individuals within the travel industry, and job satisfaction traditionally has been higher among airline personnel than with individuals in most other industries. Competition for airline jobs, an attractive employment arena for thousands of individuals, is high and attrition is low. Except for retirees, few people voluntarily leave their airline jobs for other employment opportunities. Competition for such jobs is particularly intense during economic downturns which also become periods of consolidation.

Positions

Positions within the airline industry are generally divided into the following six areas:

1. **Flight Operations:** includes a variety of jobs essential for flight operations, from pilots and flight attendants to baggage handlers and meteorologists. The major such positions include:

   - Captain
   - Co-Pilot
   - Second Officer/Flight Engineer
   - Flight Attendant
   - Operations Agent
   - Flight Dispatcher
   - Meteorologist

2. **Maintenance and Engineering:** Includes several major positions for ensuring the proper maintenance and mechanical operations of aircraft:

   - Maintenance Inspector
   - Airframe and Power Plant (Engineer A&P) Mechanic
   - Instrument Technician
   - Radio Technician
   - Engineer

3. **Administration, Sales, and Marketing:** Includes numerous positions central for maintaining day-to-day operations and the competitive position of airlines. Good entry-level opportunities, which tend to expand during periods of consolidation, include:

   - Reservations Agent
   - Ticket Agent
   - Airport Operations Agent
   - Passenger Service Agent
   - Fleet Service Employee
   - Sales Representative

- District Sales Manager
- District Operations Manager
- Freight Airport Operations Agent
- Freight Telephone Sales Representative
- Fleet Service Clerk

4. **Management/Special Positions:** Includes a variety of positions that may overlap with other positions and which may be particular to a specific airline. Among these are:

- Crew Scheduler
- Incentive Sales Representative
- Inspector
- Instructor
- Programmer/Analyst
- Purchasing Agent
- Supervisor
- Industrial Engineer
- Foreman
- Executive Secretary
- Passenger Service Manager
- Personnel Representative
- Web Developer

Depending on the airline, numerous specialty areas offer a variety of job opportunities:

- Tour Operations
- Aircraft Purchase and Sales
- Charters
- Freight/Cargo
- Insurance
- Properties and Facilities
- Labor Relations
- Community and Environmental Affairs
- Purchasing
- Internet

5. **Computer Reservation Systems:** The lifeblood of the airline industry is its reservation system. Several positions relate to the operations of the four major systems – Sabre (America), Apollo (United), and Worldspan (Delta):

   - Computer Programmer
   - Technician
   - Sales Representative
   - Marketing Representative

6. **Food, Beverage, and Catering Services:** While most airlines contract for their food and beverage services, American Airlines operates its own meal service (Sky Chef). They hire for a variety of positions for handling their in-flight kitchen operations, from chefs to salad makers.

Benefits

Many positions with the airlines, especially pilots and flight attendants, involve extensive travel. Other positions may involve little or no on-the-job travel. Compensation with major airlines has been generally good compared to jobs in other segments of the travel industry, but this situation is changing given the economic crises of airlines. Salaries and benefits have recently been cut, and many airline personnel have sought second careers in light of cutbacks in hours and jobs. Airline personnel and their families still receive excellent travel benefits – free or nearly free travel on a standby, space-available basis as well as major discounts on confirmed reserved space.

Breaking In

Breaking into the airline industry depends on your particular skills and perseverance as well as the state of the economy. Most jobs are highly competitive, with some positions generating 1,000 applicants for every vacancy. Many positions require specialized education and training. The best job opportunities that also offer good career advancement opportunities will be disproportionately found at the hubs of the three major airlines (Chicago, Atlanta, Dallas/Ft. Worth) that hire over 60 percent of airline personnel.

Don't forget the dozens of smaller national and regional airlines in the U.S. Many offer excellent job opportunities and are easier to break into than the major airlines. Indeed, Dallas-based Southwest Airlines (www. southwest.com) is considered by many informed observers of the airline industry to be the best place for airline professionals to work. It remains one of America's best managed organizations that also boasts extremely high employee morale and job satisfaction. Relatively new, rapidly expanding, and profitable Salt Lake City- and New York-based JetBlue Airways (www.jetblue.com) also offers numerous job opportunities.

Small airlines headquartered abroad, many in Third World countries, offer opportunities for enterprising and highly skilled job seekers. While the pay may not be great and the equipment may be antiquated – pilots in Papua New Guinea, for example, may earn less than $40,000 a year, fly questionably maintained aircraft, and operate aircraft without a co-pilot – such airlines do offer opportunities to gain experience. And experience increasingly counts in this highly competitive global industry.

Resources

Several major trade publications provide useful information on developments within the airline industry as well as job information:

- *Air Transport World*   www.atwonline.com
- *AviationNow*   www.aviationnow.com
- *Aviation Week's AVweb*   www.avweb.com
- *Commuter/Regional Airline News* www.aviationtoday.com
- *Travel Agent Magazine*   www.travelagentcentral.com
- *Travel Trade*   www.traveltrade.com
- *Travel Weekly*   www.travelweekly.com

The following gateway site provides contact information and links to hundreds of aviation magazines, newspapers, and newsletters around the world: www.aero.com/publications/magazine.htm.

The following books examine job and career opportunities within the airline industry:

Inside Secrets to Finding a Career in Travel, Karen Rubin (JIST Publishing, 2001)

Opportunities in Travel Careers, Robert Scott Milne and
Marguerite Backhausen (McGraw-Hill, 2003)

Useful Websites

Several websites provide a wealth of information on career opportunities
in the airline industry. Some specialize in flight attendant (www.airline
career.com) and pilot (www.pilotswanted.com) positions while others
include a wide variety of ground and air crew positions (www.aviation
jobsonline.com):

AirlineCareer.com	www.airlinecareer.com
Airline Employee Placement Service	www.aeps.com
Airline Job Site	www.airlinejobsite.com
Airport Job Hub	www.airportjobhub.com
Airport Job Kiosk	www.airportjobkiosk.com
AviationNet	www.aviationnet.com
Aviation Information Resources	www.jet-jobs.com
Aviation Job Search	www.aviationjobsearch.com
AviationJobsOnline	www.aviationjobsonline.com
AVJobs	www.avjobs.com
Find a Pilot	www.findapilot.com
Flight Deck Recruitment	www.flightdeckrecruitment.com
Flying Talent	www.flyingtalent.com
Jet Careers	www.jetcareers.com
Jobs in Aviation	www.jobsinaviation.com
Pilots Wanted	www.pilotswanted.com
Traveljobz.net	www.traveljobz.net

Flight Attendant

Primarily responsible for the safety and comfort of passengers, flight
attendants represent much of the airline industry to the traveling public.
Approximately 100,000 flight attendants are employed by airlines in the
U.S. The airlines hire nearly 12,000 flight attendants each year. The
following airlines employ the largest number of flight attendants:

Airlines	Flight Attendants (est.)
American Airlines	23,000
Continental Airlines	10,000
Delta Airlines	15,000
Northwest Airlines	10,000
Southwest Airlines	5,000
United Airlines	21,000
USAir	9,000
Other	7,000

The Work

Often viewed as working in a glamorous job, flight attendants do travel a great deal and have flexible work schedules. However, starting pay tends to be low (lowest 10 percent earned $23,450 in 2004). Median annual earnings of flight attendants in 2004 were $43,440. The work of flight attendants can be very demanding and stressful. Flight attendants are responsible for ensuring the proper boarding and deplaning of passengers, preparing passengers for take-offs and landings, providing safety briefings, serving food and beverages, and responding to passenger requests for information and additional services. Despite the modest pay and stressful working conditions, many flight attendants simply love their work, especially their traveling lifestyle and being part of the airline culture.

Benefits

Few jobs offer so many opportunities to travel both on and off the job. Flight attendants by definition are constantly traveling on the job. They may work a four-day schedule during which time they might visit eight or ten cities. They may then have the next five or six days off before returning to work another four-day schedule. During off days and vacations they may choose to travel for pleasure.

One of the major benefits of being a flight attendant is free and discounted travel. Flight attendants can travel free – on a space-available basis, and often in business or first class – with their airline. If their airline has reciprocal agreements with other airlines, they can travel on these other carriers with special deeply discounted tickets. Hotels normally offer airline discounts to flight attendants – often 50 percent. These same travel benefits are usually extended to the flight attendant's family.

While starting pay is low, flight attendants with several years experience receive more adequate compensation. For example, 50 percent of flight attendants in 2004 earned between $31,310 and $67,590 a year. The highest 10 percent earn more than $95,850 a year. In general, however, this is not a well paid profession. The real benefits lie in the lifestyle of this segment of the travel industry.

The combination of constant travel, flexible work schedules, and free and discounted travel makes this a very attractive job for many individuals. It is so attractive that competition for flight attendant positions is very keen. Indeed, some airlines receive 100 or more applications for each flight attendant position.

Breaking In

Flight attendants are required to meet certain age, education, height, and communication requirements and attend tuition-based training programs. Nearly 50 percent of all flight attendants have a four-year college degree; 70 percent have some college experience.

For application information with the major airlines, visit their websites. Many airlines have online application forms or request faxed or mailed resumes. Check out the websites of these airlines for application information:

- Air Transport International   www.airtransport.cc
- Air Wisconsin   www.airwis.com
- AirTran Airways   www.airtran.com/jobs/employ ment_opportunitis.aspx
- Alaska Airlines   www.alaskaair.com
- Allegheny Airlines   www.alleghenyairlines.com
- Allegiant Air   www.allegiantair.com
- Aloha Airlines   www.alohaair.com
- American Airlines   www.aa.com
- American Eagle Airlines   www.americaneaglecareers.com
- American Trans Air   www.ata.com

- Atlantic Southeast Airlines   www.delta.com/asa
- Caribbean Star Airlines, Inc.   www.flycaribbeanstar.com
- Champion Air   www.championair.com
- Colgan Air   www.colganair.com
- Comair   www.comair.com
- Continental Airlines   www.continental.com
- Delta Air Lines   www.delta.com
- Era Aviation   www.flyera.com
- Express Jet   www.expressjetair.com
- Falcon Air Express   www.falconairexpress.net
- Frontier Airlines   www.flyfrontier.com
- Gulfstream International   www.gulfstreamair.com
- Hawaiian Airlines   www.hawaiianair.com
- Horizon Air   www.horizonair.com
- Island Air   www.islandair.com
- JetBlue Airways   www.jetblue.com
- Mesa Airlines   www.mesa-air.com
- Mesaba Airlines   www.mesaba.com
- Miami Air   www.miamiair.com
- Midwest Airlines   www.midwest-express.com
- National Airlines   www.nationalairlines.com
- North American Airlines   www.northamericanair.com
- Northwest Airlines   www.nwa.com
- Omni Air International   www.omniairintl.com
- Pace Airlines   www.paceairline.com
- PenAir   www.penair.com
- Piedmont Airlines   www.piedmont-airlines.com
- Pinnacle Airlines   www.nwairlink.com
- Ryan International   www.flyryan.com
- Shuttle America   www.shuttleamerica.com
- Skywest Airlines   www.skywest.com
- Southwest Airlines   www.southwest.com
- Spirit Airlines   www.spiritair.com
- Sun Country Airlines   www.suncountry.com
- Trans States   www.transstates.net
- United Airlines   www.united.com
- US Airways   www.usairways.com
- USA 3000 Airlines   www.usa3000.com

- World Airways   www.worldair.com

These three organizations provide job search and placement assistance for flight attendants. Each charges user fees to access their databases:

- AirlineCareer.com   www.airlinecareer.com
- Airline Employee
  Placement Service   www.aeps.com
- AVjobs.com   www.avjobs.com

Resources

For information on flight attendant opportunities, refer to the following books which provide details on how to become a flight attendant, including lots of contact information:

The Essential Guide to Becoming a Flight Attendant, Kiki Ward (Kiki Productions, 2001)

Flight Attendant Job Finder and Career Guide, Tim Kirkwood, 2nd Edition (Planning/Communication, 2002)

Vault Guide to Flight Attendant Careers, Mark Gazdik (Vault, Inc., 2005)

Welcome Aboard! Your Career as a Flight Attendant, Becky S. Bock and Cheryl A. Cage (Cage Consulting, 2000)

For humorous stories about the trials and tribulations of working at 35,000 feet as a flight attendant, which also give a revealing look at the work of flight attendants, be sure to read these four delightful books:

The Air Traveler Tales From the Flight Crew: The Plane Truth At 35,000 Feet, A. Frank Steward (Impact Publications, 2006)

Around the World in a Bad Mood! Confessions of a Flight Attendant, Rene Foss (Theia, 2002)

The Plane Truth: Shift Happens At 35,000 Feet, A. Frank Steward (Impact Publications, 2003)

Plane Insanity, Elliott Hester (Griffin Trade, 2003)

Pilot

If you want a job that enables you to travel a lot, being a pilot is the ultimate job. Holding one of the most respected positions in the airline culture, you're in charge. Better still, you receive excellent salary and benefits for your travel passion!

Airline pilots have one of the most prestigious and well paid jobs in the airline industry. They fly airplanes and helicopters in the process of hauling millions of passengers and tons of cargo and mail. They dust crops, reseed forests, take photographs, test aircraft, fight fires, assist with police and rescue work, and engage in logging, offshore natural resource exploration, and weather operations.

Approximately 110,000 civilian pilots are employed in the United States. Nearly 60 percent are employed with the airlines.

Requirements and Outlook

Licensed by the FAA, pilots must meet certain age (18-32), physical (excellent), and flight experience (3,000+ hours) requirements. Most have college educations, and the airlines prefer to hire college graduates.

Nearly 75 percent of all pilots receive their training through the military. Given the continuing shakeout of the airline industry, the job outlook for budding commercial pilots does not appear to be good. As in the 1990s, many pilots leaving the military in the hopes of finding jobs as commercial pilots will be disappointed with their poor job prospects; since 2001 airlines have been cutting back rather than hiring new pilots. Many of these highly motivated and skilled job seekers will miss the small window of opportunity they must have (prime age and experience levels) when making the transition from military to civilian aviation. Civilian trained pilots face an equally poor job market.

However, there are a few bright spots in this industry for experienced pilots. The job outlook for commercial pilots with experience improved somewhat in recent years as the airline industry continued to expand due to a strong economy. Much of the expansion took place with small regional airlines which pay much less than the major airlines. However, competition for these jobs will remain very keen because of low turnover. The good news is that many senior pilots are retiring. Their continuing departure will provide new opportunities for entry-level pilots. Expect the employment environment to be very competitive within the next few years as airlines continue to struggle with over-capacity and shrinking business travel which had fueled commercial travel in recent years.

Positions and Benefits

The major pilot positions include Captain, First Officer (Co-Pilot), and Second Officer (Flight Engineer). Individuals in each of these positions must be certified by the Federal Aviation Administration as well as have a current medical certificate.

Airline pilots with the major airlines earn some of the highest salaries of any occupation. However, most pilots do not work for those airlines. The median annual earnings of commercial pilots were $53,870 in May 2004. The lowest 10 percent earned less than $26,300. The highest 10 percent earned more then $110,070. Pilots working with jet aircraft and with the major airlines receive higher salaries than those working with nonjet aircraft and with regional airlines. Pilots working with noncommercial airlines receive lower salaries.

Airline pilots receive a host of excellent benefits, ranging from life, health, and disability insurance to free or reduced fares on their own or other airlines.

Resources

If you are interested in becoming an airline pilot, contact the following organizations for information on training opportunities, requirements, salaries, and job opportunities:

The Aerospace Education Foundation
1501 Lee Highway
Arlington, VA 22209-1198
Website: www.aef.org
Tel. 800-291-8480 or Fax 703-247-5853

Air Transport Association of America, Inc
1301 Pennsylvania Avenue, NW, Suite 1100
Washington, DC 20004-1707
Website: www.airlines.org
Tel. 202-626-4000

Air Line Pilots Association
Pilot Information Program
Education Department
1625 Massachusetts Avenue, NW
Washington, DC 20036
Website: www.alpa.org
Tel. 703-689-2270

Helicopter Association International
1635 Prince Street
Alexandria, VA 22314-2818
Website: www.ROTOR.com
Tel. 703-683-4646

Regional Airline Association
2025 M Street, NW, Suite 800
Washington, DC 20036-3309
Website: www.raa.org
Tel. 202-367-1170

Several books also provide useful information for individuals interested in becoming an airline pilot:

Airline Pilot Interviews, Irv Jasinski (Aviation Book Co., 2002)

Flight Guide to Success: Tips and Tactics for the Aspiring Airline Pilot, Karen M. Kahn (Cheltenham Publishing Co., 2004)

Flying the Big Birds: On Becoming An Airline Pilot, Sylvia J. Otypka (Leading Edge Publishing, 1998)

Get It! A Pocket Pilot Career and Job Search Navigation Guide, Ruth Ann Trent (AuthorHouse, 2003)

Job Hunting for Pilots: Networking Your Way to a Flying Job, Gregory N. Brown (Iowa State University Press, 2002)

Professional Pilot Career Guide, Robert P. Mark (McGraw-Hill, 1999)

Working in Aviation, Verite Reily Collins (Vacation Work Publications, 2005)

Cruise Lines

Have you ever dreamed of working on the Love Boat? Put in exotic ports two or three times each week? Explore the Seven Seas, retracing the routes of some of the world's great explorers and writers? Eat great food, enjoy terrific entertainment, and party all day long? Do you want to combine your work and play in a truly hedonistic manner, travel free, and make great money at the same time?

These are stereotypical dreams of many individuals who see cruise ship work as the really glamorous end of the travel industry. Filled with numerous myths, but also involving many sobering realities, cruise ship jobs offer a very special worklife of hard work and play centered on a great deal of ocean travel. It is more a life than just another travel job. Work on a cruise ship and you will certainly travel a great deal. Best of all, you'll travel, eat, and sleep free while making a living!

Growing Industry

The cruise industry has experienced phenomenal growth during the past decade as interest in cruise vacations has increased and as more and more mega-cruise ships have come online. Each year cruise ships carry nearly 8 million North American passengers. The number of passengers is likely to double over the coming decade as more and more people choose cruise ships as their favorite mode of vacation-resort travel. In response to this projected growth in passengers, nearly 50 new cruise ships have come online during the past five years. Even Disney has launched its own cruise ships (Big Red Boat Cruises) as it continues to diversify its already substantial travel empire. Such growth translates into more and more jobs in this much sought-after industry.

Myths and Realities

There are many myths about cruise line jobs. The biggest myths are that these jobs are all fun and games, they pay well, and there are plenty of opportunities available onboard for Americans. The realities are that most cruise line jobs are hard work and do not pay well. And few Americans find jobs onboard. Cruise ship jobs involve long hours, a great deal of stress, a willingness to work with a diverse multinational team, an ability to please all types of passengers, and the willingness to give exceptional and exacting service. Above all, you must be people-oriented, tolerant, flexible,

> *Few Americans work on board. Most are found in entertainment, physical fitness, and sports.*

and handle stress well. You must have the disposition of a servant – the customer is always right, even though he may be a jerk!

If you have a family, an onboard cruise ship job is likely to involve long separations. For many Americans, it's the type of job best enjoyed by young single individuals who see cruise ship jobs as short-term travel positions or entry-level positions for moving within the larger travel and hospitality industry. Many Americans will spend three to five years working with cruise lines – accumulating valuable travel and resort experience – before "settling down" to more stable family-oriented jobs on shore.

But our myths become important realities for individuals from many other nations that make up the diverse multinational crews of most cruise ships. With foreign ownership and registry, most cruise ships are operated with crews from Greece, Italy, Portugal, Indonesia, and the Philippines. These nationals tend to work for low wages, with many primarily surviving on passenger tips. Few Americans work onboard, and those that do tend to be found in a very limited number of "American" positions – entertainment, gift shop, youth counselor, physical fitness, and sports. You won't find many Americans piloting ships, managing restaurants, serving tables, cooking food, or making beds. These positions tend to be dominated by other nationals. Most American cruise ship involvement tends to be on shore – in marketing, sales, and computer reservation systems.

The significance of such employment within a multinational context has different meanings for different nationals. For many nationals, cruise ship jobs are more than just short-term travel jobs; they are great job opportunities – well paid, secure, and prestigious compared to the limited job opportunities back home. While many foreign nationals – especially those from such Third World countries as the Philippines and Indonesia who occupy numerous low-paying positions in housekeeping and the kitchen – make cruise ship jobs a long-term career, few Americans pursue such jobs as a career. Greeks and Italians tend to be in charge of food and beverage services and general ship operations. Given their limited job options back home, cruise ship jobs for such nationals are considered excellent paying, secure, and prestigious jobs. They can save money to support their families back home. Americans, who consider such employment to be low-paying, don't last long in such crew environments.

Americans tend to be disproportionately found in the entertainment, physical fitness, public relations, youth counseling, spa, shop, casino, and marketing and sales end of cruise ship jobs. Despite all the glamour, cruise ship pay and lifestyles simply are not sufficiently attractive for many Americans to continue long-term in this industry. Americans also are not noted for their talent in dispensing exceptional, exacting, and high-level service that is the hallmark of many cruise lines. Many Americans most typically pursue cruise ship jobs in the hopes of moving on to other jobs within the travel and hospitality industry, especially with hotels, resorts, restaurants, casinos, and night clubs. A cruise ship job is often a short stop along the way to other more rewarding jobs and careers.

Positions and Benefits

Cruise ship jobs are highly competitive. Operating like large resorts whose main purpose is to pamper their guests during short three- to 14-day cruises, most cruise ships maintain a high staff-per-passenger ratio. They hire for every type of department and position you would find in five-star resorts – housekeeping, kitchen, entertainment, health, fitness, tours, gaming, guest relations, engineering, maintenance, hair salon, and gift shop. They hire accountants, cooks, waiters, engineers, casino operators, pursers, photographers, massage therapists, cosmetologists, doctors, nurses, entertainers, youth counselors, water sports instructors, fitness instructors, and lecturers. However, they disproportionately hire crew members from Southern Europe and Asia.

While the pay may not be great for many Americans, cruise ship jobs offer numerous other benefits that can outweigh the limited financial rewards. The major benefits are free travel, food, and accommodations – unusual benefits for any job! In addition, cruise ship jobs can provide valuable experience that can be transferred to numerous other jobs in the travel and hospitality industry, especially in hotel management, food and beverage service, entertainment, and public relations. Individuals working in this industry are well positioned to work in resort operations.

Breaking In

Breaking into the cruise industry is relatively easy given the high turnover rate of personnel and the availability of numerous entry-level positions. Functioning as a combination floating city, resort, and hotel, most cruise shops operate with a staff of 300 to 900 who provide a wide range of services. As a result, cruise lines are constantly hiring for all types of positions. The most common shipboard opportunities are found in:

- **Front desk/purser's desk:** Positions include chief purser, assistant purser, guest services staff members.

- **Boutiques/shops:** sales staff and cashiers.

- **Restaurants and bars:** Chef, sous chef, pastry cook, baker, wine steward, buffet staff, food and beverage staff, bartender, Maitre d', wait staff, busboy, butcher, ice carver, dishwasher.

- **Casino:** Cashier, dealer, slot technician.

- **Salon and spa:** Massage therapist, cosmetologist, hair stylist, nail technician, masseur/masseuse.

- **Operations:** Computer specialist, electrician, machinist, and painter.

- **Show lounges:** Dancer, singer, comedian, magician, lecturer, sound technician, band member, disk jockey, and other types of entertainers.

- **Activities:** Youth counselor, activities coordinator, instructor (yoga, chess, bridge, diving, golf, tennis, dance, water sports), shore excursion, sports director, swimming pool/deck attendant.

- **Photography:** Photographer.

- **Medical:** Physician, dentist, and nurse.

The cruise industry is a great entry point into the travel industry. Most positions require little or no experience, although a few positions require many years of experience. If you target your job search, make the right contacts, and are persistent, you should be able to land a job with a cruise line.

As you conduct a job search, you should be aware that many onboard positions are not controlled by the cruise lines. Gift shops, beauty salons, casinos, sports and recreation, and entertainment are often concessions operated by contractors or concessionaires. For example, dancers, musicians, singers, massage therapists, cosmetologists, and medical doctors are often hired through firms that control these onboard concessions. If a position you desire relates to these concessions, you will need to make employment contacts with the appropriate concessionaire rather than the cruise line.

Your best approach to landing a job in this segment of the travel industry is to become knowledgeable about particular cruise lines, make the right contacts with that cruise line or concessionaire, and offer these employers the desired combination of skills and experience. It's always best to know someone working with a cruise line or concessionaire – a friend, for example, who already works on the cruise ship – who knows when vacancies occur and a ship needs to quickly hire. In many cases cruise lines place classified ads in magazines and newspapers or post vacancy announcements online to recruit needed personnel. If you visit their websites, they will have a "Job Opportunities" or "Employment" section which is often found under "About Us." Here you will find vacancy announcements and instructions for submitting an online application. Most cruise lines require an online application or a mailed, faxed, or e-mailed resume and cover letter. Another approach is to send a copy of your resume, along with an accompanying cover letter, directly to the personnel office of a cruise line. Specify on the envelope whether you are applying for a "Shipside" or a "Shoreside" position, identify which department you wish to work for, and/or call ahead to get the name of the department or person you should address your correspondence to.

Cruise lines recruit individuals for both shoreside and shipboard positions. The four largest cruise lines, which employ the largest staffs, include the following:

- **Carnival Cruise Lines**   www.carnival.com
- **Princess Cruises**   www.princess.com
- **Royal Caribbean International** www.royalcaribbean.com
- **Star Cruise/Norwegian**   www.starcruises.com
  Cruise Lines/Orient Lines   www.ncl.com
                                     www.orientlines.com

Other major cruise lines you may want to direct your job search toward include:

- **American Cruise Lines**   www.americancruiselines.com
- **Celebrity Cruises**   www.celebrity.com
- **Clipper Cruise Line**   www.clippercruise.com
- **Costa Cruises**   www.costacruises.com
- **Crystal Cruises**   www.crystalcruises.com
- **Cunard**   www.cunard.com
- **Delta Queen Steamboat Co.**   www.deltaqueen.com
- **Disney Cruise Line**   www.disneycruise.com
- **Freighter World Cruises**   www.freighterworld.com
- **Galapagos Tours and Cruises**   www.galapagos-inc.com
- **Holland America Line**   www.hollandamerica.com
- **Lindblad Special Expeditions**   www.specialexpeditions.com
- **Radisson Seven Seas Cruises**   www.rssc.com
- **Regal Cruise Lines**   www.regalcruises.com
- **ResidenSea**   www.residensea.com
- **Royal Olympic Cruises**   www.royal-olympic-cruises.com

- Seabourn Cruise Line   www.seabourn.com
- Sea Cloud Cruises   www.seacloud.com
- Silversea Cruises   www.silversea.com
- Tall Ship Adventures   www.tallshipadventures.on.ca
- Viking River Cruises   www.vikingrivercruises.com
- Windjammer Barefoot Cruises   www.windjammer.com
- Windstar Cruises   www.windstarcruises.com

Be sure to familiarize yourself with each cruise line's operations. For example, the Disney Cruise Lines and Carnival Cruises are very family- and youth-oriented, requiring many youth counselors. Crystal and Seabourn Cruises are very upscale, offering many five-star amenities and the services of spa personnel and academic lecturers. Norwegian Cruise Lines is noted for its sports programs and theme cruises. If you survey the companies' websites, you should get a good idea of various opportunities available with particular companies. Best of all, you can apply for jobs online 24 hours a day!

Several companies have concessions with cruise lines or recruit personnel for particular positions. Many concessionaires and recruitment agencies are responsible for staffing a number of onboard positions and operations – photographers, casino personnel, cruise staff, entertainers, waiters, room stewards, deck and engine crew, hairdressers, beauticians, and duty-free and gift shop personnel. A cruise line may give such companies the sole responsibility for staffing various departments rather than recruit such personnel directly. Depending on your area of interest and experience, you may want to contact these companies directly:

All Positions

- Berkeley Scott Group   www.berkeley-scott.co.uk
- Cruise Placement   www.cruiseplacement.com

Entertainment

- Branson Entertainment   630 Ninth Avenue, Suite 203
                                New York, NY 10036
                                Tel. 212-265-3500
                                www.branson.com

- Fiesta Fantastica

  230 SW 8th Street
  Miami, FL 33130

- Jean Ann Ryan Productions

  308 SE 14th Street
  Ft. Lauderdale, FL 33316
  Tel. 954-523-6399
  ww.jeanannryanproductions.com

Casinos

- Atlantic Maritime Services

  990 NW 166th Street
  Miami, FL 33169
  Tel. 305-625-7113

- Casinos Austria

  555 NE 15th Street
  Plaza Venetia, Penth D/E
  Miami, FL 33132

- Princess Cruises

  Fleet Personnel Department
  24844 Avenue Rockefeller
  Santa Clarita, CA 91355-4999

- Shore Side Consultants

  1007 North America Way
  Suite 305
  Miami, FL 33132
  Tel. 305-381-9544

- Triton Cruise Services

  1007 N. America Way, #407
  Miami, FL 33132
  Tel. 305-358-7860
  www.cruisecatering.com

Port Lecturers

- International Voyager Media

  11900 Biscayne Blvd., Suite 300
  Miami, FL 33181
  Tel. 305-892-6644

- Lectures International

  P.O. Box 35446
  Tucson, AZ 85740
  Tel. 520-297-1145

- On Board Promotions

  777 Arthur Godfrey Blvd., #320
  Miami Beach, FL 33140
  Tel. 305-673-0400

- Panoff Publishing Inc.

  10 Fairway Drive, Suite 200
  Deerfield Beach, FL 33441

Hairdressers/Masseuse/Fitness

- Steiner Leisure, Ltd.

  1007 N. America Way, 4th Floor
  Miami, FL 33132
  www.steinerleisure.com
  Tel. 305-594-6460

Gift Shops/Duty Free

- Grayhound Leisure

  8052 NW 14th Street
  Miami, FL 33126-33126
  Tel. 305-592-6460

- Princess Cruises

  Fleet Personnel Department
  24844 Avenue Rockefeller
  Santa Clarita, CA 91355-4999

- Starboard Cruise Services

  8052 NW 14th Street
  Miami, FL 33126
  Tel. 305-592-6460

Photographers

- Cruise Ship Picture Co.

  1177 South America Way
  Miami, Fl 33132
  Tel. 305-539-1903

- Ocean Images Ltd.

  c/o Shoreside Florida Inc.
  Atlantic Bldg. 2800 SW 4ᵗʰ Ave.
  Bay 5
  Fort Lauderdale, FL 33350
  Tel. 954-523-2308

- Trans-Ocean Photo Inc.

  711 12ᵗʰ Avenue, Berth One
  New York, NY 10019
  Tel. 212-757-2707

Caterers/Chandlers/Waiters/Room Stewards

- Apollo Ship Chandlers

  1775 NW 70ᵗʰ Avenue
  Miami, FL 33126
  Tel. 305-592-8790

- Cruise Ship Catering
  Services

  100 S. Biscayne Blvd., Suite 700
  Miami, Fl 33131
  Tel. 305-377-4510

- CTI Recruitment and
  Placement Agency Inc.

  1439 SE 17ᵗʰ St.
  The South Port Center
  Ft. Lauderdale, FL 33316-1709

- Princess Cruises

  Fleet Personnel Department
  24844 Avenue Rockefeller
  Santa Clarita, CA 91355-4999

- Triton Cruise Services

  1007 N. America Way
  Suite 407
  Miami, FL 33132
  Tel. 305-358-7860
  www.cruisecatering.com

- Zerbone Cruise Ship
  Catering Services

  100 S. Biscayne Blvd., Suite 700
  Miami, FL 33131

Deck and Engineering

- BlueSeas International, Inc.   www.jobxchange.com

- Global Ship Services   141 NE 3rd Avenue, Suite 203
  Miami, FL 33132
  Tel. 305-374-8649

- Marine and Mercantile   6925 Biscayne Blvd.
  Miami, FL 33138
  Tel. 305-759-5900

Watersports Staff

- Aqua Fun Adventures Inc.   5821 NE 15th Avenue
  Fort Lauderdale, FL 33341
  Tel. 305-776-1469

- Worldwide Ship Services   1177 South America Way
  Pier 2
  Miami, FL 33132

Cruise Staff and Front Desk Staff

- BlueSeas International   530 East 84th Street
  Suite 5-R
  New York, NY 10028
  Tel. 212-734-7156

- Global Ship Services   141 NE 3rd Avenue
  Suite 203
  Miami, FL 33132
  Tel. 305-374-8649

- Ship Services International   370 West Camino Gardens
  Blvd., Third Floor
  Boca Raton, FL 33432

Resources

One of the best resources for surveying job opportunities in the cruise industry is Mary Fallon Miller's *How to Get a Job With a Cruise Line,* 5th Edition (Ticket to Adventure, 2001). The book is filled with useful tips on how to land a cruise job. It includes a comprehensive survey of the major cruise lines and concessionaires, descriptions of positions, information on training opportunities and special programs, insiders' stories, tips on writing resumes and completing applications, and names, addresses, and phone numbers for contacting potential employers. Other useful books for landing a cruise ship job include:

American and Canadian Cruise Ship Employment Manual, John Degolacao Rodrigues (C.E.I., 2000)

The Back Door Guide to Short-Term Job Adventures, Michael Landes (Ten Speed Press, 2005)

Cruise Ship Jobs!, Cynthia Ossenfort (Write Hand Publishing, 2000)

How to Get a Job on a Cruise Ship, Steve Hines and Don H. Kennedy (Careersource Publications, 2000)

Working on Cruise Ships, 3rd Edition, Sandra Bow (Vacation-Work, 2003)

Several websites also offer books and application packages for cruise ship jobs which include job search tips and addresses of major cruise employers and employment firms:

- Cruise Jobs   www.cruisejobs.com
- Cruise Line Jobs   www.cruiselinejobs.com
- Cruise Ship Entertainment   www.cruiseshipentertainment. com
- Cruise Ship Jobs   www.shipjobs.com
- CruiseJobFinder   www.cruisejobfinder.com

To keep abreast of developments in the cruise industry, as well as to learn more about particular cruise lines, we recommend surveying such trade magazines as *Cruise Desk, Cruise Trade, Cruise and Vacation Views, Leisure Travel News, Tour and Travel News, The Travel Counselor, Travel Trade,* and *Travel Weekly.* Several online publications also cover the cruise industry:

- Cruise News   www.cruise-news.com
- Cruise News Daily   www.cruisenewsdaily.com
- Cruise Week News   www.cruise-week.com
- CruiseMates   www.cruisemates.com

Several associations focus on cruise lines. You may want to contact these associations for information on cruise lines as well as develop useful contacts for networking within the industry:

- Cruise Lines International Association   www.cruising.org
- International Council of Cruise Lines   www.iccl.org
- Niche Cruising Marketing Alliance   www.nichecruise.com
- North West Cruiseship Association   https://nwcruiseship.org

Useful Websites

Several websites provide job search assistance. Some of the sites charge job seekers for marketing their resumes to cruise lines and concessionaires. Others are free to job seekers:

- Cruise Employment Databank   www.nwcruisejobs.com
- Cruise-Jobs   www.cruise-jobs.com
- CruiseJobFinder.com   www.cruisejobfinder.com
- CruiseJobLine.com   www.cruisejobline.com
- CruiseJobLink   www.cruisejoblink.com
- Cruiselinejob.com   www.cruiselinejob.com
- Cruiselinejobs.com   www.cruiselinejobs.com

- Cruiseshipjob.com   www.cruiseshipjob.com
- Hospitality Careers   www.hcareers.com
- Job Monkey   www.jobmonkey.com/cruise
- Jobs on Cruise Ships   www.jobsonships.com
- My Cruise Ship Job   www.mycruiseshipjob.com
- New World Cruise Ship
  Employment Agency   www.cruiseshipjob.com
- ShipJobs.com   www.shipjobs.com

Several e-travel companies function as online travel agencies for selling cruise packages. Many of these companies offer affiliate and outside sales opportunities for enterprising online job seekers and entrepreneurs:

- 1-800-Cruise.com   www.1-800CRUISE.com
- 7 Seas Cruises   http://7seascruises.com
- 11th Hour Vacations   www.11thhourvacations.com
- Air Cruise Savings   www.aircruisesavings.com
- Best Price Cruises   www.bestpricecruises.com
- Cheap Cruise Deals   www.cheap-cruise-deals.com
- Cruise411   www.cruise411.com
- Cruise4Fun   www.cruise4fun.com
- Cruise Adventure   www.cruiseadventure.com
- Cruise Café   www.cruisecafe.com
- Cruise Connections   www.cruiseconnections.com
- Cruise Newsletter   www.cruisenewsletter.com
- Cruise One   www.cruiseone.com
- Cruise Server   www.cruiseserver.net
- Cruises Inc.   www.cruisesinc.com
- Moment's Notice   www.moments-notice.com
- My Travel   www.mytravel.com
- Vacations To Go   www.vacationstogo.com

Rail Services

Ever dream of hopping on a train and heading off into the sunset? It's a dream thousands of individuals realize each day as locomotive engineers, railyard engineers, conductors, or brakemen on freight and passenger trains, or as cooks, bartenders, waiters, waitresses, hosts, and hostesses on

Amtrak passenger trains. Riding the rails is the ultimate travel high for many individuals pursuing jobs and careers in the travel industry. For them, rail work is similar to airline or cruise line work – it literally gets into their blood. They become addicted to the work-travel lifestyle. Following a family tradition, members of their family often pursue careers in the rail industry.

Nearly 78 percent of all rail transportation jobs are with the railroads. In 2004 approximately 112,000 individuals worked in rail transportation. This included 40,000 locomotive engineers and operators; 38,000 railroad conductors and yardmasters; 17,000 railroad brake, single, and switch operators; 9,200 subway and streetcar operators; and 8,100 rail transportation workers and others. The remaining jobs were with state and local governments and mining and manufacturing firms that operate their own railroad cars to carry freight.

Opportunities

Which end of the rail industry most appeals to you – freight or passenger service? If you are primarily interested in jobs involving travel on freight trains, you should focus on the positions of engineer, conductor, and brake, signal, and switch operator.

Passenger train service in the United States is operated by Amtrak, a quasi-government organization. Staffed by a workforce of nearly 25,000, Amtrak transports about 25 million passengers each year. Approximately 90 percent of Amtrak workers are union members; the remaining 10 percent are nonunionized management employees. While many positions with Amtrak, such as ticket agents and station personnel, involve little or no rail travel, those involving frequent travel relate to onboard services: porters, conductors, dining-car employees (chefs, waiters, waitresses), bartenders, and sleeping car personnel (hosts and hostesses). The work of other support personnel, such as inspectors and investigators, does involve frequent and interesting travel.

Competition for jobs will remain keen within this changing industry. Basically requiring a high school education, railway jobs tend to be well paying and secure. However, job opportunities in rail transportation will continue to decline in the coming decade even though the demand for railroad freight service will increase. The only job growth will be for locomotive engineers and subway and streetcar operators. The increased efficiency of railroad operators along with larger, faster, and more fuel-efficient trains and computerized classification yards will continue to eliminate many traditional jobs. Amtrak will continue to downsize its workforce as it eliminates several routes. Employment of subway operators will increase, and competition is expected to be keen for what are relatively high-paying subway operator positions for jobs requiring limited educational requirements.

Benefits

Except for management personnel, most rail workers are unionized. As such, their salaries and benefits tend to be good to excellent with both freight and passenger rail services. In 2004, the median hourly earnings for locomotive engineers was $24.30; for subway and streetcar operators it was $23.70; for railroad conductors and yardmasters it was $22.28; and for railroad brake, signal, and switch operators it was $21.46.

As unionized workers, most railway employees receive good health and retirement benefits.

Breaking In

Most railway workers start out as trainees for either engineer or brake operator jobs. Applicants generally need a high school education, good health and eyesight, and demonstrate mechanical aptitude. Beginning engineers usually undergo a six-month training program. Brake operators learn their job by working closely with experienced conductors and operators as well as participate in some classroom training. Conductors are usually hired from the ranks of experienced brake operators who have sufficient seniority to move into vacant conductor positions.

Applicants for subway operator positions normally need a high school education and must be in good health and have good judgment. They receive from a few weeks to six months of classroom and on-the-job training.

Numerous craft unions represent railway workers. However, most engineers belong to the Brotherhood of Locomotive Engineers; other railway workers tend to belong to the United Transportation Union. Most subway workers are represented by either the Amalgamated Transit Union or the Transport Workers Union of North America.

If you are interested in working for the railways, it's best to contact the employment offices of various railways or the appropriate craft unions for information on requirements and applications. For a list of addresses, telephone numbers, and websites of the major railroads, contact:

Association of American Railroads
Communications Department
50 F Street, NW
Washington, DC 20001
Website: www.aar.org
Tel. 202-639-2100

For application and vacancy information relating to passenger service jobs, contact:

Amtrak National Railroad Passenger Corporation
60 Massachusetts Avenue, NE
Washington, DC 20002
Website: http://jobs.amtrak.com

Amtrak also has a toll-free job line with information on current job openings: 1-877-268-7251. You must call this number to get a job title and posting number for submitting a mailed resume. Amtrak does not accept faxed or e-mailed resumes at present.

Local offices of rail transit systems and state employment services also have information on job opportunities in rail transportation. For general information on career opportunities in passenger transportation, contact:

American Public Transportation Association
1666 K Street, NW, Suite 1100
Washington, DC 20006
Website: www.apta.com
Tel. 202-496-4800

For information on rail transportation occupations and career opportunities as a locomotive engineer, contact:

Brotherhood of Locomotive Engineers and Trainmen
1370 Ontario Street, Mezzanine
Cleveland, OH 44113-1702
Website: www.ble.org
Tel. 216-241-2630

Bus Lines and Motorcoach Industry

One position in the bus industry involves extensive travel – bus driver. In 2004 bus drivers held 653,000 jobs and worked for nearly 4,000 companies. About 35 percent worked part-time. Nearly 71 percent worked for school systems or companies providing school bus services; 17 percent worked as local transit bus drivers. Four percent worked as intercity bus drivers. Five percent worked as for charter, tour, commuter service, package express, feeder service, and other types of private companies.

Opportunities

Employment opportunities for bus drivers in the decade ahead should grow as fast as the average for most occupations. This is primarily due to the coming growth in elementary and secondary school enrollments and the consequent need for more buses and bus drivers. Indeed, it's easiest to find a job as a school bus driver because most of these positions are part-time and experience a high turnover rate. These also are low-paid and seasonal positions. Opportunities for bus drivers with local transit and intercity bus systems will gradually grow as bus ridership increases. However, expect high competition for these jobs because many of these positions are well paid and come with excellent benefits for individuals with limited educational achievement. Opportunities also should be excellent for bus drivers with tour and charter companies – one of the fastest growing and most innovative segments of the industry.

Benefits

The nature of this business is such that bus drivers often work part-time and experience seasonal layoffs. Seniority tends to determine the extent of part-time and full-time employment for bus drivers. Salaries are often low but more than adequate in many communities.

Salaries of bus drivers vary greatly. The median hourly earnings of transit and intercity bus drivers were $14.30 in May 2004. The highest 10 percent earned $23.53 an hour. School bus drivers earned $11.97 an hour.

Fringe benefits also vary greatly from employer to employer. Most intercity and local transit bus drivers receive paid health and life insurance, sick leave, and free bus rides. Most full-time bus drivers annually receive four weeks vacation. Most intercity and many local transit bus drivers belong to the Amalgamated Transit Union. Local transit bus drivers in New York and many other large cities belong to the Transport Workers Union of America. Some drivers belong to the United Transportation Union and the International Brotherhood of Teamsters, Chauffeurs, Warehousemen and Helpers of America.

Resources

Information on employment opportunities for bus drivers is available by directly contacting local transit systems, intercity bus lines, school systems, tour and charter companies, or the local offices of the state employment service. For general information on bus driving, contact the following association:

American Bus Association
700 13th Street, NW, Suite 575
Washington, DC 20005-5923
Website: www.buses.org
Tel. 202-842-1645

For information on school bus driving, contact:

National School Transportation Association
113 South West Street, 4th Floor
Alexandria, VA 22314
Website: www.yellowbuses.org
Tel. 1-800-222-NSTA

School Bus Fleet
www.schoolbusfleet.com

For information on local transit bus driving, contact:

> **American Public Transportation Association**
> 1666 K Street, NW, Suite 1100
> Washington, DC 20006
> Website: www.apta.com
> Tel. 202-496-4800

General information on motorcoach driving is available from:

> **United Motorcoach Association**
> 113 S. West Street, 4th Floor
> Alexandria, VA 22314-2824
> Website: www.uma.org
> Tel. 800-424-8262

For information on opportunities with the growing tour and charter bus companies, contact:

> **National Motorcoach Marketing Network**
> P.O. Box 1088
> Mount Jackson, VA 22842
> Website: www.motorcoach.com
> Tel. 540-477-3323

> **National Tour Foundation**
> 546 E. Main Street
> Lexington, KY 40508
> Website: www.ntaonline.com
> Tel. 800-682-8886

Tour Operators and Guides

One of the most exciting ends of the travel industry are the numerous companies that organize and conduct tours. They produce travel products which they market to travel agencies, corporations, and individuals. Highly specialized, entrepreneurial, and competitive, these companies are responsible for putting together packaged tours as well as providing both outbound and inbound tour services. Jobs involve everything from organizing packages, marketing tours, and selling services to making reservations, coordinating inbound ground services, and actually conducting tours. People who like to travel love these jobs!

Opportunities

During the past 20 years the number of specialty tour operators has increased dramatically. Most are small two- to seven-person operations specializing in destinations (Europe, the Caribbean, Asia, Africa, Latin America); activities (ballooning, mountain climbing, white water rafting, safaris, bicycling, scuba diving, voluntourism); educational experiences (museums, archeological ruins, culture, university courses); lifestyle choices (environment, habitats, nudism, cooking, shopping, crafts); and markets (women, youth, retirees, teachers, singles, religious groups, people with disabilities, grandparents, gays, ethnic groups, alumni, veterans). Others are large well established firms, such as American Express, Travcoa, Abercrombie & Kent, and Globus, which offer hundreds of tour options to special destinations. The average firm is run by four full-time and two part-time employees and sells 80 different tours to 2,500 clients a year. In the larger scheme of things, these are small travel operations. For a good overview of this industry, subscribe to the biannual *Special Travel Index*, which includes 500+ tour operators that offer more than 1,000 specialty tours:

Specialty Travel Index
P.O. Box 458
San Anselmo, CA 94979
Website: www.spectrav.com
Tel. 415-455-1743

Tour managers – also known as tour guides or tour escorts – experience the greatest amount of on-the-job travel. The work is very demanding. Tour managers must be well organized, responsible, and great diplomats who handle a host of daily demands. Given the seasonal nature of this business, most tour managers are freelancers who are hired by tour operators for specific itineraries. Many individuals prefer this lifestyle because it enables them to travel as well as have several months off each year to pursue other interests.

The specialty tour business should continue to expand in the decade ahead as more and more people choose to go beyond the standard destinations and sightseeing that has largely defined tour operations during the past 30 years. At the same time, many travel agencies, faced with a declining general travel market, have developed new niche markets centered on specialty travel. Accordingly, job opportunities will continue to expand for individuals with expertise in specialty travel and for entrepreneurs interested in starting their own specialty travel agency.

Benefits and Salaries

The major benefits for tour operators are the ability to travel free or at low cost to exciting destinations, participate in stimulating programs, and work with interesting people. Salaries of tour operators and tour guides are relatively low. However, many talented tour guides do very well on tips from satisfied clients. Most make $55,000 a year or more – with tips comprising two-thirds of their earnings. Given the highly competitive nature of the industry and the pressure to offer good value to clients, profit margins for tour operators tend to be very narrow.

Most individuals working in this end of the travel business, including presidents and managers of tour firms, earn under $55,000 a year; many earn under $40,000 a year. This is the type of industry many people enter because they primarily enjoy the non-monetary benefits of the business.

Resources

If you are interested in pursuing jobs with tour operators, you should refer to some of the following publications. A few have online editions:

- *International Travel News*   www.intltravelnews.com
- *Specialty Travel Index*   www.spectrav.com
- *Travel Agent*   www.travelagentcentral.com
- *Travel Weekly*   www.travelweekly.com

For good overviews of the growing specialty travel business, we recommend these guides and directories:

The Back Door Guide to Short-Term Job Adventures, Michael Landes (Ten Speed Press, 2005)

Start Your Own Specialty Travel and Tour Business (Entrepreneur Press, 2003)

Volunteer Vacations, 9th Edition, Bill McMillon (Chicago Review Press, 2006)

For a good online directory to specialty travel firms and activities, be sure to explore Google's directory to nearly 25,000 such firms:

http://directory.google.com/Top/Recreation/Travel/Specialty_Travel/

The following organizations provide information on opportunities with tour operators:

American Sightseeing International
2727 Steeles Avenue West, Suite 301
Toronto, Ontario M3J 3G9
Website: www.americansightseeing.org
Tel. 416-736-4432

American Society of Travel Agents
1101 King Street, Suite 200
Alexandria, VA 22314
Website: www.astanet.com
Tel. 703-739-2782

National Tour Foundation
546 East Main Street
Lexington, KY 40508
Website: www.ntaonline.com
Tel. 800-682-8886

Travel Industry Association of America
1100 New York Ave., NW, Suite 450
Washington, DC 20005
Website: www.tia.org
Tel. 202-408-8422

U.S. Tour Operators Association
275 Madison Avenue, Suite 2014
New York, NY 10016
Website: www.ustoa.com
Tel. 212-599-6744

Convention, Meeting, and Event Planners

Do you like to party? What about organizing the largest party you've ever seen? And travel to great places at the same time? That's what meeting planners do – throw really big parties that can involve a great deal of travel to exciting places.

> *Meeting planners spend a great deal of time traveling to meeting sites.*

Who's in charge of putting on nearly 300,000 meetings, conferences, conventions, and workshops attended by over 60 million people spending over $80 billion each year? Nearly 35,000 meeting and convention planners in the United States. If you work for an association, incentive house, travel agency, hotel, conference center, convention bureau, or a consulting firm specializing in organizing meetings, you may have one of the most enjoyable and challenging jobs that also involves a great deal of travel. Indeed, as much as 75 percent of your time may be spent traveling. This a very big, exciting, and rewarding business that lies at the heart of business travel. Unfortunately, many people who love to travel overlook this employment field.

Being a meeting planner is not the same as working in Hollywood. But you are in charge of putting on a major production that may last only one day or as long as one week. From start to finish, you want a flawless production in which everyone knows their part and plays it well. If not, you must be well prepared to deal with problems and crises.

Meeting planners are in charge of nearly every aspect of organizing and conducting professional meetings of groups as small as 50 or as large as 50,000. They select sites, plan programs, negotiate facilities, publicize events, block space, make hotel and airline reservations, organize food and beverages, set up registration, arrange equipment and security, organize shipping and exhibits, schedule speakers, and attend to 1,001 other logistic details necessary for operating successful meetings.

Meeting planners must have excellent communication, organization, negotiating, planning, and management skills as well as exhibit a great deal of initiative, creativity, and attention to detail. They are constantly on the telephone and on the Internet, planning and coordinating events. The nature of their jobs involves traveling a great deal to meeting sites. The larger the meeting, the more likely it will be held in a large city that offers adequate facilities to accommodate attendees. Large associations, for example, can only be accommodated at huge convention centers which are primarily found in New York City, Miami, Chicago, San Francisco, Los Angeles, Las Vegas, and Washington, DC.

Benefits

Salaries and travel are the major benefits of the meeting business. Median annual earnings of meeting and convention planners in May 2004 were $39,620. The lowest 10 percent earned less than $24,660, and the highest 10 percent earned more than $65,060.

Many people go into this business because of the travel benefits. Meeting planners are constantly traveling because of their need to examine sites, plan and negotiate facilities, and oversee the conduct of meetings. However, the travel benefits can become a negative for some individuals who discover they are traveling too much. The demands of the job are great – long hours and stress – and thus most appealing for certain types of individuals at certain stages of their lives.

Breaking In

Given the seemingly glamorous nature of these jobs as well as the extensive travel involved, competition for jobs in the meeting business is high. Many of the jobs are found with associations, which must plan annual conventions, while others are found with convention bureaus, incentive houses, travel agencies, hotels, and corporations.

Entry into this career field requires excellent communication and management skills. Most meeting planners have at least a bachelor's degree, preferably in business administration. Many have attended degree programs in hotel/motel management as well as special training programs in meeting management.

The best way to break into this business is to learn as much as possible about employers and contact them directly. The following organizations specialize in recruiting meeting planners:

- **American Society of Association Executives**
  www.asaenet.org
  Tel. 202-626-2723

- **Association of Destination Management Executives**
  www.adme.org
  Tel. 303-394-3905

- **B-There.com**
  www.b-there.com
  Tel. 1-877-828-4373

- **International Association of Conference Centers**
  www.iacconline.com
  Tel. 314-993-8575

- **International Association of Exposition Management**
  www.iaem.org
  Tel. 972-458-8002

- **International Society of Meeting Planners**
  www.iami.org/ismp.home.cfm
  Tel. 320-763-4919

- **Meeting Professionals International**
  www.mpiweb.org
  Tel. 972-702-3000

- **Professional Convention Management Association**
  www.pcma.org
  Tel. 312-423-7262

- **Society of Corporate Meeting Professionals**
  www.scmp.org
  Tel. 210-822-6522

Some of these associations provide job and career information as well as sponsor job banks.

Resources

If you are interested in opportunities in the meeting business, you should consult several of the following trade publications. Most are available in both print and online versions:

- *Association Trends*   www.associationtrends.com
- *Business Travel News*   www.btonline.com
- *Convene*   www.pcma.org/resources/
                                 convene/

- *Corporate Meetings &*
  Incentives   www.meetingsnet.com
- *Meeting News*   www.meetingnews.com
- *Meetings and Conventions*   www.meetings-conventions.com
- *Meetings Industry Megasite*   www.mimegasite.com
- *MeetingsNet*   www.meetingsnet.com
- *Tradeshow Week*   www.TradeshowWeek.com

The following organizations can provide you with information on opportunities for meeting planners:

Convention Industry Council
8201 Greensboro Drive, Suite 300
McLean, VA 22102
Website: www.conventionindustry.org
Tel. 800-725-8982

International Society of Meeting Planners
1224 North Nokomis NE
Alexandria, MN 56308
Website: www.iami.org/ismp.html
Tel. 320-763-4919

Meeting Professionals International
4455 LBJ Freeway, Suite 1700
Dallas, TX 75244-5903
Website: www.mpiweb.org
Tel. 972-702-3000

Society of Corporate Meeting Professionals
217 Ridgemont Avenue
San Antonio, TX 78209
Website: www.scmp.org
Tel. 201-822-6522

Useful Websites

The following websites specialize in jobs in the meeting industry:

- Meeting Jobs   www.meetingjobs.com
- Meeting Professionals
  International   www.mpiweb.org

Incentive Travel Planners

Closely related to the work of convention, meeting, and event planners is the incentive travel business. Each year thousands of companies offer their employees, primarily those in sales, incentive trips as rewards for reaching certain performance targets. Insurance agents, for example, who sell $10 million in insurance a year may be eligible for an all-expense paid incentive trip to places such as Hawaii or Hong Kong. Altogether, U.S. companies spend over $10 billion a year on incentive travel.

Incentive travel planners work either within companies as in-house travel agents or for a company specializing in the incentive travel business. They organize trips, plan meetings, and ensure that incentive trips become dream vacations for participants.

The major incentive travel companies include:

- Maritz   www.maritztravel.com
- Carlson   www.carlsonconnected.com
- The Journeymasters   www.journeymasters.com

Most companies specializing in incentive travel belong to:

- Events Industry Association   www.eventia.org.uk
- Society of Incentive &
  Travel Executives (SITE)   www.site-intl.org

Major publications in this field include:

- **Corporate & Incentive Travel** www.corporate-inc-travel.com
- **Incentive Magazine**   www.incentivemag.com
- **Meetings & Conventions**   www.meetings-conventions.com

Accommodations and Lodging Industry

One does not normally think of the accommodations and lodging industry offering travel opportunities. Jobs in this industry appear to be specific to individual properties. However, many jobs, especially with major international hotel chains, offer some wonderful opportunities that also involve frequent travel and residence abroad.

The lodging industry employs the largest number of people in the travel industry. In 2004 approximately 1.8 million people worked in approximately 62,000 hotels, motels, and other accommodations in the United States. Many millions more work in hotels and resorts abroad. More than eight out of 10 workers are employed in service and office and administrative support occupations.

Until 2001, the accommodations industry in the United States was one of the fastest growing segments of the travel industry. But in 2002 this industry witnessed a 4.5 percent decline in employment attributed to the combined impact of a recession and the post-9/11 slowdown in business travel. Depending on the overall conditions of the U.S. economy, the accommodations industry in the United States is expected to experience better than average growth in the decade ahead – increase by 17 percent from 2004 to 2014. Much of this growth will be due to gradual increases that will exceed pre-2002 levels of business and leisure travel.

Opportunities

The lodging or hospitality industry offers numerous job opportunities for people with a variety of skills, interests, educational backgrounds, and motivations. While desk clerks, housekeepers, and managers are most evident in small hotels and motels, large hotels and resorts hire numerous other individuals to staff their extensive operations and departments – food and beverage, restaurant, front office, accounting, engineering, public relations, convention and meeting rooms, tours, fitness center, business center, sales and marketing, security, laundry, purchasing, computer systems, maintenance, and operations.

Hotels with 800 rooms may be operated by a staff of over 1,000. Positions with these properties are numerous: front-office manager, room clerk, reservation clerk, cashier, telephone operator, concierge, bell captain, doorperson, controller, credit manager, purchasing agent, accounts payable supervisor, payroll supervisor, night auditor, catering manager, waiter/waitress, bartender, dietician, food/beverage manager, executive chef, fry cook, pastry chef, butcher, steward, executive housekeeper, room attendant, houseperson, marketing director, sales director, group sales coordinator, banquet manager, public relations manager, chief engineer, plumber, carpenter, and electrician.

Hotels and motels are not the only sources for jobs in this industry. Numerous parallel jobs also are available with firms managing condominiums, time-share facilities, and senior communities as well as with bed-and-breakfast operations, inns, and campgrounds.

Many jobs should be available in the decade ahead for entry-level personnel in the lodging industry. Many of these jobs only require a high school education and little or no experience. Individuals receive on-the-job training, and many employees quickly move from entry-level positions to management positions – within five years and with significant increases in salary. Other jobs require extensive experience in the lodging and travel industries as well as high levels of education and training. Overall, however, this is one of the few industries where individuals with high school educations can enter and rapidly advance to positions of major responsibility within the industry.

Benefits

Earnings in hotels and other accommodations are lower than the average for all industries. In 2004, average earnings for all nonsupervisory workers in this industry were $10.58 an hour, or $317 a week, compared with $15.78 an hour, or $529 a week, for workers throughout private industry. Many workers in this industry earn the federal minimum wage of $5.15 an hour. However, salaries and benefits of those working in the lodging industry can vary greatly. Entry-level personnel receive relatively low wages, but mid- and upper-level management can earn above-average salaries. The median annual earnings for lodging managers in May 2004 were $37,660. The lowest 10 percent earned less than $22,680, whereas the highest 10 percent earned more than $72,160. General managers of large properties earn considerably more.

Working in the lodging industry has numerous benefits. Many employees simply love this industry because of the constantly changing nature of the business, the interesting guests they meet, the opportunities to frequently travel and relocate, and the fast-track career advancement they experience. Public relations managers in major international hotels, for example, feel they have one of the best jobs in the world – they work in a first-class environment and are constantly meeting and dining with celebrities and other VIPs. And they have opportunities to transfer to other properties within the hotel chain.

One of the major benefits for many individuals working in this industry is travel and relocation. After working three or four years with one hotel, one can move on to another hotel. Management personnel interested in international operations frequently relocate to hotels in different countries. Indeed, for many people, working in a major hotel or resort in Tahiti, Hong Kong, Bangkok, Singapore, Bali, Sydney, Rome, Madrid, Paris, London, Bermuda, or Anguilla is a dream come true. And to work in several of these exciting locations for a major hotel chain is the ultimate career high!

Breaking In

The lodging industry has a tradition of advancing individuals from entry-level positions to higher level management positions. Many of the major hotel chains, such as Hyatt, Marriott, Hilton, Sheraton, and Ritz-Carlton, offer outstanding in-house training and career development programs, and they transfer personnel to various properties. Getting a job with one of these companies can lead to an excellent career up the corporate ladder and within the larger travel industry. Indeed, it's not unusual to discover managers of major hotel chains began their careers as front desk clerks.

Employers in the accommodations industry look for candidates who demonstrate a willingness to work hard, the ability to learn, and enthusiasm for working with people. If you possess these traits, you may be a good candidate for the accommodations industry.

Entry into the lodging industry can be difficult, especially with major hotel chains where competition is very high. In fact, many hotels are inundated with resumes and applications for a limited number of positions.

The best way to break into this industry is to apply directly to individual hotels. If you don't have a personal contact, start by contacting the Human Resources Department by telephone or the Internet, as well as send a copy of your resume for their files. You also should monitor classified job ads in newspapers, trade publications, and on the Internet. Many hotels will advertise vacancies in local newspapers. Some employment firms specialize in recruiting hotel personnel.

If you follow this industry and individual hotels closely, you should be able to identify when and where new properties will open. A new 500-room ho tel or resort, for example, may need to quickly staff itself with nearly 500 employees two or three months before its grand opening. You may want to include several of these properties in your job search.

> _The best way to break into this industry is to make direct applications to individual hotels._

While many hotels continue to hire individuals with little experience for entry-level positions, your chances of getting a job are better if you have some formal training in the industry. Nearly 1,000 schools, colleges, and universities offer a variety of programs for careers in the accommodations industry. Some of the best four-year programs in hotel and restaurant management are offered by Cornell University, Michigan State, Pennsylvania State University, University of Houston, University of Denver, Florida International, and Johnson and Wales. One of the best sources for identifying many of these programs is CHRIE's *A Guide to College Programs in Hospitality, Tourism, and Culinary Arts*, which includes over 550 institutions offering programs in the culinary arts, restaurant management, food service, hotel and motel management, and travel and tourism. It's available in both downloadable and CD-ROM formats through CHRIE (www.chrie.org).

The websites of these three professional associations also identify education and training programs for individuals interested in careers with this industry:

- **Educational Institute of the American Hotel & Lodging**   www.ei-ahma.org

- International Council on Hotel,
  Restaurant, and Institutional
  Education (CHRIE)   www.chrie.org

- International Society of Travel
  and Tourism Educators   www.istte.org

Travel opportunities in the accommodations industry are best with large international hotel chains with 15 or more properties. Some of the largest or best international hotel chains include Ritz-Carlton, Hyatt, Sheraton, Regent, Four Seasons, Mandarin Oriental, Holiday Inn, Intercontinental, Novotel, Shangri-La, Oberoi, Hilton, Amanresorts, Marriott, Ramada, Taj International, and Westin.

Resources

For more information on opportunities in the accommodations and lodging industry, contact:

American Hotel and Lodging Association
1201 New York Ave., NW, Suite 600
Washington, DC 20005-3931
Website: www.ahma.com
Tel. 202-289-3100

American Resort Development Association
1201 15th Street, NW, Suite 400
Washington, DC 20005-2842
Website: www.arda.org
Tel. 202-371-6700

Useful Websites

The following trade publications focus on the lodging industry:

- Hotel & Motel Management   www.hotelmotel.com
- Hotel Business   www.hotelbusiness.com
- Lodging Magazine   www.lodgingmagazine.com
- Resorts and Great Hotels   www.resortsgreathotels.com

Several recruiters specializing on the hospitality industry can be found on this website: www.hospitalityonline.com/career-links/recruiters. Other recruiters and websites specializing on jobs in the hospitality industry include:

■ Action Jobs	www.actionjobs.com
■ Adventures in Hospitality Careers	www.hospitalityadventures.com
■ Casino Careers Online	www.casinocareers.com
■ Chef Job	www.chefjob.com
■ Chef Jobs Network	www.chefjobsnetwork.com
■ Cool Works	www.coolworks.com
■ e-Hospitality.com	www.e-hospitality.com
■ Escoffier.com	www.escoffier.com
■ Food Industry Jobs.com	www.foodindustryjobs.com
■ Food Management Search	www.foodmanagementsearch.com
■ Food Service.com	www.foodservice.com
■ Foodservice Central	www.foodservicecentral.com
■ Harrison Business Group	www.harrisonbusinessgroup.com
■ Hospitality Careers	www.hospitalitycareers.net
■ Hospitality Careers Online	www.hcareers.com
■ Hospitality Link	www.hospitalitylink.com
■ Hospitality Net	www.hospitalitynet.org
■ HospitalityJobs Online	www.hospitalityonline.com
■ Hospitality Recruiters	www.hospitalityrecruiters.com
■ Hotel Job Resource	www.hoteljobresource.com
■ Hotel Jobs Network	www.hoteljobsnetwork.com
■ Hotel Online Classifieds	www.hotel-online.com
■ Hotel Resource	www.hotelresource.com
■ Hoteljobs.com	www.hoteljobs.com
■ iHire Hospitality	www.ihirehospitality.com
■ iHire Hospitality Services	www.ihirehospitalityservices.com
■ International Seafarers	www.jobxchange.com
■ Job Monkey	www.jobmonkey.com
■ Jobs in Paradise	www.jobsinparadise.com

- Resort Jobs   www.resortjobs.com
- Resort Recruitment   www.resortrecruitment.com.au
- Restaurant Manager.net   www.restaurantmanager.net
- SkiTown.com   http://skitown.com/skitownjobs
- Spa Jobs   www.spajobs.com
- Travel Jobs   www.traveljobs.com
- Traveljobz.net   www.traveljobz.net
- Wine & Hospitality Jobs   www.wineandhospitalityjobs.
                                       com
- Workamper.com   www.workamper.com
- Working Vacation   www.theworkingvacation.com

Travel Writers and Photographers

Travel writers and photographers appear to have some of the most glamorous jobs in the travel industry. Unlike others, they seem to have the ultimate freedom to set their own schedules, choose their own locations, and receive a variety of discounted and free travel benefits.

Travel writers come in several forms. Many are freelance writers who produce articles for magazines and newspapers and write travel books. These individuals are usually paid for each article they write or given royalties for books they produce. The pay is usually very low – $30 for a short article or $150 for a two-page article is typical. Other travel writers are salaried employees of major trade publications, commercial magazines, and newspapers. Indeed, over 300 weekly and monthly magazines employ travel editors. Over 400 newspapers have full- or part-time travel editors.

The Life

Do you want to travel free and do so in first-class style? You can if you become a travel writer.

Travel writing is as much a lifestyle as an occupation. Many people become travel writers because travel is in their blood and they love the wonderful benefits given to travel writers. Except for full-time travel editors who may combine their travel writing responsibilities with other editorial duties, most travel writers simply love to travel and write about it at the same time. Getting paid for it, however minimal, is even better.

The real benefits of a travel writer do not lie in direct compensation in the form of salaries, fees, or royalties. As most travel writers know, the real benefits come in the form of complimentary or discounted air transportation and accommodations. Many airlines, hotels, restaurants, and travel wholesalers routinely give travel writers "freebies" in exchange for free publicity. An all-inclusive 10-day trip that might normally cost $5,000 may be given free to a travel writer in exchange for receiving major coverage in an article or travel book. Consequently, many travel articles and books tend to be biased toward those airlines, hotels, travel wholesalers, and restaurants that provide the writer with freebies. Only a few travel writers claim to pay their own way and refuse to accept the perks that come with the job.

Opportunities

Freelance travel writers are basically travel entrepreneurs who become travel writers by getting travel articles published. Their major qualification is persuading editors to accept their work. They take trips, write about them, and submit their articles for publication in major magazines and newspapers. While this is the easiest way to break into travel writing – declare yourself a travel writer and get published – it can also be the most frustrating. Competition among freelance writers is great. Many publications prefer publishing pieces produced by their own staff rather than purchase freelance articles. Those that do publish outside articles usually rely on a core of established travel writers.

Given the nominal fees paid for freelance travel articles, it is extremely difficult to make a living as a freelance travel writer. As a result, many freelance travel writers do this type of work as a sideline to some other occupation or "real job."

Numerous opportunities for travel writers are available with trade publications. Most professional travel associations publish newspapers and magazines. Their staffs report on developments within their respective associations. Major trade publications include:

- *ASTA Agency Management*   www.astanet.com
- *Aviation Week*   www.aviationnow.com
- *Business Travel News*   www.btnonline.com
- *Lodging Magazine*   www.lodgingmagazine.com

- *Meeting News*   www.meetingnews.com
- *Meetings & Conventions* www.meetings-conventions.com
- *Successful Meetings*   www.mimegasite.com
- *Travel Age West*   www.travelagewest.com
- *Travel Agent*   www.travelagentcentral.com
- *Travel Trade*   www.traveltrade.com
- *Travel Weekly*   www.travelweekly.com

Numerous magazines also hire travel writers as well as work with freelance travel writers. The two major travel magazines include:

- *Conde Nast Traveler*   www.concierge.com
- *Travel & Leisure*   www.travelandleisure.com

Afar magazine

Other well-known magazines which have travel sections and articles include:

- *Cosmopolitan*   www.cosmopolitan.com
- *Glamour*   www.glamour.com
- *Gourmet*   www.epicurious.com/gourmet
- *Seventeen*   www.seventeen.com
- *Town & Country*   www.hearstcorp.com
- *Vogue*   www.style.com

Over 400 newspapers either have a travel section or regularly include travel articles. The major position with these newspapers is Travel Editor. However, many individuals in these positions previously held other editorial responsibilities before being assigned to the travel desk. Few travel editors are hired directly from outside the newspaper. Newspapers normally buy freelance travel articles to supplement the writings of their travel editor and staff members. Newspapers with some of the most extensive and influential travel sections include:

- *Chicago Tribune*   www.chicagotribune.com/travel/
- *Los Angeles Times* www.latimes.com/travel/
- *New York Times*   www.nytimes.com
- *Washington Post*   www.washingtonpost.com

Travel guidebook writing tends to be dominated by a few publishing houses that offer major travel series; most are published annually. The major travel series include:

- **Fodor's Guides**   www.fodors.com
- **Frommer's Guides**   www.frommers.com
- **Globe Pequot**   www.globe-pequot.com
- **Hunter Publishing**   www.hunterpublishing.com
- **Insight Guides**   www.insightguides.com
- **Let's Go Guides**   www.letsgo.com
- **Lonely Planet Guides**   www.lonelyplanet.com
- **Moon Guides**   www.moon.com
- **Rough Guides**   www.roughguides.com

Most travel guide publishers work with a core of writers who are assigned to complete specific travel volumes in a series. While many of their writers used to be paid on a royalty basis (8-20 percent of net receipts), more and more travel publishers now commission "works for hire." Rather than pay royalties to authors, they offer travel writers flat fees for producing a travel guide. Most of their fees are very low – $3,000 to $8,000 – to produce a complete travel guidebook, which also includes all travel expenses. As a result, many experienced travel writers no longer work for such publishers. Indeed, travel writing for many of the major guidebook series is increasingly a young person's activity commissioned on a shoestring budget. It attracts individuals with little travel experience who are willing to work for next to nothing in order to break into the travel field. The bias of these writers is generally toward the budget side of travel given their limited financial resources to conduct such research. Accordingly, the quality of guidebook travel writing has decreased in recent years.

Smaller publishers may offer less extensive and more specialized travel series, and some publish books submitted by freelance writers. However, most smaller publishers tend to specialize in particular travel areas and work with their own group of established writers.

It is very difficult to break into guidebook travel writing. The competition is extremely keen and the financial rewards are not particularly impressive, except for a few bestselling books – mostly on Europe and the Caribbean – that appear in the major travel series. Nonetheless, each year many people manage to break into this rather exclusive group of travel professionals. Only a few people develop long-term careers as guidebook travel writers. Many quickly find what ostensibly seemed to be an exciting job becomes boring after a few years, and compensation tends to be too low to support a long-term career.

Travel Photographers

Travel photographers face an even more competitive environment than travel writers. While magazines and newspapers use photographs, they often get them directly from the authors of articles, tourist offices, or photo bureaus. Rarely do editors give photo assignments to photographers. Consequently, most travel photographers tend to be freelance photographers who are constantly frustrated in trying to market their photos to travel publications. Many travel photographers find it easier to sell their photos to stock houses, such as New York-based Black Star, Freelance Photographers Guild, and Gamma/Liaison.

Resources

If you want to become a travel writer or photographer, you might begin by consulting the following books:

How to Make a Living as a Travel Writer, Susan Farewell (Marlowe & Co., 1997)

Travel Photography, Susan McCarthey (Allsworth Press, 1999)

Travel Writer's Handbook, 5th Edition, Louise Purwin Zobel (Surrey Books, 2002)

Travel Writer's Guide, 3rd Edition, Gordon Burgett (Communication Unlimited, 2002)

Writer's Market (Writer's Digest, annual)

Several open universities offer intensive three- to eight-hour courses on travel writing. Most are "how to" courses on how to travel free by becoming a travel writer. Most people attending these courses are probably more interested in learning how to travel free than becoming a legitimate travel writer.

Unfortunately, some travel writing books and short courses tend to abuse the hospitality of the travel industry as well as give travel writing a bad name – encourage individuals to rip off the travel industry for freebies. As a result, many sponsors of travel writers are understandably suspicious of anyone claiming to be a travel writer. They usually want to see evidence of previous travel writing (clippings) as well as a letter from an editor confirming the fact that the writer is on a specific research/ writing assignment. The days when anyone could just declare themselves a travel writer – perhaps print their own "Travel Writer" stationery and business cards – and expect to get travel freebies for ostensibly being "on assignment" are largely gone. Nonetheless, some enterprising groups have gone into the questionable business of selling travel writer press credentials to anyone who pays them an annual fee for an "International Correspondent's Kit," which includes a laminated card and phony documents. For around $500 you can become an instant travel writer!

> *Many members of the travel industry prefer channeling promotional efforts through the SATW because members are considered legitimate travel writers.*

Many established travel writers belong to the Society of American Travel Writers (1500 Sunday Drive, Suite 102, Raleigh, NC 27607, Tel. 919-861-5586, www.satw.org). Membership in this organization, however, is very restrictive, confined mainly to public relations directors with major airlines and travel editors and writers with years of experience. You must be sponsored by three members in order to be considered for membership in SATW. One of the major benefits of being a member of this organization is that most travel wholesalers, hotels, and airlines routinely offer free trips to members. Indeed, the SATW's monthly newsletter lists upcoming "fam" (familiarization) trips its members are encouraged to take advantage of. Many members of the travel industry prefer channeling such promotional efforts through the Society of American Travel Writers because members of this organization are considered legitimate travel writers who are constantly "on assignment." Confining promotional efforts through the SATW reduces the chances of being ripped off by an enterprising and instant "travel writer" who may have just completed a "travel free" book or how-to course.

Useful Websites

If you're interested in joining a network of travel guidebook writers, be sure to sign up for this mailing list:

http://lists.topica.com/lists/tgw

Members of this list exchange ideas on a wide variety of subjects and issues affecting travel writers. It's an excellent list for making contacts and gaining useful information on travel writing.

Many travel writers join the following organizations that help promote their services:

■ Freelance Success	www.freelancesuccess.com
■ Guide Book Writers	www.guidebookwriters.com
■ International Food, Wine, and Travel Writers Association	www.ifwtwa.org
■ North American Travel Journalists Association	www.natja.org
■ Travelwriters	www.travelwriters.com
■ Writers Marketplace	www.writersmarketplace.com

Useful Resources

You will find numerous resources available to assist you with a job search within the travel industry, from general job and career books to directories and publications of professional associations. In addition to the specific books mentioned throughout this chapter, you may want to refer to two books which give a good overview of opportunities in the travel industry:

Guiding Your Entry Into Hospitality, Recreation, and Tourism Mega-Profession, Jack B. Samuels and Reginald Foucar-Szocki (Prentice-Hall, 1998)

Hospitality and Tourism Careers: A Blueprint for Success, Carl
Riegel and Melissa Dallas (Prentice-Hall, 1998)

Each book has informative chapters on various segments of the travel
industry. You will also find a few other career books that deal with
specific segments of the industry, such as travel agents, airline pilots,
travel writers, or in hotel management and cruise lines. Many of these
books should be available in your local library and a few bookstores.

You should also begin reading several of the trade publications and
following developments within the professional travel associations.
Magazines such as *Travel Digest, Travel Weekly, Hotel and Resort
Industry, Meetings and Conventions, Successful Meetings,* and *Tour and
Travel News* will keep you abreast of developments in the travel industry.
Professional associations such as the Institute of Certified Travel Agents,
International Association of Convention and Visitors Bureaus, Meeting
Professionals International, and the Society of Incentive Travel Executives
provide information on their organization and membership. Since all of
these organizations have websites (see previous sections on these
subjects), you can learn more about them by visiting their sites on the
Internet.

Internet Travel Specialists

Like so many other businesses today, more and more of the travel and
hospitality industry is engaged in e-commerce. All major industry players
have their own websites from which they provide information and
promote their products and services. Indeed, the Internet is the perfect
medium for the travel and hospitality industry. Bypassing traditional
commissioned gatekeepers, individuals and companies can now directly
purchase products and services from the producers.

We anticipate a tremendous growth of e-commerce in the travel and
hospitality industry. In fact, you may want to consider staking out an
exciting e-commerce career within this industry. For starters, visit some
of the major websites that specialize in consumer travel information and
services:

- Away.com   www.away.com
- Cruise411   www.cruise411.com

- Expedia   www.expedia.com
- Fodor's   www.fodors.com
- Frommer's   www.frommers.com
- Hotwire   www.hotwire.com
- iExplore.com   www.iexplore.com
- JohnnyJet   www.johnnyjet.com
- My Travel   www.mytravel.com
- Orbitz   www.orbitz.com
- Priceline   www.priceline.com
- Quikbook   www.quikbook.com
- SideStep   www.sidestep.com
- Site59   www.site59.com
- Smarter Living   www.smarterliving.com
- Travelocity   www.travelocity.com
- USA Hotel Guide   www.usahotelguide.com

Behind each of these websites are web designers, web programmers, managers of client services, customer service representatives, business developers, hotel and cruise specialists, partnership marketers, content providers, and accountants. While many people working in this end of the travel business do little travel, they are in the exciting business of selling travel dreams via the Internet.

Our sample websites should give you an idea of what's in store for the future of the travel and hospitality industry on the Internet. Many websites specialize in key sectors of this industry: air, hotels, car rentals, cruises, tours, and insurance. By using various search engines, you should be able to explore hundreds of other travel and hospitality sites on the Internet. Individuals first entering the travel and hospitality industry are well advised to become Internet savvy. For, in the end, much of the future of this industry will be found online engaged in billions of dollars of e-commerce.

The following books provide good overviews of the many travel-oriented websites involved in e-commerce:

Michael Shapiro's Internet Travel Planner, 2nd Edition, Michael Shapiro (Globe Pequot, 2002)

Practical Nomad Guide to the Online Travel Marketplace, Edward Hasbrouck (Avalon Travel Publishing, 2001)

The Rough Guide to Travel Online, Samantha Cook and Greg Ward (Rough Guides, 2002)

Travel Planning on the Internet: The Click and Easy Guide, Ron and Caryl Krannich (Impact Publications, 2001)

5

✈

Federal, State, and Local Governments

FEDERAL, STATE, AND LOCAL governments offer numerous on-the-job opportunities to travel at home and abroad. Whether you travel or live overseas through the U.S. Agency for International Development, the Peace Corps, or the Departments of State, Defense, Homeland Security, Commerce, and Justice, or inspect projects, field offices, or products within the United States through the Departments of Agriculture, Transportation, Energy, or Interior, the federal government can be one of the best employers for travel. Even within state and local (city and county) governments, opportunities abound to travel at home and abroad.

International Travel and Opportunities

The largest number of international job opportunities in the United States are found with various agencies of the federal government. Approximately 120,000 federal civilian employees work overseas. Another 500,000 U.S. military work in overseas U.S. installations.

But these numbers represent less than half of all government employees working in international affairs. Indeed, the federal government employs nearly 680,000 individuals in positions relating to national defense and international relations (for a statistical overview of the federal government, see www.opm.gov/feddata/index.asp). The majority of international-related government jobs are based in the United States. These jobs either provide support for agency field operations, or they direct international operations from U.S.-based offices. Each agency has some international interest and staffs itself accordingly. At the same time, many state and local governments offer international job opportunities because of their involvement in international trade and investment.

While many of the federal government's international jobs are based in the United States and require occasional travel abroad, many other international jobs require residence in foreign countries and rotation from one field site to another as well as between field and headquarters. Many individuals working in the U.S. Department of State and the U.S. Agency for International Development, for example, experience frequent moves.

Definitions and Distinctions

The federal government hires all types of individuals for international positions, ranging from highly skilled intelligence specialists to administrative support personnel. Most positions deal with security, international politics, economics, administrative relations, commercial activities, nation building, and information affairs, as well as all support services required to perform numerous international activities.

The distinction between what is an international or a non-international job is not always clear. For example, one may be employed as a Department of State librarian in charge of developing and maintaining an excellent international resource collection. While this position involves a great deal of knowledge and skill concerning international affairs, it does not require overseas travel nor the use of foreign languages. Yet, the position could lead to other international positions requiring overseas travel and knowledge of foreign languages.

For our purposes, we consider any position which to some degree involves international or global affairs to be an international position. This broad definition includes Foreign Service Officers, Peace Corps Volunteers and staff, U.S. Agency for International Development employees, members of intelligence and immigration agencies (CIA, DIA, FBI, DEA, INS), as well as thousands of individuals in other agencies promoting foreign, military, economic, commercial, and social goals in both policy and support staff positions at the federal, state, and local levels. Some agencies and positions are primarily oriented toward foreign policy, whereas others are mainly concerned with promoting domestic policies, especially security, trade, and economic development, through the use of international resources.

The "Big Six" Federal Employers

The federal government offers thousands of international job opportunities. The largest number of international jobs are found with the "Big Six" federal agencies that have major international missions:

- Department of State   www.state.gov
- Department of Defense   www.defenselink.mil
- Department of Homeland
  Security   www.dhs.gov
- U.S. Agency for International
  Development (USAID)   www.usaid.gov
- Peace Corps   www.peacecorps.gov
- Central Intelligence Agency   www.cia.gov

The "Big Six" offer the largest number of international positions. They are an important "network" for job seekers who want to live and travel abroad.

Thousands of additional international positions are found in the Executive Office of the President, within other executive departments and agencies, and throughout various congressional agencies, committees, and personal staffs.

But most international job seekers interested in government work set their sights on the "Big Six" agencies, because these agencies offer the largest number of international positions. In addition, these agencies constitute one of the most important "networks" for job seekers who want to live and travel abroad. Many former Peace Corps Volunteers, for example, move into positions in the U.S. Agency for International Development and other agencies within the Department of State. Within the intelligence community, individuals who work for the Defense Intelligence Agency (DIA) or the Federal Bureau of Investigation (FBI) also find international job opportunities with the Central Intelligence Agency (CIA) and the Drug Enforcement Agency (DEA). Many other federal agencies have international interests, offices, and positions. Some of them, such as international agencies within the Department of Agriculture and Department of Commerce, hire a large number of international specialists. Other agencies only have a small number of international positions.

Other Agencies With International Positions

Other federal government departments and agencies offering international opportunities include the following:

- African Development
  Foundation   www.adf.gov
- Consumer Product Safety
  Commission   www.cpsc.gov
- Department of Agriculture   www.usda.gov
- Department of Commerce   www.doc.gov
- Department of Energy   www.energy.gov
- Department of Health
  and Human Services   www.os.dhhs.gov
- Department of Justice   www.usdoj.gov
- Department of Transportation   www.dot.gov
- Environmental Protection
  Agency   www.epa.gov
- Export-Import Bank   www.exim.gov
- Federal Communications
  Commission   www.fcc.gov
- General Services
  Administration   www.gsa.gov
- Inter-American Foundation   www.iaf.gov
- Internal Revenue Service   www.irs.ustreas.gov
- Smithsonian Institution   www.si.edu
- U.S. Postal Service   www.usps.gov

For additional information on U.S. government involvement in defense and global affairs, follow this link which is available through the General Services Administration's (GSA) useful gateway website, FirstGov.com:

www.firstgov.gov/Citizen/Topics/Defense.shtml

Let's briefly review each of the major departments and agencies that offer international job opportunities. Most are headquartered in the Washington, DC metropolitan area. Since the federal government is highly wired via the Internet, be sure to explore each of our recommended websites, which include a wealth of information on various federal employers. Many of these websites will point you directly to an agency's international operations as well as its key personnel and vacancy announcements.

Key Departments and Agencies

Making Contacts

You can easily access information on the federal government by going directly to the White House's gateway website:

www.whitehouse.gov

Start by clicking on to "Your Government" and then "More Offices" which takes you directly to "The Executive Office of the President." From here, just click on the particular office you are interested in, such as the National Security Council. You'll go to a section that includes information on the National Security Council:

www.whitehouse.gov/nsc

Do the same type of search for other offices in the Executive Office of the President. To access information on other executive agencies, click on to "Citizens' Handbook," which takes you to another useful gateway site (www.firstgov.gov operated by the GSA), and "Federal Agencies and Commissions" under the "Government Connections" section. The "Federal Agencies and Commissions" lists all offices in alphabetical order.

If you click on to the linkage to the Federal Citizen Information Center (FCIC) National Contact Center (www.info.gov), you will go to a gateway site that takes you to a telephone directory to all government agencies:

<u>www.pueblo.gsa.gov/call/phone.htm</u>

Therefore, if you need current telephone numbers of federal agencies, go to this useful website.

If you explore the White House's website (www.whitehouse.gov), you'll discover this is one of the most useful gateway sites for accessing information, including vacancy announcements, on agencies.

Executive Office of the President

The Executive Office of the President is a relatively small employer (fewer than 2,000 full-time employees) compared to various executive branch departments and independent agencies. Nonetheless, it employs several international specialists. The major offices involved with international affairs include:

Council of Economic Advisors
www.whitehouse.gov/cea

Analyzes the economy and makes policy recommendations to the President for economic growth and stability. Covers both domestic and international economic policy issues.

National Security Council (NSC)
www.whitehouse.gov/nsc

Advises the President on all policy matters (domestic, foreign, military) relating to national security. Includes area (Asia, Africa, Europe, Russia, the former Soviet republics, Near East, and South Asia) and policy (arms control, intelligence, economic affairs, and legislative affairs) divisions.

Office of Management and Budget (OMB)
www.whitehouse.gov/omb

Assists the President in preparing and formulating the federal budget as well as controlling the administration of the budget. Informs the President on the progress of government agencies. Within the National Security Programs Office, it includes a **National Security Division** and an **International Affairs Division**.

Office of National Drug Control Policy
www.whitehousedrugpolicy.gov

Coordinates federal, state, and local efforts to control illegal drugs as well as devises national strategies relating to anti-drug activities. While primarily oriented toward domestic drug control, this office's international interests include dealing with Mexico, Colombia, international money laundering and asset forfeiture, and cocaine interdiction.

Office of Science and Technology Policy
www.ostp.gov

Advises the President on all matters relating to science, engineering, and technology relevant to the economy, national security, health, foreign relations, and the environment.

Office of the United States Trade Representative
www.ustr.gov

Responsible for formulating and coordinating all trade policy for the U.S. Functions as the country's chief trade representative and negotiator for all multinational (WTO, OECD, FTAA, APEC, NAFTA, CAFTA, UNCTAD, UNEP) and bilateral trade matters. Many former employees who worked in this office as U.S. trade negotiators are noted for playing the "revolving door" game by becoming highly paid consultants to foreign governments on U.S. trade matters after working in this office.

White House Office

Provides the President with staff assistance necessary for the orderly day-to-day administration of the Office of President. Includes such divisions as Chief of Staff, Counsel to the President, Press Secretary, Presidential Personnel, Communications, Presidential Advance, Presidential Scheduling, Legislative Affairs, Economic and Domestic Policy, Public Liaison, Administration, National Service, Military, Office of the First Lady, Cabinet Affairs, Domestic Policy Council, Economic Policy Council, and Agriculture, Trade, Food Assistance.

The Departments

For linkages to the various federal government departments, check out GSA's useful gateway site:

www.firstgov.gov/Agencies/Federal/index.shtml

If you wish to contact agencies by phone, use this site in conjunction with GSA's gateway telephone directory to the federal government:

www.pueblo.gsa.gov/call/phone.htm

Department of Agriculture
www.usda.gov

The Department of Agriculture is one of the largest employers of international specialists who are involved with foreign agricultural issues affecting U.S. agricultural and trade policies. The **Foreign Agricultural Service** (FSA), for example, posts nearly 100 agricultural specialists in more than 60 American embassies and consulates worldwide. It monitors foreign agriculture policies and commercial trade relations and promotes U.S. agricultural products. Other offices and divisions within the department deal with specific policy matters (conservation, forestry, inspection, transportation) or provide policy support services (research, marketing, information). The major international-related agencies within the department include:

- Foreign Agricultural Service   www.fas.usda.gov
- Agricultural Research Service   www.ars.usda.gov
- Food Safety and Inspection
  Service   www.fsis.usda.gov
- Forest Service   www.fs.fed.us
- World Agricultural Outlook   www.usda.gov/commodity/
  Board   index.htm

Department of Commerce
www.doc.gov or www.commerce.gov

The mission of this department is to promote the nation's international trade, economic growth, and technological advancement. Its international interests and activities are extensive, from encouraging competitive foreign trade, standardization, and telecommunications to protecting U.S. trademarks and copyrights and promoting U.S. exports. The major international employers within the Department of Commerce include:

- International Trade
  Administration   www.ita.doc.gov
- U.S. Commercial Service   www.export.gov/comm_svc/
- U.S. Census Bureau   www.census.gov
- Market Access and Compliance   www.mac.doc.gov
- Trade Compliance Center   www.tcc.mac.doc.gov
- Bureau of Industry and Security   www.bis.doc.gov
- Import Administration   www.ia.ita.doc.gov
- Trade Information Center   www.trade.gov/td/tic
- Manufacturing and Services   www.ita.doc.gov/td
- National Oceanic and
  Atmospheric Administration   www.noaa.gov
- Bureau of Economic Analysis   www.bea.gov
- Technology Administration   www.technology.gov
- National Institute of
  Standards and Technology   www.nist.gov
- National Technical
  Information Service   www.ntis.gov
- United States Patent and
  Trademark Office   www.uspto.gov

Department of Defense and Related Agencies
www.defenselink.mil

The Department of Defense is by definition extensively involved in international affairs. Its activities involve everything from defense and security matters to educating the children of U.S. military personnel assigned abroad. International-related jobs in this department range from high-level policy, information, and security positions based in Washington, DC to blue-collar positions at U.S. military bases abroad. A few of the major offices that hire international specialists include:

- Africa Center for Strategic Studies — www.africacenter.org
- Asia-Pacific Center for Security Studies — www.apcss.org
- Defense Security Cooperation Agency — www.dsca.mil
- Defense Advanced Research Projects Agency — www.darpa.mil
- Defense Information Systems Agency — www.disa.mil
- Defense Intelligence Agency — www.dia.mil
- Defense Security Service — www.dss.mil
- National Geospatial-Intelligence Agency — www.nima.mil
- National Reconnaissance Office — www.nro.gov
- National Security Agency — www.nsa.gov
- Near East South Asia Center for Strategies Studies — www.ndu.edu/nesa
- Undersecretary for Defense (Policy) — www.dod.gov/policy

Many civilian government positions are available with U.S. military bases in Europe, Asia, and the Pacific. For information on the various services attached to the Departments of Army, Navy, and Air Force, please visit these relevant websites:

- Department of Air Force   www.af.mil
- Department of Army   www.army.mil
- Department of Navy   www.navy.mil
- U.S. Marine Corps   www.usmc.mil

The U.S. Coast Guard, which used to be part of the Department of Transportation, has now been absorbed into the Department of Homeland Security: www.uscg.mil.

Teachers who wish to work with Department of Defense schools abroad should contact this office:

- Department of Defense
  Educational Activity   www.dodea.edu

Department of Energy
www.doe.gov

The Department of Energy is responsible for developing a comprehensive national energy plan, promoting energy technology, marketing federal power, conserving energy, operating the nuclear weapons program, and collecting and analyzing data on energy. This is a unique department in which over 80 percent of its personnel are private contractors. Since energy policy has important international dimensions, the department has numerous international interests. The major agencies and offices within the department hiring international specialists include:

- Energy Information
  Administration   www.eia.doe.gov
- International Nuclear
  Safety Center   www.insc.anl.gov
- Office of Science   www.er.doe.gov
- Office of Nuclear Energy,
  Science and Technology   www.ne.doe.gov
- Office of Policy and
  International Affairs   www.pi.energy.gov

Department of Health and Human Services
www.os.dhhs.gov

The Department of Health and Human Services is responsible for promoting the nation's health and welfare. Extensively involved in international health matters, its international activities involve conducting research and promoting health policy. The major agencies and offices within the department with international interests and which tend to hire international specialists include:

- Centers for Disease Control
  and Prevention   www.cdc.gov
- National Cancer Institute   www.cancer.gov
- National Institute of
  Environmental Health Sciences   www.niehs.nih.gov
- National Institute of
  Mental Health   www.nimh.nih.gov
- National Institutes of Health   www.nih.gov
- Office of Global Health   www.globalhealth.gov
- Substance Abuse and Mental
  Health Services Administration   www.samhsa.gov

Department of Homeland Security
www.dhs.gov

The Department of Homeland Security was created in 2003 from agencies which were formerly part of the Departments of Treasury, Justice, Transportation, Agriculture, Health and Human Services, Energy, Defense, Commerce, FBI, and GSA. Hailed by the White House as "the most significant transformation of the U.S. government in over a half-century," the mission of this huge department (180,000 employees, which makes it the fourth largest U.S. government agency) is to prevent terrorist attacks within the United States, reduce America's vulnerability to terrorism, and minimize the damage and recover from attacks that do occur. The department includes four major divisions consisting of several agencies merged from 12 different departments and agencies:

Border and Transportation Security   Old Agency

- Animal and Plant Health Inspection Service   Agriculture
- Federal Law Enforcement Training Center   Treasury
- Federal Protective Service   GSA
- Immigration and Naturalization Service   Justice
- Office of Domestic Preparedness   Justice
- Transportation Security Administration   Transportation
- U.S. Customs Service   Treasury

Emergency Preparedness and Response

- Domestic Emergency Support Team   Justice
- Federal Emergency Management Agency   Independent
- National Disaster Medical System   HHS
- National Domestic Preparedness Office   FBI
- Nuclear Incident Response Team   Energy
- Strategic National Stockpile   HHS

Science and Technology

- CBRN Countermeasures Programs   Energy
- Environmental Measurements Laboratory   Energy
- National BW Defense Analysis Center   Defense
- Plum Island Animal Disease Center   Agriculture

Information Analysis and Infrastructure Protection

- Critical Infrastructure Assurance Office   Commerce
- Energy Security and Assurance Program   Energy
- Federal Computer Incident Response Center   GSA
- National Communications System   Defense
- National Infrastructure Protection Center   FBI

The department also includes these two agencies:

- U.S. Coast Guard   Transportation
- U.S. Secret Service   Treasury

Many individuals working for the former agencies that constitute this new department, especially the U.S. Coast Guard, U.S. Customs Service, Immigration and Naturalization Service, Border Patrol, and the Federal Emergency Management Agency (FEMA), have jobs involving travel. Key national security agencies, such as the Central Intelligence Agency (CIA), Federal Bureau of Investigation (FBI), and the National Security Agency (NSA), remain outside the control of the Department of Homeland Security.

Based on the federal government's past experience in creating new departments, we expect it may take at least 10 years before this department becomes effective. In the meantime, expect a great deal of confusion as the department navigates through a minefield of bureaucratic turf wars.

If you are interested in jobs relating to national security and foreign intelligence, focus your job search on the various agencies that fall under this new department umbrella, as well as on the Central Intelligence Agency (independent agency), Federal Bureau of Investigation (Department of Justice), and the Department of Defense's National Security Agency, Defense Intelligence Agency, and the National Reconnaissance Office. A good resource for exploring 14 key agencies involved in intelligence work is the U.S. Intelligence Community's website:

www.intelligence.gov

Many of these agencies expect to expand their operations during the next few years as the federal government gives greater budgetary priority to national security and terrorism issues. Mark Merritt's *Alternative Careers in Secret Operations* (Impact Publications, 1999) also outlines the extensive network of employment and professional relationships that make up the "intelligence community."

Department of the Interior
www.doi.gov

The Department of the Interior is responsible for protecting and managing federally owned lands and natural resources. It is also responsible for American Indian reservation communities and for the peoples populating island territories under U.S. jurisdiction. For a summary of the Department's international programs, which employ about 141 out of 70,600 (about 0.02%) employees, visit this website:

www.doi.gov/intl/

The major agencies and offices within the department with international interests include:

- **Bureau of Land Management**   www.blm.gov
- **Bureau of Reclamation**   www.usbr.gov
- **Minerals Management Service**   www.mms.gov
- **National Park Service**   www.nps.gov
- **Office of Insular Affairs**   www.doi.gov/oia
- **U.S. Fish and Wildlife Service**   www.fws.gov
- **U.S. Geological Survey**   www.usgs.gov

Department of Justice and Related Agencies
www.usdoj.gov

One of the fastest growing federal departments, the Department of Justice is responsible for enforcing federal laws. Its thousands of lawyers, investigators, and agents are involved in protecting citizens from criminals and subversion, ensuring business competition, safeguarding consumers, and enforcing drug, immigration, and naturalization laws. Its international interests are especially pronounced in the areas of drug enforcement and immigration. The major offices and agencies within the Department of Justice with international interests include:

- **Antitrust Division**   www.usdoj.gov/atr/
- **Bureau of Alcohol, Tobacco, Firearms, and Explosives**   www.atf.gov
- **Civil Division**   www.usdoj.gov/civil/home.html
- **Criminal Division**   www.usdoj.gov/criminal/criminal-home.html
- **Drug Enforcement Administration**   www.usdoj.gov/dea

- Federal Bureau of Investigation   www.fbi.gov
- Foreign Claims Settlement
  Commission of the U.S.   www.usdoj.gov/fcsc
- INTERPOL-U.S. National
  Central Bureau   www.usdoj.gov/usncb
- U.S. Marshals Service   www.usdoj.gov/marshals

Department of Labor
www.dol.gov

The Department of Labor is responsible for the welfare of wage earners. It administers federal labor laws on safety, welfare, and compensation of workers, including unemployment insurance and workers' compensation. The major agencies and offices with international interests include:

- Bureau of International
  Labor Affairs   www.dol.gov/ilab
- Office of the Solicitor   www.dol.gov/sol/

Department of State
www.state.gov

The Department of State is responsible for advising the President on foreign policy matters and for implementing U.S. foreign policy. It represents the U.S. abroad through its network of embassies and consulates and participates in the United Nations and over 50 major international organizations. It is the federal government's major employer of international specialists, with a total personnel level of nearly 34,000. Entry into many positions within this department involves taking the Foreign Service examination which is given each year in April:

http://careers.state.gov/officer/join/examinfo.html

The examination also is used for several Foreign Service Officer (FSO – www.careers.state.gov/officer) positions with the U.S. Agency for International Development (USAID) and the U.S. Department of Commerce.

The Foreign Service constitutes a separate personnel system within the federal government with its own rules, regulations, and procedures. Other positions within the Department of State fall under the personnel system administered by the Office of Personnel Management (OPM) and its General Schedule (GS) salary scale. Some of the most interesting agencies and offices in this department include:

- Bureau of African Affairs — www.state.gov/p/af
- Bureau of Consular Affairs — www.travel.state.gov
- Bureau of East Asian and Pacific Affairs — www.state.gov/p/eap
- Bureau of European and Eurasian Affairs — www.state.gov/p/eur
- Bureau of Intelligence and Research — www.state.gov/s/inr
- Bureau of the International Narcotics and Law Enforcement Affairs — www.state.gov/p/inl
- Bureau of Near Eastern Affairs — www.state.gov/p/nea
- Bureau of Oceans and International Environmental and Scientific Affairs — www.state.gov/g/oes
- Bureau of Political-Military Affairs — www.state.gov/t/pm
- Bureau of Population, Refugees, and Migration — www.state.gov/g/prm
- Bureau of South and Central Asian Affairs — www.state.gov/p/sa
- Bureau of Western Hemisphere Affairs — www.state.gov/p/wha

Department of Transportation
www.dot.gov

The Department of Transportation is responsible for the nation's overall transportation policy in the areas of highways, mass transit, railways, aviation, waterways, and ports. It is also responsible for the safety of oil and gas pipelines. Its international transportation interests focus on aviation, maritime, and trade issues. These are centered in the following agencies and offices:

- Federal Aviation Administration   www.faa.gov
- Maritime Administration   www.marad.dot.gov
- Office of Intelligence
  and Security   http://152.122.41.10
- Office of the Assistant Secretary
  for Aviation and International   http://ostpxweb.dot.gov/
  Affairs   aviation/index.html
- Saint Lawrence Seaway
  Development Corporation   www.seaway.dot.gov

Department of Treasury
www.ustreas.gov

The Department of Treasury is responsible for formulating and recommending economic, financial, tax, and fiscal policies. It is the federal government's chief financial agent enforcing tax laws and manufacturing coins and currency. Its international interests focus on international tax and revenue, monetary, finance, trade, investment, and banking issues. The major offices and agencies involved with international issues and affairs include:

- Bureau of Alcohol, Tobacco,
  and Firearms   www.atf.treas.gov
- Financial Crimes
  Enforcement Network   www.fincen.gov
- Internal Revenue Service   www.irs.gov
- Office of International Affairs   www.ustreas.gov/offices/
    international-affairs/index
    .html
- Office of the Comptroller
  of the Currency   www.occ.treas.gov

Independent Agencies and
Government Corporations
www.whitehouse.gov/government/independent-agencies.html

The following independent agencies and government corporations offer numerous international job opportunities. Inquiries and applications should be addressed directly to each organization. Start by visiting the website of each organization. In most cases, the website will provide information on vacancies as well as application procedures. Some sites, such as the Central Intelligence Agency (www.cia.gov), will supply linkages to other related agencies.

African Development Foundation
www.adf.gov

This nonprofit, government corporation promotes broad-based sustainable development in sub-Saharan Africa. Established by Congress in 1980 as both a federal agency and a public corporation, ADF has funded over 1,500 projects in 34 African countries during the past 25 years. It provides grants, loans, and loan guarantees to private African groups, associations, and other organizations engaged in self-help activities. ADF is headquartered in Washington, DC and operates with a staff of 35.

Central Intelligence Agency (CIA)
www.cia.gov

The Central Intelligence Agency is one of three major federal intelligence agencies involved in collecting, evaluating, and disseminating information on political, military, economic, and scientific developments relevant to national security. Employing over 35,000 individuals (actual numbers remain classified), it hires numerous international specialists with area and foreign language skills who become intelligence officers and analysts. The CIA is linked to 15 other federal agencies that define the federal government's "Intelligence Community":

www.intelligence.gov

For travel lovers, the CIA publishes annually a very useful directory on countries around the world – *The World Factbook*. It can be downloaded by going to this section of the CIA website:

www.cia.gov/cia/publications/factbook/index.html

Consumer Product Safety Commission
www.cpsc.gov

The Consumer Product Safety Commission is responsible for maintaining the safety of consumer products. It does this by setting uniform product safety standards and by conducting research and investigating the causes and prevention of product-related deaths, illnesses, and injuries. It is involved in some international activities through its **Office of International Affairs**.

Environmental Protection Agency
www.epa.gov

The Environmental Protection Agency is responsible for controlling and abating pollution in the areas of air, water, solid waste, pesticides, radiation, and toxic substances. While most of its activities center on coordinating federal, state, and local government efforts, it has become increasingly involved in international environmental issues. Its international interests and activities are centered in the **Office of International Affairs**:

www.epa.gov/oia

Export-Import Bank of the United States
www.exim.gov

The Export-Import Bank is responsible for promoting the export of U.S. products. It does this by assisting private firms with commercial export financing involving loans, guarantees, and insurance. Most offices and positions within this organization involve international activities. Includes eight regional offices, from New York to California, that provide expert assistance and access to export financing in every state.

Federal Communications Commission
www.fcc.gov

The Federal Communications Commission is responsible for regulating interstate and international communications by radio, television, wire, satellite, and cable. Its jurisdiction covers the 50 states, the District of Columbia, and U.S. possessions. Its international interests are primarily centered in the **International Bureau:**

www.fcc.gov/ib

Federal Reserve System
www.federalreserve.gov

As the central bank of the United States, the Federal Reserve System is responsible for administering and making policy for the nation's credit and monetary affairs. It is responsible for promoting a sound banking system that is responsive to both domestic and international needs of the nation.

General Services Administration
www.gsa.gov

The General Services Administration establishes policy for and provides economical and efficient management of government property and records, including construction and operation of buildings, procurement and distribution of supplies, utilization and disposal of property; transportation, traffic, and communications management; and management of the government-wide automatic data processing resources program.

Inter-American Foundation
www.iaf.gov

This independent government corporation is responsible for supporting social and economic activities in Latin America and the Caribbean by providing grants to nongovernmental and community-based organizations that operate innovative, sustainable, and participatory self-help projects aimed at improving the quality of life of poor people. Primarily funds partnerships among grassroots and nonprofit organizations, businesses, and local governments.

National Aeronautics and Space Administration
www.nasa.gov

The National Aeronautics and Space Administration (NASA) conducts research and operates programs relating to flight within and outside the Earth's atmosphere, including the nation's major space programs and centers. Its international interests involve working with Russia and several other countries in developing the space program.

National Science Foundation
www.nsf.gov

The National Science Foundation is responsible for promoting research and education programs in science and engineering. It does this through grants, contracts, and cooperative agreements with universities, university consortia, and nonprofit and other research organizations. Its international interests center on several offices and divisions that deal with international programs within the **Office of International Science and Engineering**. For information on NSF's international interests, visit this section of their website:

www.nsf.gov/div/index.jsp?div=OISE

Nuclear Regulatory Commission
www.nrc.gov

The Nuclear Regulatory Commission is responsible for licensing and regulating civilian use of nuclear energy to protect public health and safety and the environment. Makes rules, sets standards, and inspects those licensed to build and operate nuclear reactors and other facilities as well as to own and use nuclear materials. Its international interests center on the **International Programs Office:**

www.nrc.gov/what-we-do/international.html

Overseas Private Investment Corporation
www.opic.gov

The Overseas Private Investment Corporation assists U.S. companies in making profitable investments in approximately 150 emerging markets and developing nations. While helping companies minimize investment risks abroad, the Corporation also encourages investment projects that will assist countries with social and economic development. It provides U.S. investors with assistance in finding investment opportunities, insurance to protect investments (political risk insurance), and loans and loan guaranties to help finance their projects.

Peace Corps
www.peacecorps.gov

Since its establishment in 1961, the Peace Corps has sent 182,000 volunteers to work in 138 host countries. Today, this organization, with a staff of 1,072, promotes world peace, friendship, and understanding by providing 7,810 volunteers and trainees to work in nearly 100 developing countries for periods of two to three years. Volunteers work in a variety of programs, from teaching English to community development, health care, and small enterprise development. For many individuals interested in international jobs and careers, the Peace Corps offers excellent "entry-level" opportunities to get international experience that will become invaluable for later finding jobs with the U.S. State Department, U.S.

Agency for International Development, private contractors and consultants, nonprofit organizations, and private voluntary organizations (PVOs). All positions within the Peace Corps, either Volunteer or staff, should be considered "international" positions because they involve international operations.

Securities and Exchange Commission
www.sec.gov

The Securities and Exchange Commission is responsible for administering federal securities laws that protect investors and ensure that the securities markets are operated fairly and honestly. Its international interests center on the following offices and divisions:

- Corporation Finance   www.sea.gov/divisions/corpfin.shtml
- Enforcement   www.sec.gov/divisions/enforce.shtml

Smithsonian Institution
www.si.edu

The Smithsonian Institution is responsible for promoting historical, technological, scientific, and artistic knowledge of the nation. It does this by presenting exhibits, conducting research, publishing studies, and participating in cooperative international programs of scholarly exchange. Its international-related activities are found in numerous positions throughout the organization, including the museums and galleries. However, the largest number of international specialists are found in:

- Smithsonian Journeys   http://smithsonianjourneys.org
- Woodrow Wilson International Center for Scholars   www.wilsoncenter.org

U.S. Agency for International Development (USAID)
www.usaid.gov

The Agency for International Development is an independent federal government agency responsible for developing and implementing U.S. economic assistance programs. Receiving its foreign policy guidance from the Secretary of State, this is the single most important U.S. government agency involved in the developing world, which encompasses nearly 75 percent of the world's population. It defines the focus and provides the funding for a great deal of public and private sector development efforts in Third and Fourth World countries. It presently emphasizes economic growth, agricultural development, global health, democracy, conflict prevention, humanitarian assistance, and sustainable development.

Through its Global Development Alliance (GDA), it works with more than 3,500 American companies and over 300 U.S.-based private voluntary organizations (PVOs), including indigenous organizations, universities, international agencies, other governments, and other U.S. government organizations. USAID missions abroad are staffed with project officers and specialists in agriculture, rural development, health, nutrition, population planning, education, human resource development, private sector development, environment, and energy. It provides billions of dollars in funds for projects that are implemented by the many private contractors and nonprofit organizations.

Although USAID is not yet a part of the U.S. Department of State (plans are underway to absorb it), entry into most USAID positions is via the Foreign Service. USAID is primarily organized by geographic bureaus (Sub-Saharan Africa; Asia and Near East; Europe and Eurasia; Latin America and the Caribbean), functional bureaus (Global Health; Economic Growth, Agriculture, and Trade; and Democracy, Conflict, and Humanitarian Assistance), and headquarters bureaus (Management; Legislative and Public Affairs; and Policy and Program Coordination).

U.S. Institute of Peace
www.usip.org

Created in 1984, the U.S. Institute of Peace, an independent, nonpartisan federal institution created and funded by Congress, is responsible for strengthening the nation's ability to promote international peace and the peaceful resolution of conflicts throughout the world. It does this by providing grants and fellowships to individual scholars, conducting in-house research, and sponsoring educational activities.

U.S. Trade and Development Agency (USTDA)
www.tda.gov

Established in 1981 as an independent agency within the International Development Cooperation Agency, the U.S. Trade and Development Agency promotes economic development and U.S. commercial interests in developing and middle-income countries through the export of U.S. goods and services. It assists U.S. companies in doing business overseas. It funds various forms of technical assistance, feasibility studies, training, orientation visits, and business workshops that support the development of a modern infrastructure and a fair and open trading environment. This is a small agency with only 51 employees who direct activities in 69 host countries around the world.

U.S. International Trade Commission
www.usitc.gov

The International Trade Commission is responsible for providing the President, Congress, and other government agencies with studies, reports, and recommendations relating to international trade and tariffs. It determines the impact of imports on U.S. industries and directs actions against certain unfair trade practices, such as patent, trademark, and copyright infringement. Its major activities involve conducting investigations, public hearings, and research projects concerning the international policies of the U.S. as well as the trade and tariff policies of other countries that affect U.S. trade and trade negotiations. For example, the Commission's work plays an important role in selecting items included in the Generalized System of Preferences (GSP), identifying unfair import practices, and interference with U.S. agricultural programs. Since much of its work involves laws, rules, and regulations, this organization is heavily staffed with lawyers.

U.S. Postal Service

www.usps.com

The U.S. Postal Service is responsible for the orderly processing and delivery of mail. Since its work involves international mail – individuals, businesses, and military – the U.S. Postal Service is increasingly involved in international matters. Its major international interests are centered in the **International and Military Mail Operations Division**. The U.S. Postal Service operates its own personnel system separate from other government agencies.

U.S. Congress

The U.S. Congress is very much involved in the international arena. International job opportunities are found on Capitol Hill (Senate and House personal and committee staffs) as well as among congressional agencies. While not as numerous as executive departments and agencies, nonetheless, many international positions are available in this branch of government. These positions often become stepping stones to other international positions in agencies of the executive branch of government and with private firms.

Finding a job with a congressional agency is similar to finding a job with an executive agency – contact the agency directly for information on vacancies and application procedures. It's best to start with the agency's website for vacancy and application information.

Congressional Agencies

Congressional agencies are the bureaucratic equivalent to executive agencies. They are responsible to and under the control of Congress rather than the Executive branch. Reflecting the international interests and work of Congress, these agencies offer several international opportunities for enterprising job seekers. Congressional agencies with the largest number of international activities include the Library of Congress, Congressional Budget Office, and the General Accounting Office.

Library of Congress
www.loc.gov

The Library of Congress is the national library. It maintains an extensive collection o f do cuments, pro vides impo rtant publishing and library services, and serves as the critical public policy research arm of the U.S. Congress. Its international activities are found in several offices but especially in the Foreign Affairs, Defense, and Trade Division of the **Congressional Research Service** (www.loc.gov/crsinfo), which provides congressional committees and members of Congress with information on questions relating to their day-to-day work, including foreign policy matters. Other offices involved in international matters include several divisions within **Acquisitions** and **Area Studies Collections**. For travel lovers who want background information on countries, the Library of Congress website includes a useful linkage to its Country Studies/Area Handbook Program (formerly the Army Area Handbook Program) which is part of the Area Studies Collections. Go to this website to view the contents of handbooks on 101 countries and regions published by the Federal Research Division (www.loc.gov/rr/frd) of the Library of Congress under the Country Studies Program:

http://lcweb2.loc.gov/frd/cs/profiles.html

Congressional Budget Office
www.cbo.gov

The Congressional Budget Office is Congress's counterpart to the Executive branch's Office of Management and Budget. It provides Congress with basic budget data as well as analyzes alternative fiscal, budgetary, and programmatic policy issues. Its international activities are centered in:

- Budget Analysis Unit
- Microeconomic and Financial Studies Division
- National Security Division

General Accounting Office (GAO)
www.gao.gov

The General Accounting Office is the investigative arm of Congress which is responsible for examining all matters relating to the receipt and disbursement of public funds. As such, it closely monitors and audits all Executive agencies involved in international matters, especially the Department of State, the U.S. Agency for International Development, the Office of the U.S. Trade Representative, the World Bank, the International Monetary Fund, the United Nations, and some Department of Defense functions. Its major international activities are centered in the office of **International Affairs and Trade**. However, other offices within GAO also have international responsibilities.

Congressional Staffs

International positions within Congress are found in two different areas:

- on personal staffs of members of the House and Senate
- on committee staffs within both the House and Senate

Both the House and Senate have their own administrative staffs, but these have little to do with international matters other than foreign travel.

Senate
www.senate.gov

International job opportunities in the U.S. Senate center on the staffs of these committees and subcommittees:

- **Appropriations:** Foreign Operations
- **Banking, House, and Urban Affairs:** International Finance and Monetary Policy
- **Budget**
- **Commerce, Science, and Transportation:** Consumer Affairs, Foreign Commerce, and Tourism
- **Finance:** International Trade

- **Foreign Relations:** All subcommittees
- **Judiciary:** Immigration

Senators who chair or are members of these committees and subcommittees also hire staff members who are responsible for international-related issues. Each senator hires one to four legislative assistants and other staffers who are responsible for foreign affairs, foreign relations, foreign trade, military, arms control, intelligence, human rights, immigration, refugee, and international drug and terrorism issues.

House of Representatives
www.house.gov

International positions in the House of Representatives follow the same pattern as in the Senate – committee and subcommittee staffs and personal staffs. For information on house committees and subcommittees, including members and staff personnel, visit this section of the House's website: www.house.gov/house/CommitteeWWW.html. House committees and subcommittees with international specialists include the following:

- **Agriculture:** Department of Operations, Oversight, Nutrition, and Forestry; and Specialty Crops and Foreign Agriculture Programs
- **Appropriations:** Defense; and Foreign Operations
- **Armed Services:** All subcommittees
- **Budget**
- **Finance Services:** Domestic and International Monetary Policy, Trade, and Technology
- **International Relations:** All subcommittees
- **Judiciary:** Immigration, Border Security, and Claims
- **Ways and Means:** Trade

Several members of the House of Representatives also designate one to three legislative assistants or other staff members to handle international-related issues. Like their Senate counterparts, these individuals are also responsible for other policy areas which may or may not be related to international concerns.

Federal Job Finding Strategies

When looking to the government for international employment opportunities, be sure to do your homework. Learn as much as possible about the agencies by visiting their websites and by networking with individuals who are familiar with the agency. Keep in mind that government agencies contract out a great deal. Try to discover whom they work with on international matters.

Unfortunately, many federal government agencies experience temporary hiring freezes that both delay and disappoint job seekers. USAID, for example, has undergone a great deal of downsizing and experiences frequent hiring freezes. Indeed, this agency is a shadow of what it used to be a decade or two ago. Much of its work is contracted out. Therefore, you may want to contact many of the firms that do work with USAID (see Chapter 8). Many contractors offer

> *Some agencies have their own hiring procedures and personnel systems.*

excellent international job opportunities. You can identify these firms through USAID's website (www.usaid.gov), which lists its contractors in the *USAID Yellow Book* (www.usaid.gov/business/yellowbook). USAID also maintains a useful list of "Development Links" on its website:

www.usaid.gov/about/resources

This invaluable network section will take you directly to many of the major federal government agencies, nongovernmental and private voluntary organizations, international and regional organizations, and foreign government agencies that work with USAID.

Finding an international job with the federal government requires carefully observing the formal hiring procedures as well as making personal contacts within targeted agencies. In most cases, hiring takes place at the agency level. Once a vacancy is announced, individuals should submit an application package. In most cases, the requested application package consists of a completed OF-612 or federal-style resume – two application options permitted by most federal agencies. You must complete these applications in reference to the qualifications specified in the vacancy announcement. Consequently, the more you know about the agency and position and tailor your application to the position, the better your chances of getting the job.

Some agencies have their own hiring procedures and personnel systems. For example, entry into many positions in the U.S. Department of State and the U.S. Agency for International Development is via the Foreign Service. Applicants must pass the Foreign Service Exam which is given each year in April. Other agencies, such as the Central Intelligence Agency, Defense Intelligence Agency, Smithsonian Institution, and the Library of Congress, also have their own application procedures and personnel systems.

The above federal agencies and congressional organizations are the major sources for international employment within the federal government. We recommend that you use the referenced websites for gathering information on the various agencies. When vacancies occur, they will be announced through the agency personnel office in the form of a position vacancy announcement. The position may also be listed through the Office of Personnel Management's website (www.usajobs.opm.gov), the agency's website, or published in printed job listings such as *Federal Career Opportunities* and *Federal Jobs Digest*. However, coverage of vacancies is not always complete nor timely through published sources.

It is always best to keep in close contact with the hiring agency in order to learn about impending vacancies. Start by going directly to the agency's website. All federal agencies have their own websites which include vacancy announcements and information on the agency's operations. Five good starting places for accessing information via the Internet on agencies are these key gateway websites:

www.firstgov.gov
www.whitehouse.gov
www.fedworld.gov
www.usajobs.opm.gov

You also may wish to call the agency personnel office for information on current vacancies. Better still, make contact with the hiring officials within the agency to learn if and when a vacancy will become available.

Key Federal Resources

If you are interested in pursuing international jobs with the federal government, we recommend the following books and computer software programs:

The Book of U.S. Government Jobs, 9th Edition, Dennis V. Damp (Bookhaven Press, 2005)

The Directory of Federal Jobs and Employers, Ron and Caryl Krannich (Impact Publications, 1996)

Electronic Federal Resume Guidebook, Kathryn Kraemer Troutman (JIST Publishing, 2001)

FBI Careers, Thomas Ackerman (JIST Publishing, 2005)

Federal Applications That Get Results, Russ Smith (Impact Publications, 1996)

Federal Career Opportunities (Federal Research Service, biweekly subscription service)

Federal Jobs Digest (Breakthrough Publications, biweekly subscription service)

Federal Resume Guidebook, Kathryn Kraemer Troutman (JIST Publishing, 2004)

Find a Federal Job Fast: How to Cut the Red Tape and Get Hired, 4th Edition, Ron and Caryl Krannich (Impact Publications, 1999)

Government Job Finder, 4th Edition, Daniel Lauber and Deborah Verlench (Planning/Communications, 2006)

Guide to America's Federal Jobs, Bruce Maxwell, ed. (JIST Publishing, 2005)

Guide to Homeland Security Jobs, Dnald B. Hutton and Anna Mydlarz (Barrons Educational Series, 2003)

Quick and Easy Federal Jobs Kit, software (DataTech, 2006)

Guide to Careers in Federal Law Enforcement, Thomas H. Ackerman (JIST Works, 1999)

Ten Steps to a Federal Job, Kathryn Kraemer Troutman (JIST Works, 2002)

Several directories also are available for researching different federal agencies:

Federal Executive Directory (Washington, DC: Carroll Publishing Co., annual)

Federal Personnel Guide (Bethesda, MD: Key Communications, annual)

Federal Yellow Book (Washington, DC: Monitor Publishing Co., annual)

Government Phone Book (Detroit, MI: Omnigraphics, annual)

The United States Government Manual (Washington, DC: U.S. Government Printing Office, annual)

Washington Information Directory (Washington, DC: Congressional Quarterly, Inc., annual)

Each of these books and directories provides names, addresses, and telephone numbers for locating the right offices and individuals you should contact for employment information.

Most of these resources are available in major public and university libraries, bookstores, and through Impact Publications (see the order form at the end of this book or visit the "CareerStore" section of their website: www.impactpublications.com).

State and Local Governments

International opportunities with state and local governments are both relatively unknown and widely overlooked among most international specialists. This is in part due to the expectation that only the federal government engages in foreign policy and international affairs.

During the past two decades, state and city governments have increasingly become involved in international affairs. Many have their own foreign policies involving:

- Trade promotion
- Tourism
- Local economic development
- Immigration
- International shipping

Florida, for example, maintains a state tourism agency which attempts to promote travel to Florida among European tourists. Virginia Beach maintains sister city relationships and promotes foreign industrial investment in the city through their Department of Economic Development. In certain areas, regional economic development authorities, tourism boards, and port authorities perform international functions for several units of government.

State and local governments offer unique international opportunities. They combine local economic issues with international development activities. For individuals who want to be involved in international affairs but wish to avoid many of the negative aspects of international careers – such as living abroad and transfers – these positions may be ideal.

Finding an international job with state and local governments requires a great deal of research and initiative on your part. Your best approach will be to identify which city or state governments you would like to work with and then research the organizations to find the offices involved in international affairs. Both the national and local branches of the World Affairs Councils of America (www.worldaffairscouncils.org) may be helpful in uncovering international positions with these governmental units.

Domestic Opportunities

Government also offers numerous opportunities to travel within the United States. Most agencies within the federal government, for example, have extensive field operations. Indeed, only 12 percent of federal government employees work in the Washington, DC metropolitan area.

Many federal government jobs involve frequent travel between headquarters offices in Washington, DC and field offices spread throughout the continental United States, Alaska, Hawaii, Puerto Rico, and other U.S. territories. Individuals in positions involving inspections, audits, and extension work tend to travel most frequently between field and headquarter offices.

Federal employees who travel the most frequently are U.S. postal workers who have local delivery routes or move the mail by truck between cities and regions each day. If you want a government job that constantly lets you travel, though perhaps not far from home, set your sights on your local post office.

Many federal jobs relating to law enforcement involve frequent travel. Federal agencies such as the Federal Bureau of Investigation (FBI), Central Intelligence Agency (CIA), Environmental Protection Agency (EPA), Immigration and Naturalization Service (INS), INTERPOL, National Security Agency, Bureau of Alcohol, Tobacco and Firearms (ATF), Customs Service, and the Secret Service, have numerous investigative positions involving travel. For information on how to land a job with these agencies, see Thomas H. Ackerman's *FBI Careers* (JIST Publishing, 2005); *John Douglas's Guide to Landing a Career in Law Enforcement* (McGraw-Hill, 2005); *John Douglas's Guide to Careers in the FBI* (Kaplan, 2005); Russ Smith's *Federal Jobs in Law Enforcement* (Impact Publications, 1995); and John W. Warner, Jr.'s *Federal Jobs in Law Enforcement*, 2nd Edition (Arco Publishing, 2001).

Many state and local government positions also involve frequent travel. State agencies with field offices or operations, especially in law enforcement, agriculture, and transportation, will have many positions that permit you to regularly travel. At the local level, police officers, building and health inspectors, and maintenance workers are constantly traveling on the job. For information on jobs at the state and local level, we recommend Daniel Lauber's latest edition of *Government Job Finder* (Planning/Communications, 2006) and www.lawenforcementjobs.com.

6

✈

International Education and Internships

FOR MANY PEOPLE, education is synonymous with travel. Indeed, numerous people got their first taste for travel because of a particularly inspiring teacher or an educational program they participated in during their high school, undergraduate, or graduate years. Perhaps it was a particular foreign language, history, political science, anthropology, business, or interdisciplinary course that motivated them to travel, work, or study abroad. Such experiences often represent the best and most memorable experiences for graduates when recalling their finest college moments. Some get struck with a long-term case of wanderlust because of such experiences.

Many students have an opportunity to participate in exchange programs, attend semester or summer abroad programs, acquire international internships, or become involved in off-campus field research. For them, combining education with travel is an exciting experience.

Whatever the particular experience, for many individuals it is their key years in education that often convinced them to pursue educational careers in specialties that also permit them to engage in frequent travel at home and abroad. Many literally become travel junkies within education, spending two or more months a year traveling "on assignment" for professional development purposes – be it teaching, research, attending conferences, or acquiring new subject matter or administrative skills. Some even become involved in sponsoring travel abroad programs for students, faculty, and alumni.

Travel As Education

Whether you are teaching, conducting research, or administering education programs in the United States or abroad, education offers numerous travel opportunities. Teachers and education administrators regularly attend professional meetings, participate in special programs and seminars, study for higher degrees, and deliver educational services in many different locations. While most teachers working in the traditional classroom, housed in a single school building, travel very little on a daily basis, others who provide outreach, tutorial, adult, and special education services travel daily from one location to another.

Higher education researchers in biology, ecology, geology, geography, oceanography, anthropology, and international relations may spend weeks and months conducting research in remote and exotic locations both at home and abroad. Studying on-site environmental problems along the Amazon River, the family structure of tribal groups in Papua New Guinea, volcanic eruptions in Hawaii and the Philippines, or the latest political developments in Moscow and Beijing can be some of the most exhilarating moments in the lives of educators. This type of work, involving travel, rather than classroom teaching or administration, is what draws and keeps many educators in education. For them, one of the major benefits of a job in education is the ability to frequently travel to the "field." Best of all, they often travel free – transportation and per diem expenses – because their projects are frequently funded through grants, contracts, research awards, and seed money provided by foundations, corporations, government, or their educational institution.

International Education

Educational institutions have always been a major avenue for acquiring international experience as well as for pursuing education-related jobs and careers. One of the best ways to break into the international arena is through an educational program. Numerous colleges and universities offer area studies programs as well as internships and semester abroad programs which enable students to acquire first-hand experience in living and studying abroad. Some programs even involve working abroad as part of an internship experience.

For information on thousands of scholarships for such programs as well as over 3,000 study abroad opportunities, consult these books:

Alternative Travel Directory: The Complete Guide to Work, Study, Travel Overseas, 7th Edition, Clayton Hubbs, ed. (Transitions Abroad Publishing, 2002)

Financial Aid for Research and Creative Activities Abroad 2006-2008, Gail A. Schlachter and R. David Weber (Reference Service Press, 2005)

Financial Aid for Study and Training Abroad 2006-2008, Gail A. Schlachter and R. David Weber (Reference Service Press, 2006)

Peterson's Study Abroad (Peterson's, annual)

Peterson's Summer Study Abroad (Peterson's, annual)

Study Abroad: How to Get the Most Out of Your Experience, Michele-Marie Dowell and Kelly P. Mirsky (Prentice Hall, 2002)

Study Abroad 101, Wendy Williamson (Agapy Publishing, 2004)

Study Abroad for Dummies, Erin Sullivan (John Wiley & Sons, 2003)

Study Away: The Unauthorized Guide to College Abroad, Mariah Balaban and Jennifer Shields (Anchor, 2003)

You should also review several issues of *Transitions Abroad,* the authoritative bimonthly magazine which is jam-packed with information on travel, work, living, and study abroad. Special issues focus on study abroad programs, budget travel, language vacations, working abroad, internships, and responsible travel. If you can't find it in your local library or on the newsstand, visit the Transitions Abroad website (www.Transi tionsAbroad.com), write (Dept. TRA, Box 3000, Denville, NJ 07834), call (866-760-5340), or e-mail (info@TransitionsAbroad.com) them for information. Another publication, *Abroad View* (www.abroadviewmagazine. com), which is published twice a year and emphasizes students' international and cross-cultural experiences and perspectives, is also useful for anyone interested in work, study, and travel abroad.

Several websites also offer a wealth of information for anyone interested in study abroad programs. Explore a few of these websites and you'll quickly uncover a very competitive world of study abroad:

- AIFS Study Abroad   www.aifsabroad.com
- Allen's Guide   www.allensguide.com
- Center for Study Abroad   www.centerforstudyabroad. com
- Council on International Educational Exchange   www.ciee.org
- Go Abroad   www.goabroad.com
- Cultural Experiences Abroad   www.gowithcea.com
- Global Learning Semesters   www.globalsemesters.com
- iAgora   www.iagora.com
- IES Abroad   www.iesabroad.org
- Institute for Shipboard Education   www.seamester.com
- Institute of International Education Passport   www.iiepassport.org
- International Education Site   www.intstudy.com
- International Student   www.internationalstudent. com
- LanguagesAbroad.com   www.languagesabroad.com
- NAFSA: Association of International Educators   www.nafsa.org
- National Registration Center for Study Abroad   www.nrcsa.com
- North American Institute for Study Abroad   www.naisa.com
- Scholar Stuff   www.scholarstuff.com/ netguide/studyabroad.htm

- School for International
  Training   www.sit.edu
- Sea-mester Programs   www.seamester.com
- Studies Abroad   www.studiesabroad.com
- Study Abroad   www.studyabroad.com
- Study Abroad Directory   www.studyabroaddirectory.
                                    com
- Study Abroad Links   www.studyabroadlinks.com
- Study Abroad Programs
  in Spain   www.foreignstudy.com
- Study Abroad Worldwide   www.studyabroadworldwide.
                                    com
- Study Overseas   www.studyoverseas.com
- Transitions Abroad   www.transitionsabroad.com
- TransWorld Education   www.transworldeducation.
                                    com
- University Studies
  Abroad Consortium   http://usac.unr.edu
- World Learning   www.worldlearning.org
- World Study   www.worldstudy.gov
- Worldwide Classroom   www.worldwide.edu

Internships

Internships both in the United States and abroad provide excellent entry into the international job market. With an internship you may gain valuable international work experience as well as develop important contacts for gaining full-time international employment. Many internships also provide unique opportunities to study and travel while working abroad. Sponsoring internship organizations normally arrange all the details for placement, travel, and accommodations. Upon completing the internship, participants can expect the sponsoring organization to arrange for letters of recommendation from the interns' employers.

International internships come in several forms. Ideally, most people would like to find paid internships with organizations overseas that might lead to being hired on a full-time basis. Some internships come in this form, especially those for business, engineering, and science majors sponsored by the International Association of Students in Economics and

Business Management (AIESEC) and the Association for International Practical Training (AIPT). These are the two premier international internship organizations that offer paid internships with major international companies.

Most internships, however, tend to be nonpaid, volunteer positions sponsored by colleges and universities or nonprofit organizations. Many of these internships require enrollment, tuition, or program fees to participate in the program. Some of these internship experiences are basically study abroad programs which include a short work experience. Most such programs are designed for students in linguistics, social sciences, and the humanities. If sponsored by a college or university, students can usually earn academic credits while participating in the internship program. A three- to twelve-month internship program may cost participants between $4,000 and $8,000, including international transportation, insurance, visas, and room and board. Like many volunteer positions, these internships may involve basic living and working conditions, such as participating in homestays and workcamps.

> *Most internships tend to be nonpaid, volunteer positions sponsored by colleges and universities or nonprofit organizations.*

Other international internships are based in the United States with nonprofit public interest, education, and research organizations. While these groups give interns an opportunity to work with important international organizations and issues, they involve little or no international travel. Many of these internships will involve basic research, copyediting, and clerical tasks, but they also offer opportunities to attend seminars, conferences, and make important international contacts.

Many internships are for two- to three-month periods while others run for six to twelve months or coincide with regular or summer college semester programs. Others may be flexible, depending on the individual intern's interests and skills. Many internships can lead to full-time employment with the sponsoring organization.

Most international internship programs tend to be centered in Washington, DC, the center for hundreds of government, nonprofit, consulting, and contracting organizations involved in international affairs.

Internship programs typically have application deadlines, and several charge both application and placement fees. Some require an application package consisting of a resume, transcript, writing sample, recommendations, and a letter of availability and interest. Be sure to check websites first for detailed information and then call, fax, e-mail, or write the organization for current application details.

If you are interested in an internship or volunteer position with an organization involved in the international arena, do not restrict your search efforts only to the organizations included in this chapter. You should be creative, aggressive, and persistent. Many of the organizations and employers listed in previous chapters, especially nonprofit organizations and consultants, are open to enterprising individuals who approach them with a **proposal for an internship**. In other words, you can create your own internship by directly approaching an organization with a detailed proposal. Do your homework on the organization. Identify what knowledge and skills you can bring to such a position as well as the experience you hope to acquire from such an experience. You may be surprised how many employers will be interested in your proposal. In the process you will gain invaluable international work experience specifically tailored to your needs and long-term international career goals.

Major Internship Organizations and Programs

The following businesses, government agencies, nonprofit organizations, and educational institutions offer a variety of internship experiences throughout the world. Many of the internships are based in the United States while others involve working overseas.

- Acción — www.accion.org
- AIESEC International — www.aiesec.org
- American Institute for Foreign Study — www.aifs.com
- American-Scandinavian Foundation — www.amscan.org
- Amnesty International USA — www.amnestyusa.org
- Arms Control Association — www.armscontrol.org
- Ashoka — www.ashoka.org

- Association for International
  Practical Training   www.aipt.org
- Atlantic Council of the
  United States   www.acus.org
- Acadia University Center
  for Education Abroad   www.arcadia.edu/cea
- Brethren Volunteer Service   www.brethren.org/genbd/bvs
- Bunac   www.bunac.org
- CDS International   www.cdsintl.org
- Center for the Study of Conflict   www.angelfire.com/mt/
    internships/72.htm
- Committee for National
  Security   www.angelfire.com/mt/
    internships/12.htm
- Council on International
  Educational Exchange (CIEE)   www.ciee.org
- Cross-Cultural Solutions   www.crossculturalsolutions.
    com
- Delegation of the European
  Commission to the U.S.A.   www.eurunion.org
- Educational Programs Abroad   www.epa-internships.org
- Export-Import Bank of the U.S.   www.exim.gov
- General Electric Company   www.ge.com
- Human Rights Watch   www.hrw.org
- InterExchange   www.interexchange.org
- Intern in Asia   www.interninasia.com
- International Cooperative
  Education Program   www.icemenlo.com
- International Education
  Programs, Foothill College   www.foothill.fhda.edu
- Internships International   www.rtpnet.org/~intintl
- People to People International   www.ptpi.org
- Quaker Information Center   www.quakerinfo.org
- Radio Free Europe/Radio Liberty   www.rferl.org
- School for International Training   www.sit.edu/studyabroad
- Sister Cities International   www.sister-cities.org
- United Nations Association
  of the USA   www.unausa.org
- U.S. Chamber of Commerce   www.uschamber.com

- U.S. State Department — www.state.gov
- Visions in Action — www.visionsinaction.org
- World Federalist Movement — www.wfm.org
- Youth for Understanding — www.yfu.org

Other Internship Opportunities

Numerous other organizations – from government agencies to private companies and nonprofit firms – offer internship opportunities. You may want to contact some of the following "internship friendly" organizations. Start by exploring these websites:

- African Wildlife Foundation — www.awf.org
- Amigos De Las Americas — www.amigoslink.org
- The Brookings Institution — www.brook.edu
- CARE — www.care.org
- Center for Strategic and International Studies — www.csis.org
- Central Intelligence Agency — www.cia.gov
- Freedom House — www.freedomhouse.org
- Habitat for Humanity — www.habitat.org
- International Finance Corporation — www.ifc.org
- International Monetary Fund — www.imf.org
- MAP International — www.map.org
- Organization of American States — www.oas.org
- United Nations — www.un.org
- World Bank — www.worldbank.org
- Population Connection — www.populationconnection.org

For more information on internships and volunteer opportunities, see the following publications which identify thousands of opportunities for enterprising job seekers. They are available through the publishers and Impact Publications (www.impactpublications.com or at the end of this book). The most comprehensive listing of internships – over 50,000 paid and unpaid in the U.S. and abroad – can be found in this popular directory, which was discontinued with the last edition in 2005: *Peterson's*

Internships (Peterson's). Other useful internship guides include *The Internship Bible* (Princeton Review), *Best 109 Internships* (Princeton Review), and *Vault Guide to Top Internships* (Vault, Inc, 2005). Students interested in international internships should acquire a copy of Charles Gliozzo's latest edition of the *Directory of International Internships* (Michigan State University). Several websites primarily focus on internship opportunities:

- Intern Abroad   www.internabroad.com
- Intern Jobs   www.internjobs.com
- Intern Web   www.internweb.com
- International Internships   www.umich.edu/~icenter/
                                         overseas/work/internships1.html
- International Internships   www.career.ucsb.edu/students/
                                         internships/international.html
- Internship Database   www.angelfire.com/mt/
                                         internships/home.htm
- Internship Programs   www.internshipprograms.com
- Internship4America   www.internship4america.com
- Internships.com   www.internships.com
- Internships-USA   www.internships-usa.com
- Rising Star Internships   www.rsinternships.com
- Study Abroad   www.studyabroad.com
- Volunteer Study Abroad   www.volunteerstudyabroad.org

While you will discover numerous competitive sponsored internship programs through the above resources, many students easily find internships on their own by approaching employers directly with an **internship proposal**. They network through their contacts or make cold calls to employers inquiring about internship opportunities. Indeed, this is one of the best ways to get into the doors of employers and acquire experience. Consider contacting employers directly with a proposal. If you are willing to volunteer your time as an unpaid intern, you may find many employers will be receptive to your approach. Best of all, many students report receiving job offers from employers they worked for as interns. The internship experience gives both the intern and employer an excellent opportunity to examine each other carefully to determine whether or not they wish to work together in the future.

7

✈

Teaching and Traveling Abroad

I F YOU LOVE TO TRAVEL ABROAD but lack international job skills and experience, or if you are primarily interested in gaining short-term (less than two years) international work experience that satisfies your curiosity for travel and living abroad, here's the best kept global employment secret – **become an international teacher.**

This chapter may turn out to be your best friend! Teaching is the easiest and quickest way to break into the international employment arena with little previous work experience. In fact, thousands of young and inexperienced individuals choose this employment route each year, especially if they are looking for short-term jobs rather than long-term professional employment. It's a good way to acquire international experience without having to invest a great deal of time and money in acquiring specialized skills, education, and foreign language expertise required by many employers identified in previous chapters.

Teaching Opportunities Galore

Numerous teaching opportunities exist in schools throughout the world. Many of these jobs are for certified teachers who teach in the U.S. Department of State schools, U.S. Department of Defense schools, or international schools. Teaching jobs with these schools include all subject matters as well as administrative positions. These teaching positions offer pay comparable to that of teaching positions in the United States. Moving from one country to another every three to six years, many education professionals decide to make a career of teaching in these overseas schools. Others may only teach in these schools for two to five years.

However, the largest number of overseas teaching positions are for teachers of English who work in local schools, institutes, or universities on either a short- or long-term basis. While many of these positions require some teaching experience or teacher certification, many do not. Some teacher training is advisable for landing such teaching positions. Several universities, for example, offer special training as well as overseas placements for individuals interested in teaching English as a foreign language. Earnings for these types of teaching positions vary greatly. Most such positions are low-paying or volunteer positions, but earnings can be very good in such countries as Japan, Korea, or Taiwan.

Teaching English as a Foreign Language

If you are willing to teach English as a foreign language, you can easily find a job abroad. Indeed, the worldwide demand for English language teachers remains high and the jobs are plentiful. During the past 15 years, the demand for English teachers has increased substantially in Eastern Europe, Russia, and the former Soviet republics.

If you are willing to teach English as a foreign language, you can easily find a job abroad.

The first thing you need to do is to understand the specialized language, training requirements, and certification options of this particular occupational group. Teachers of English language usually refer to themselves and their training programs in the following abbreviated terms:

- **TEFL or TFL:** teaching English as a foreign language

- **TESL or TSL:** teaching English as a second language

- **TESOL:** teaching English to speakers of other languages

- **RSA/Cambridge CELTA:** Cambridge/RSA Certificate Course in English Language Teaching to Adults

- **CTEFL:** Certificate in Teaching English as a Foreign Language

Several universities in the United States, Canada, and Europe provide degree programs in TEFL or TESOL, and many institutes and schools offer teacher training courses and certification in TEFL or TESOL. While you are well advised to participate in such a program, be sure to check out their credibility. Some schools and institutes offering quick and easy online certification may be of questionable value. Teaching English as a foreign language involves specific methodologies you should be familiar with before venturing into this field. Fortunately you can participate in several short intensive TEFL or TESOL training programs that will get you up and running quickly for English language teaching. Many of these programs can be identified through ads in the bimonthly issues of *Transitions Abroad* magazine and on its related website (www.transitions abroad.com).

> *You are well advised to participate in a TEFL or TESOL program which prepares you for teaching in this field.*

You basically have two approaches to landing an English language teaching position abroad – either apply through a U.S.-based organization specializing in the training and placement of English language teachers or apply directly to an overseas school, institute, or university. It is probably easier to work through a U.S.-based organization, since most handle placements and arrange other details such as visas, work permits, housing, and transportation. A third option is to become a freelance teacher of English, offering your services to individuals and groups at an hourly rate.

During the past 45 years the U.S. Peace Corps has trained thousands of Volunteers to teach English in many Third and Fourth World countries throughout the world. While today's Peace Corps places Volunteers in many technical and business fields, it still recruits Volunteers to teach English and other subjects in over 100 countries. In fact, nearly 40 percent of all Volunteers serve in the field of education; most are English teachers. Volunteer assignments are for two years. Since the Peace Corps continues to expand its Volunteer presence abroad, more teaching opportunities should be available with the Peace Corps in the coming years. A great deal of information on Volunteer opportunities with the Peace Corps can be found on its very informative website. For more information on the Peace Corps program, contact:

Peace Corps
1111 20th Street, NW
Washington, DC 20526
Tel. 800-424-8580
www.peacecorps.org

Teaching Abroad

Several private, nonprofit, and educational organizations also recruit, train, and place college graduates who are interested in teaching English and other subjects abroad. Many are volunteer positions, similar to internships, while others are salaried positions. Contact the following organizations for information on their placement programs. The first three organizations sponsor job fairs for teachers interested in working overseas – a great way to quickly network, interview, and land a job:

INTERNATIONAL SCHOOLS SERVICES
15 Roszel Road, Box 5910, Princeton, NJ 08543, Tel. 609-452-0990, Fax 609-452-2690, or e-mail: iss@iss.edu. Website: www.iss.edu. This is the premier elementary through secondary international education placement and consulting organization. It places nearly 700 teachers and administrators in 200 international and American schools around the world each year primarily in the fields of math, science, computers, library science, and elementary teaching. Teaching salaries in 2006 ranged from $14,000 to $84,500 annually; administrative salaries ranged from $24,000 to over $121,000 annually. Requires a registration or reactivation fee of $175. Applications should have two years of current full-time elementary or secondary school experience (no certification required by ISS, but 85 percent of all schools recruiting through ISS do require certification), but this experience requirement may be waived in the case of "teaching teams" (spouses) who are certified, or in a few other cases. Math and science teachers with

certification but no experience are eligible for consideration. Sponsors four annual International Recruitment Centers fairs in the winter (January in Bangkok, February in Boston and Vancouver) and summer (June in Philadelphia) which require a $200 fee per fair. Publishes an annual directory of international schools: *The ISS Directory of Overseas Schools*. Interested candidates can apply online through this section of ISS's website: www.iss.edu/edustaff/candidate/index.html.

OVERSEAS PLACEMENT SERVICE FOR EDUCATORS
University of Northern Iowa Career Center, 242 Gilchrist Hall, Cedar Falls, IA 50614-0390, Tel. 319-273-2083, Fax 319-273-6998, or e-mail: overseas.placement@uni.edu. Website: www.uni.edu/placement/ overseas. This is one of the major annual overseas education recruiting events in the United States for American and international schools around the world – from representatives of the Department of Defense overseas schools to international schools from Shanghai, Bangkok, Abu Dhabi, Cairo, Mexico City, and Haiti. The University of Northern Iowa sponsors an annual UNI Overseas Recruiting Fair in late February ($5 fee for pre-registration packet required plus a registration fee) for over 700 positions relevant to international teachers and administrators. In 2006, for example, over 500 registered candidates attended and had an average of six interviews with the over 100 international schools registered, which represented 65 countries. The most successful candidates (90 percent) "are single with no dependents or part of a certified married teaching team." Only current certified elementary or secondary teachers or administrators can attend this event. Offers a placement service that also includes an Overseas Credential Service that keeps a candidate's credentials on file for three years. Publishes a popular 200+ page book entitled *UNI Overseas Fact Sheet Book* ($30.00) that includes useful information on international schools and the job search process. Also publishes a newsletter ($30.00 if not registered for the job fair) which includes listings of overseas teaching vacancies.

TESOL INC.
Teachers of English to Speakers of Other Languages, 700 South Washington Street, Suite 200, Alexandria, VA 22314, Tel. 888-547-3369, 703-836-0774, or 703-836-6447. Website: www.tesol.org. This 23,000-member nonprofit organization includes a placement service for its members. Membership dues are $75 for regular members and $51.00 for students. Members can subscribe to the *Placement E-Bulletin*, which includes biweekly job postings, and access an online job search tool, the *JobFinder*. Members attending the annual conference also can participate in the popular annual job fair (Employment

Clearinghouse) that provides a great opportunity to network with employers and fellow professionals.

JET PROGRAMME

JET Office, Embassy of Japan, 2520 Massachusetts Ave., NW, Washington, DC 20008, Tel. 202-939-6772, 202-939-6773, Fax 202-265-9484, or e-mail: eojjet@erols.com. Website: www.mofa.go.jp/ j_info/visit/jet/. U.S. citizens also can apply through 16 Japanese consulates operating in major cities throughout the country. Do you want to live and work in Japan as an English teacher? Here's the one of the best programs to make this happen. The JET (Japan Exchange and Teaching) Programme is a popular Japanese government-sponsored program that places young college and university graduates from overseas as English teachers in Japanese schools and government offices (2,200 contracting organizations) throughout Japan for one-year assignments. Participants are assigned to one of three positions:

- Assistant Language Teacher (ALT)
- Coordinator for International Relations (CIR)
- Sports Exchange Advisor (SEA)

In 2006, nearly 6,000 individuals work in Japan through this program (44,000 participants from 44 countries since the program began in 1987). Application deadline is early December for positions beginning in July of the following year. Application deadlines and forms are usually posted on the JET website in September of each year. For inside information on the hiring process, including sample interview questions (*"What would you do if you came to a class and the teacher wasn't there, and you weren't ready for that?"* – something that frequently happens to JET Programme participants who serve as an Assistant Language Teacher), visit this JET-related website run by previous JET Programme participants: www.jet-program.com.

WORLDTEACH

Center for International Development, Harvard University, 79 John F. Kennedy Street, Cambridge, MA 02138, Tel. 800-483-2240, 617-495-5527, Fax 617-495-1599, e-mail: info@worldteach.org. Website: www.worldteach.org. Each year places nearly 200 volunteer teachers in the local schools of Chile, China, Costa Rica, Ecuador, Guyana, Micronesia, the Marshall Islands, Namibia, Poland, and South Africa. Operates one-year, six-mouth, summer, and nature guide training programs. Participants pay program fees ranging from $1,990 to $5,990, depending on the country and length of program. The fees typically cover the cost of airfare, health insurance, training, and administration. Offers a limited number of scholarships for qualifying participants. Local employers provide room and board.

BRETHREN VOLUNTEER SERVICES
1451 Dundee Ave., Elgin, IL 60120, Tel. 847-742-5100, 800-323-8039, or Fax 847-742-0278, e-mail: bvs_gb@brethren.org. Website: www.brethren.org/genbd/bvs. This faith-based Quaker organization places English teachers (volunteers) for two-year assignments primarily in Dominican Republic, Nicaragua, Nigeria, but also includes 17 other countries. Provides expenses plus a $60-$80 monthly stipend. Includes other types of overseas volunteer experiences, including health care, peacekeeping, housing, refugees, agriculture, community development, and environment. Recruits young adults, middle-aged adults, and retirees.

CENTRAL EUROPEAN TEACHING PROGRAM
3800 NE 72nd Avenue, Portland, OR 97213, Tel. 503-287-4977 or e-mail: cetp@att.net. Website: www.ticon.net/~cetp. Handles placements in 100 state high schools and middle schools in Hungary and Romania and in colleges in Poland. Program fee ranges from $500 to $2,000, depending on the length of the volunteer program (summer language camp, one semester, or one complete school year). Volunteers receive a monthly stipend.

INTEREXCHANGE
161 6th Avenue, New York, NY 10013, Tel. 212-924-0446, Fax 212-974-0575, or e-mail: info@interexchange.org. Website: www.interex change.org. Includes several teaching English, au pair, internship, farm work, hotel/restaurant, volunteer, and work and travel programs. Currently operates teaching programs in Spain, which require a $495 placement fee.

PROJECT HARMONY
5197 Main Street Unit 5, Waitsfield, VT 05673, Tel. 802-496-4545, Fax 802-496-4548, e-mail: info@projectharmony.org. Website: www. projectharmony.org. Among its many international projects (Community Development, Internet Technology, Professional Development), it places English teachers with schools in Russia and the Ukraine. Also operates educator programs (Professional Development) in Finland, Ireland, Sweden, and Russia as well as school connectivity (Internet Technology) programs in Azerbaijan, Russia, and the Ukraine. Requires a program fee (around $2,000), which includes airfare and housing stipend.

SEARCH ASSOCIATES

www.search-associates.com. Each year this firm places over 1,000 teachers, administrators, and interns in international schools around the globe.

Other organizations providing placement programs for teachers or useful information on teaching abroad include:

- Friends of World Teaching   www.fowt.com
- Institute of International
  Education   www.iie.org
- Association of American
  Schools in South America   www.aassa.com
- Education Jobs in the UK   www.education-jobs.co.uk
- NAFSA: Association of
  International Educators   www.nafsa.org
- U.S. State Department
  (Office of Overseas Schools)   www.state.gov/m/a/os
- U.S. Department of Defense
  Educational Activity   www.dodea.edu
- Teach Abroad   www.teachabroad.com
- Teaching Abroad   www.teaching-abroad.co.uk
- Edufind Jobs   www.jobs.edufind.com
- TESOL   www.tesol.org
- Cactus TEFL   www.cactustefl.com
- English Job Maze   www.englishjobmaze.com
- ESLBase.com   www.eslbase.com
- ESL Employment   www.eslemployment.com
- ESL Focus   www.eslfocus.com
- ESL Job Feed   www.esljobfeed.com
- ESL Job Find   www.esljobfind.com
- ESL Worldwide   www.eslworldwide.com
- Internet/Networks (Mexico)   www.employnow.com/
                                   Mexico.htm
- Mark's ESL World   www.marksesl.com
- TESall.com   www.tesall.com
- TEFL/TESL Jobs Worldwide   www.tefl.net/jobs
- TEFL Professional Network   www.tefl.com
- TEFL.net   www.tefl.net

- Educational Services
  International (China)   www.esiadventure.org
- ELIC (China)   www.elic.org
- GlobalStudy   www.globalstudy.com
- Overseas Digest   www.overseasdigest.com
- O-Hayo Sensei (Japan)   www.ohayosensei.com
- Job Monkey   www.jobmonkey.com/
                                teaching
- Teach in Korea   www.teachkoreanz.com
- TeachOverseas.ca   www.teachoverseas.ca
- Teach in Thailand   www.thailandteacher.com
- Teach in Taiwan   www.iacc.com.tw

The following websites function as excellent gateway sites to these and many other teaching-English-abroad programs. Many of these sites provide linkages to other relevant sites, as well as include useful articles, chat groups, forums, job listings, and services. If you start with these sites, you will probably discover a wealth of information and develop some excellent contacts for launching your international teaching job search:

- Dave's ESL Cafe   www.eslcafe.com
- Teaching Jobs Overseas   http://joyjobs.com
- Transitions Abroad   www.transitionsabroad.com
- University of Michigan,   www.umich.edu/~icenter/
  International Center   overseas/work/waoverweb/
                                html
- University of California Center www.cie.uci.edu/iop/
  for International Education   teaching.html
- American University Career   www.american.edu/career
  Center Online Career Library center/students/career/
                                teachabroad.html
- iAgora   www.iagora.com

For an excellent compilation of linkages to English language teaching resources, including job boards, discussion forums, and regional and country portals, visit Transition Abroad's teaching resources section:

www.transitionsabroad.com/listings/work/esl/

Training Programs for English Teachers

The best qualified candidates possess teacher certification and are skilled in teaching English as a foreign language. Ideally, you should have a bachelor's or master's degree in TEFL or in a substantive academic field. If you lack such qualifications, don't worry. You can easily establish your teaching credentials and land an overseas teaching job by enrolling in a TEFL program that also has a good placement record. In fact, we do not recommend looking for an English-language teaching position unless you have completed a TEFL program. You will quickly discover these programs have several advantages. Many use the highly respected RSA/University of Cambridge and Trinity College London teaching methods for qualifying participants.

In the United States most TEFL programs are integrated into regular university academic programs which are usually part of an undergraduate or graduate Applied Linguistics program. A few universities and private institutes now offer intensive four-week TEFL programs modeled after the British 100-hour intensive TEFL teacher certification programs. These intensive four-week programs quickly prepare you for overseas teaching positions and thus save you time and money in the process of getting ready for an overseas job. Many of these programs also provide job assistance through their employment contacts with schools, institutes, and universities abroad.

For online information on various TEFL training options, see this section of Jeff Mohamad's useful website:

www.english-international.com/training.html

Within the United States, several public and private organizations provide training for teachers of English as a foreign language. The following universities offer degree programs, many through traditional Applied Linguistics, English, or Education departments, that require two to four years preparation; some offer graduate degrees in TEFL/TESOL:

- Ball State University (Muncie, IN)
- Brigham Young University (Laie, HI)
- Fairleigh Dickinson University (Teaneck, NJ)
- Georgetown University (Washington, DC)

- Hawaii Pacific University (Honolulu, HI)
- Portland State University (Portland, OR)
- University of California (Irvine, CA)
- University of Delaware (Newark, DE)
- University of Georgia (Athens, GA)
- University of New Hampshire (Durham, NH)
- Wright State University (Dayton, OH)

Many other public and private institutes offer certification through intensive four- to eight-week training programs. The major such programs include:

■ **AEON**	www.aeonet.com
■ **Boston Language Institute**	www.teflcertificate.com
■ **China Teaching Program**	www.ac.wwu.edu/~ctp
■ **Embassy CES**	www.embassyces.com
■ **English International**	www.english-international. com
■ **Hamline University TEFL**	www.hamline.edu/personal/ troux/index.htm
■ **International Language Institute**	www.celta.ca
■ **International TEFL Certificate**	www.itc-training.com
■ **Lado Certificate Program**	www.lado.com
■ **Seattle University TESOL**	www.seattleu.edu/soe/stesl
■ **St. Giles International**	www.stgiles-usa.com
■ **TEFL International**	www.teflintl.com
■ **Worldwide Teachers Development Institute**	www.bostontefl.com

Tuition for most of these programs runs from $2,000 to $3,000. However, English International (www.english-international.com) offers three cost-effective TEFL Certificate courses through distance learning that operate throughout the year: Introductory Certificate in TEFL ($195); Certificate in TEFL ($195); and Certificate in TEFL with Practice Teaching ($225). Participants can enroll at any time and work at their own pace. It's operated by noted TEFL trainer and author (*Teaching English Overseas: A Job Guide for Americans and Canadians*) Jeff Mohamed.

Numerous other teacher training programs are offered by universities and private institutes in Canada, England, Ireland, France, Germany, Greece, Hong Kong, Malaysia, Spain, Turkey, and Australia. The oldest, largest, and most highly respected TEFL training program awarding the RSA/University of Cambridge Certificate is operated by International House in London: www.ihlondon.com. This four-week (110-hour) program costs £1,195 (US$2,077). International House offers courses at Teacher Training Centers in its affiliated schools in Barcelona, Budapest, Cairo, Krakow, Lisbon, Madrid, New York, Paris, Poznan, Rome, San Sebastian, and Vienna. It also recruits nearly 200 teachers each year for its network of over 100 schools in 23 countries. If you want premier training in TEFL, enroll in this well established program. For more information on TEFL training programs in these and other countries, consult Susan Griffith's latest edition of *Teaching English Abroad.*

Other Teaching Opportunities

If you teach at the university level, you may find opportunities to teach and conduct research abroad through your present institution, through a regional international consortium, or through special programs such as the Fulbright Program (Council for International Exchange of Scholars). You should also monitor the job vacancy announcements appearing in *The Chronicle of Higher Education* as well as in professional journals and newsletters of your academic discipline. Occasionally overseas university vacancy announcements appear in *The New York Times, Washington Post, Wall Street Journal,* and a few other prominent newspapers. Major international magazines, such as *The Far Eastern Economic Review* and *The Economist,* regularly list university vacancy announcements.

Enterprising job seekers don't limit their search to established teaching programs, training institutes, and placement and job listing services. Numerous other teaching opportunities are available by directly applying to local schools in each country without the assistance of a U.S.-based organization or with a U.S.-sponsored school. While salaries may appear low in many of these schools, such teaching positions often come with free housing and they do offer an opportunity to gain experience in living and working abroad. They enable you to work in a truly international environment where you get to know faculty members and become a member of the local community – important international experiences which are sometimes best acquired by living off the local economy at the level of fellow faculty members.

Take, for example, one of our favorite colleges abroad with which we have been involved for years as both advisory board members and donors. If you are interested in teaching English in Thailand, you might consider applying directly to Yonok College in Northern Thailand. We know this college very well since we have been closely involved with its evolution since 1973. One of Thailand's most beautiful private colleges located in a delightful provincial town near the famous city of Chiangmai, Yonok College offers an excellent English language program for its nearly 3,000 students who are studying for bachelor's degrees in business, arts, and the sciences. It also offers an innovative summer abroad program in Thai Elephant Studies for anyone interested in learning about Lampang's famous elephant conservation camp within the context of Thai language, arts, and culture. Yonok College has an ongoing exchange program with the faculty and students of Baylor University in Waco, Texas as well as welcomes applicants from other educational institutions. Numerous Americans have taught English here for periods of one to five years. If you are interested in working at Yonok, send a cover letter and resume to:

Office of International Recruitment
YONOK COLLEGE
Vachiravudh Damnern Road
Lampang 52000, Thailand
E-mail: oir@yonok.ac.th
Website: www.yonok.ac.th

Be sure to first visit their website for information about the university, including vacancy announcements. Indicate in your letter what you would like to do and when you are available. If you e-mail, be sure to include your resume in the body of your e-mail message; do not include it as an attachment. Yonok College also welcomes applications from individuals with experience in university administration.

Key Resources on Teaching

The following books, directories, and websites provide useful information on teaching abroad. Many of them are available through Impact Publications (www.impactpublications.com or at the end of this book):

The ELT Guide (Teachers of English to Speakers of Other Languages, www.tesol.edu)

The ISS Directory of Overseas Schools (International Schools Service, annual, www.iss.edu)

Teaching English Abroad, Susan Griffith (Vacation Work, annual)

Teaching English Overseas: A Job Guide for Americans and Canadians, Jeff Mohamed (English International)

UNI Overseas Fact Sheet Book (University of Northern Iowa Career Center, annual)

Work Abroad: The Complete Guide to Finding Work Overseas. (Transitions Abroad Publishing, 2002)

The U.S. government offers useful information on teaching opportunities with the U.S. Department of State and the U.S. Department of Defense Dependents schools through the following websites:

U.S. Department of State, Office of Overseas Schools, Washington, DC 20522-0132, Tel. 202-261-8200, Fax 202-261-8224, or e-mail: OverseasSchools@state.gov. You can download all Department of State schools by clicking on the "Directory of Schools" on the left navigation bar of its website: www.state.gov/m/a/os.

Department of Defense Education Activity, Office of Personnel, Dependents Schools, 4040 N. Fairfax Drive, 6th Floor, Alexandria, VA 22203, Tel. 703-696-1352 or Recruitment@HQ.DoDEA.edu. Explore employment opportunities with over 200 Department of Defense K-12 schools servicing U.S. military bases abroad by clicking on the "Human Resources – Employment" section on the left side of this office's website: www.dodea.edu. This section of the website includes information on salaries, benefits, current vacancies, and applications.

Teaching in Higher Education

If your international education interests lie in higher education, you should check out several of the following sites. If you are a U.S. citizen and currently work at a U.S. university or are a graduate student at a participating institution, you can apply for a Fulbright teaching, research, or administrative position:

Council for International Exchange of Scholars
3007 Tilden Street, NW, Suite 5L
Washington, DC 20008-3009
Tel. 202-686-4000 or Fax 202-362-3442
www.iie.org/cies

Other resources for landing a teaching position abroad include:

- Association of Commonwealth Universities — www.acu.ac.uk
- Chronicle of Higher Education — www.chronicle.com
- Times Higher Education Supplement — www.thes.co.uk
- United Nations University — www.unu.edu
- University of Maryland (Overseas teaching program) — www.umuc.edu/faculty/employment/overseas.html

8

✈

International Organizations, Consulting Firms, and Nonprofits

ANY PEOPLE WHO LOVE TO travel are primarily interested in pursuing international jobs that enable them to either live abroad for lengthy periods of time or make frequent trips abroad. While many of these jobs are found in government, education, and business, many other jobs are found with three types of organizations:

- International organizations
- Nonprofit organizations
- Contracting and consulting firms

This chapter focuses on these organizations. In addition, we examine two U.S. government agencies which we briefly touched on in Chapter 5 – USAID and the Peace Corps – because of their close relationship to contracting firms and nonprofit organizations.

Jobs with these organizations often lead to long-term careers. Working for the United Nations, for example, becomes a career for many individuals who thrive on receiving excellent salaries, benefits, advancement

217

opportunities, and job security. Individuals working for international consulting and contracting firms often make careers of their work, even though they may change jobs many times over a 25- to 40-year period, moving from one firm to another or starting their own firm. And individuals working for nonprofit organizations often remain committed to an international career by working with several types of PVOs (private voluntary organizations) or NGOs (nongovernmental organizations) during their worklife.

International Organizations

Numerous international organizations offer job opportunities for talented individuals. Relics of the Cold War period in search of new roles in a fast-changing global arena, most of these organizations are either directly tied to the United Nations or function as regional military, political, economic, and social organizations. In most cases the United States is involved as a major bilateral or multilateral partner.

Since historically the United States has played a major role in developing international organizations and continues as a major funding source, many Americans have been employed with these groups. Yet, American participation in the day-to-day administration of international organizations is normally limited by specific hiring quotas imposed on all member nations related to population and financial contribution criteria. As a result, only certain positions requiring specific expertise will be open to American job seekers. In this sense, employment with many international organizations is very political in terms of both hiring for a position and retaining a job in competition with eager job seekers from the United States and other countries.

Future job opportunities with international organizations are difficult to predict given the ending of the Cold War, the increasing prevalence of regional conflicts and terrorism, and recent realignments within a newly emerging world order. The whole structure of multilateral and bilateral international organizations is undergoing major changes. NATO, for example, continues to expand its membership and scope of military operations throughout Europe, including membership of former communist countries, as well as deal with problematic old allies within the alliance. While the United Nations should logically play more important international peacekeeping and development roles in the future, it frequently functions like a classic Third World bureaucracy – highly politicized, unresponsive, inefficient, ineffective, and often inept and corrupt. It tends to function in the interests of its bureaucrats, who are intent on keeping and advancing their jobs, rather than in response to specific international missions. Consequently, its future direction is at best in question. Indeed, we expect major restructuring of this international institution in the aftermath of the post-2003 changes in the Middle East political map. Nonprofit organizations (PVOs and NGOs) may play a much greater role in the future than the United Nations and other bilateral and multilateral international organizations.

In this section we provide a brief overview of employment alternatives with numerous international organizations. Each organization has its own hiring system which you must understand in order to be effective in landing a job. Most important of all, each organization has a particular political environment which may or may not meet your criteria for a rewarding job or career involving travel.

Opportunities

International organizations provide numerous job opportunities for global specialists who are interested in a variety of issues relating to international economic and social development as well as regional security. The largest employer of international specialists is the United Nations (UN) bureaucracy and its complex of affiliated organizations. While the UN is headquartered in New York City, its many specialized agencies are spread throughout the world. A majority of these offices are headquartered in Geneva, Brussels, Vienna, Rome, Montreal, and Washington, DC.

Many other international organizations employ international specialists. The World Bank, for example, offers excellent job opportunities for individuals with expertise in international economics and finance. Like many other jobs in the UN system, positions with the World Bank tend to be well paid and come with numerous benefits. Compensation, benefits, and perks with these organizations are much better than with the U.S. government.

Job Outlook

Many international organizations, such as the United Nations and the World Bank, have undergone major cutbacks in personnel during the past eight years. The World Bank, for example, receives nearly 30,000 applications each year for 200 professional positions it actually fills. Many UN agencies remain under hiring freezes or are downsizing their personnel due to budgetary shortfalls and political pressure from the United States to overhaul an extremely bloated bureaucracy. Consequently, competition is very keen for what few positions become available. You'll need to put together a terrific application and hopefully have some "inside connections" to help you through these highly competitive international employment arenas.

Hiring Practices and the Internet

Each international organization has its own hiring procedures. Indeed, even within the United Nations, much of the hiring is decentralized to the individual agencies. Therefore, it's important to understand the structure and function of each organization in order to properly approach it. Many of these organizations purposefully discriminate by only hiring individuals from member states. Fortunately, most international organizations now have their own websites, which include a great deal of information on the organization as well as job vacancy announcements and applications. Some agencies accept e-mailed resumes or those transmitted in ASCII format. Since a great deal of this international hiring is wired via the Internet, it is to your advantage to conduct much of your job search on the Internet.

If you are not using the Internet in your international job search, you will simply be at a distinct disadvantage since much of the hiring process with international organizations has moved online. Internet-savvy job seekers can now quickly access employment information on the United Nations and its agencies, the World Bank, the Asian Development Bank, or the Organization of American States by visiting these organizations' websites. Writing, calling, or faxing their personnel or human resources departments for job information will be a great waste of your time and their time. Indeed, if you call these organizations for information, you will most likely be told *"All the information about our organization and employment opportunities is on our website."* As potential employers ourselves, we would not be impressed by someone who doesn't use the Internet – an indication they lack proper skills for today's job market! Do everyone a favor and follow our rule for finding an international job: *"You got to get wired if you want to get hired!"*

In this chapter we include several Internet sites to assist you in your research. Since international organizations and their employment needs are constantly changing, you are well advised to **first** visit their websites for the latest information on employment needs and opportunities. The sites will answer many of your questions. Only after reviewing the content of a site should you phone, fax, or write for information. Do not send a resume to any of the addresses we list until you understand the application procedures. In many cases, you must complete an agency application form as well as submit a lengthy curriculum vitae, which is not the same as a pithy one- or two-page American resume (see our companion volume, *Best Resumes and CVs for International Jobs*).

International organizations tend to hire professionals with a great deal of international experience and higher educational degrees. Many positions within the United Nations and the World Bank, for example,

> *International organizations tend to hire professionals with a great deal of international experience and higher educational degrees.*

involve research, writing, consulting, and meeting skills as well as knowledge of procurement – obligating funds for projects. Indeed, if you are interested in getting involved in the nitty-gritty of development – working with people at the local level on development projects – becoming employed by one of these international organizations may frustrate you. Few of these organizations are involved in implementing projects. At best, they fund the implementation activities of government agencies, contractors, and nonprofit organizations, and host frequent meetings where they function as forums for "exchanging ideas." The United Nations, for example, is well noted for its culture of meetings, reports, and consultation. However, it does get involved in many "field operations" through the United Nations Development Program (UNDP) and various peacekeeping operations. If you are interested in working for one of these organizations, you may quickly discover that you are competing with many other individuals who have lengthy resumes that demonstrate their extensive international-relevant education, research, writing, consulting, and meeting skills.

The international organizations outlined in this chapter represent the major ones employing U.S. citizens. Numerous other international organizations also provide job opportunities for enterprising job seekers. If you are interested in exploring additional international organizations, we recommend consulting the following directories:

- *Encyclopedia of Associations: International Organizations*
- *Europa World Year Book*
- *The World Factbook* (CIA)
- *Yearbook of International Organizations*

Current volumes of these directories are available in most major libraries. But if you are using the Internet, you can easily access the CIA's useful *World Factbook* online by going to the agency's website:

www.cia.gov/cia/publications/factbook/index.html

While most of this book is devoted to country profiles, Appendix B ("International Organizations and Groups") includes basic information on the UN and other major international organizations.

United Nations and Its Specialized Agencies

The United Nations offers numerous international job opportunities within the Secretariat and specialized agencies. It is the largest employer of international specialists with a bureaucracy of nearly 65,000 individuals working in over 600 duty stations throughout the world. Fewer than 10 percent of the UN civil servants are U.S. citizens.

The UN consists of six major organizational units and numerous specialized and autonomous agencies, standing committees, commissions, and other subsidiary bodies. Given the decentralized nature of the UN, all specialized agencies and related organizations recruit their own personnel. The six principal UN organs are:

- General Assembly
- Security Council
- Economic and Social Council
- Trusteeship Council

- International Court of Justice
- Secretariat

While job opportunities are available with all of these organs, the largest number of job opportunities are found with the Economic and Social Council and the UN Secretariat.

The **Economic and Social Council** is under the General Assembly. It coordinates the economic and social work of the United Nations and numerous specialized agencies, standing committees, commissions, and related organizations. The work of the Council involves international development, world trade, industrialization, natural resources, human rights, status of women, population, social welfare, science and technology, crime prevention, and other social and economic issues. Its overall goal is to promote world cooperation on economic, social, cultural, and humanitarian problems.

The Economic and Social Council is divided into a headquarters staff in New York City and five regional economic commissions:

- **Economic Commission for Africa** (Addis Ababa)
  www.uneca.org
- **Economic and Social Commission for Asia and the Pacific** (Bangkok)
  www.unescap.org
- **Economic Commission for Europe** (Geneva)
  www.unece.org
- **Economic Commission for Latin America & the Caribbean** (Santiago)
  www.eclac.cl
- **Economic and Social Commission for Western Asia** (Beirut)
  www.escwa.org.lb

Each Commission maintains a large staff of specialists. Furthermore, they promote the work of several standing committees and commissions which also have their own staffs.

Specialized or intergovernmental agencies are autonomous organizations linked to the United Nations by special intergovernmental agreements. In addition, they have their own membership, budgets, personnel systems, legislative and executive bodies, and secretariats. The Food and

Agriculture Organization (FAO), for example, consists of a staff drawn from 184 member nations. It is administered by a professional staff of nearly 3,200 which is headquartered in Rome; some employees work in FAO regional offices located in Ghana, Thailand, Chile, New York City, and Washington, DC. Each year the FAO hires nearly 500 staff members, of whom 60 to 65 are U.S. citizens.

The Economic and Social Council coordinates the work of these organizations with the United Nations as well as with each other. Altogether, there are 12 specialized agencies:

- **Food and Agriculture Organization (FAO)**
  www.fao.org
- **International Civil Aviation Organization (ICAO)**
  www.icao.int
- **International Fund for Agricultural Development (IFAD)**
  www.ifad.org
- **International Labour Organization (ILO)**
  www.ilo.org
- **International Maritime Organization (IMO)**
  www.imo.org
- **International Monetary Fund (IMF)**
  www.imf.org
- **International Telecommunication Union (ITU)**
  www.itu.int
- **United Nations Educational, Scientific, and Cultural Organization (UNESCO)**
  www.unesco.org
- **United Nations Industrial Development Organization (UNIDO)**
  www.unido.org
- **Universal Postal Union (UPU)**
  www.upu.int
- **World Health Organization (WHO)**
  www.who.org
- **World Intellectual Property Organization (WIPO)**
  www.wipo.org
- **World Meteorological Organization (WMO)**
  www.wmo.ch

Several other major organizations also are attached to the Economic and Social Council as well as the Secretariat. These consist of:

- International Atomic Energy Agency (IAEA)
  www.iaea.org
- International Bank for Reconstruction and Development (IBRD or World Bank)
  www.worldbank.org
- International Seabed Authority (ISA)
  www.isa.org.jm
- United Nations Human Settlements Programme (UN-HABITAT)
  www.unhabitat.org
- United Nations Children's Fund (UNICEF)
  www.unicef.org
- United Nations Conference on Trade and Development (UNCTAD)
  www.unctad.org
- United Nations Development Programme (UNDP)
  www.undp.org
- United Nations Environment Programme (UNEP)
  www.unep.org
- United Nations Population Fund (UNFPA)
  www.unfpa.org
- United Nations Refugee Agency (UNHCR)
  www.unhcr.org
- United Nations Industrial Development Organization (UNIDO)
  www.unido.org
- United Nations Institute for Training and Research (UNITAR)
  www.unitar.org
- United Nations Office on Drugs and Crime (UNODC)
  www.unodc.org
- United Nations Relief and Works Agency for Palestine Refugees in the Near East (UNRWA)
  www.un.org/unrwa

- World Food Programme (WFP)
  www.wfp.org
- World Trade Organization (WTO)
  www.wto.org

The UN Secretariat employs nearly 14,000 international civil servants from 160 countries. Most are stationed at the United Nations headquarters in New York City. The Secretariat is the central "bureaucracy" in charge of carrying out the day-to-day work of the United Nations.

The largest UN agencies – those employing at least 1,500 individuals – consist of the following:

- Food and Agriculture
  Organization   www.fao.org
- International Labour
  Organization   www.ilo.org
- International Monetary Fund   www.imf.org
- UNESCO   www.unesco.org
- UNICEF   www.unicef.org
- United Nations Development
  Programme   www.undp.org
- World Bank   www.worldbank.org
- World Health Organization   www.who.int

The United States is especially involved in the following United Nations organizations which are headquartered in various cities:

- Food and Agricultural Organization (Rome)
- International Atomic Energy Agency (Vienna)
- International Bank for Reconstruction and Development,
  or popularly known as the World Bank (Washington, DC)
- International Civil Aviation Organization (Montreal)
- International Finance Corporation (Washington, DC)
- International Monetary Fund (Washington, DC)
- International Telecommunication Union (Geneva)
- Universal Postal Union (Bern, Switzerland)
- World Health Organization (Geneva)

Consequently, U.S. citizens may have a much higher probability of landing jobs with these UN agencies than with other agencies that tend to favor hiring nationals from other member countries.

Hiring Process

Since the hiring process is largely decentralized within the United Nations and among the specialized agencies and related organizations, you should directly contact each agency for job vacancy information. The good news is that the UN personnel system is highly wired via the Internet. You can easily access information on agencies and job vacancies by visiting several websites. One of the first places to start is the U.S. Department of State's Bureau of International Organization Affairs and its gateway website to the UN hiring system:

www.state.gov/p/io

From here you can link to numerous websites of the United Nations:

www.state.gov/p/io/rlnks

The site also provides links to employment information, including vacancy announcements, with various United Nations agencies:

www.state.gov/p/io/empl

It also links to the UN Secretariat's Office of Human Resources Management:

https://jobs.un.org/elearn/production/home.html

This office includes a great deal of information on application procedures and vacancies. Go to this website first. Most other UN human resources offices have websites.

The U.S. Department of State assists U.S. citizens in finding employment with the United Nations, its specialized agencies, and other international organizations. Its UN Employment Information and Assistance Unit is responsible for improving American participation in UN programs by providing employment information through its "Fact Sheet" and by maintaining electronic linkages with various UN agencies. A good starting place for conducting a job search with various UN agencies is this helpful U.S. State Department website:

http://www.state.gov/p/io/empl/11076.htm

The "Fact Sheet" provides information on employment opportunities and requirements; professional and senior positions; short-term emergency relief and peacekeeping positions; translator and interpreter positions; secretary positions; other positions; grade structure, salaries, and related allowances; U.S. government assistance; and a list of U.S. government agencies involved in recruiting for UN positions. It also includes links to other international organizations relevant to the U.S. Departments of Defense and State. You'll also learn there are very few UN openings available for Junior Applicants – students, recent college graduates, or persons lacking pertinent experience or language skills. The UN regularly recruits for the following professional positions: administrative, agriculture/forestry, demography, development, economics, engineering, information systems, legal, political/international affairs, public health, public information, social welfare, statistics, teaching, and telecommunications. The UN also recruits for short-term (usually one year) relief and peacekeeping positions relating to election monitoring, emergency relief, transportation, and logistics. The UN also operates a few special employment programs: UN Guides, Intern Programs (for graduate students), and UN Volunteers. You'll need to arrange personnel interviews for these positions which usually take place in the fall.

International Financial Institutions

International financial institutions attempt to promote the economic development of Third and Fourth World countries through a variety of lending and investment strategies. The major such institutions include the following. For more information on their operations, opportunities, and hiring practices, explore their websites:

- **African Development Bank**   www.afdb.org
- **Asian Development Bank**   www.adb.org

- Inter-American Development
  Bank   www.iadb.org
- International Finance
  Corporation   www.ifc.org
- International Monetary Fund   www.imf.org
- World Bank   www.worldbank.org

Regional Organizations

Several major regional organizations provide a variety of employment opportunities in various cities as well as in island nations worldwide:

- Comprehensive Nuclear Test
  Ban Treaty Organization   www.ctbto.org
- Inter-American Institute for
  Cooperation on Agriculture   www.iica.int
- International Organization for
  Migration   www.iom.int
- North Atlantic Treaty
  Organization   www.nato.int
- Organization for Economic
  Cooperation and Development   www.oecd.org
- Organization for the Prevention
  of Chemical Weapons   www.opcw.org
- Organization of American States www.oas.org
- Pacific Community   www.spc.org.nc
- Pan American Health
  Organization   www.paho.org

The international community includes more than 1,000 additional international organizations. Some of the most important ones include:

- **Andean Community of Nations** (Lima, Peru)
  www.comunidadandina.org
- **Asian-Pacific Economic Cooperation** (Singapore)
  www.apec.org
- **Association of Southeast Asian Nations** (Jakarta, Indonesia)
  www.aseansec.org

- Common Market for Eastern and Southern Africa (Lusaka, Zambia)
  www.comesa.int
- The Commonwealth (London)
  www.thecommonwealth.org
- The Commonwealth of Independent States (Minsk, Kirava, Belarus)
  www.cis.minsk.by
- Council of Europe (Strasbourg Cedex, France)
  www.coe.int
- European Bank for Reconstruction and Development (London)
  www.ebrd.com
- European Space Agency (Paris Cedex, France)
  www.esa.int
- European Union
  www.europa.eu.int
- International Chamber of Commerce (Paris)
  www.iccwbo.org
- International Committee of the Red Cross (Geneva)
  www.icrc.org
- International Confederation of Free Trade Unions (Brussels, Belgium)
  www.icftu.org
- International Olympic Committee (Lausanne, Switzerland)
  www.olympic.org
- Nordic Council (Copenhagen, Denmark)
  www.norden.org
- Organization for Security and Co-Operation in Europe (Vienna)
  www.osce.org
- Organization of Arab Petroleum Exporting Countries (OAPEC)
  www.oapecorg.org
- Organization of Petroleum Exporting Countries (OPEC)
  www.opec.org
- South Pacific Forum Secretariat (Suva, Fiji)
  www.forumsec.org.fj
- Western European Union (Brussels, Belgium)
  www.weu.int

The Commonwealth and the European Union are two of the largest regional groups. When seeking employment with these regional international organizations, keep in mind that most of them only hire individuals who are citizens of their member states. However, there are exceptions to this hiring rule, especially if you have special skills that are not available through their own regional talent pools. Most of these organizations list job vacancies, with qualifications, on their websites.

Contractors and Consultants in Development

Although international organizations and U.S. government agencies have the greatest visibility in the international arena, numerous other organizations pursue public-related international interests. These peripheral institutions consist of consulting firms, trade and professional associations, nonprofit organizations, foundations, research organizations, and educational institutions. These organizations have international interests and interface in both the U.S. domestic and international arenas.

Much of what gets done by government and international organizations is actually done through contractors and consultants. During the past 40 years more and more public services and programs have been contracted out to private firms. This trend should continue in the future.

Consultants and contractors play important roles in providing services to government and business. Government agencies use consultants and contractors for several reasons:

- They require specialized information not available through their present staffs.

- They need special services and products only available from contractors and consultants.

- It is often more cost-effective to contract out services than to increase agency personnel to provide the services in-house.

- Many services are short term and thus can be most quickly and effectively performed by outside consultants and contractors.

At the state and local government levels, contractors may provide sanitation services, road construction, health care, and building construction and maintenance. At the federal level these firms run a variety of programs, conduct numerous studies, and regularly supply agencies with every conceivable type of durable and nondurable goods from pencil sharpeners to submarines. At the international level, contractors and consultants are involved in building and maintaining U.S. facilities abroad, implementing the U.S. foreign aid program, and providing information on international developments.

Almost every job in the private sector will be performed in government. Ironically, these government jobs are often performed by private firms on contract with government agencies. Therefore, much of the work of government employees involves obligating funds and administering contracts rather than providing direct government services.

Contractor services are performed at the contractor's or agency's site. In many cases, an agency will provide office space for a contractor's staff, which then performs services in offices adjacent to agency personnel. The extreme example of this type of relationship is found in the U.S. Department of Energy, where over 80 percent of its personnel are actually private contractors.

The Procurement Process

The work of contractors and consultants centers around the **procurement process**. Procurement is the process by which government acquires goods and services. Well defined rules and regulations govern the process by which agencies can contract out various services.

The federal government strictly regulates the procurement process through a set of general regulations. In addition, each agency develops its own more detailed regulations in reference to the general regulations. Altogether, over $800 billion a year flows from the federal government to the private sector through this process.

One major result of the federal procurement process has been to create competition among consulting and contracting firms. This normally takes the form of sealed bids for equipment or negotiations with agency personnel for services. Once a procurement need is identified and defined by agency personnel, contractors are identified and the procurement process follows specific rules and procedures. If the amount for small purchases is above $25,000, officials must issue a Request for Proposal (RFP). An announcement must be published in the *Federal Business Opportunities (FBO)* –www.fedbizopps.gov –for at least 30 days. During that time firms request copies of the solicitation which outlines the Statement of Work and evaluation criteria for judging proposals. Firms normally have 30 days to develop and submit detailed proposals. Once proposals are received and reviewed by contracting officers and technical personnel, an award is made to the firm receiving the highest evaluation on both technical and cost criteria. This may take from one to three months after the closing date for submitting proposals.

While all federal agencies are supposed to follow these rules for ensuring competition, informal systems also operate to limit competition. Many agencies prefer working with a single contractor and thus they "wire" RFPs to favor one particular contractor. This is done by specifying in both the Statement of Work and the evaluation criteria various requirements which only one firm is likely to meet. Agencies also issue IQCs (Indefinite Quantity Contracts) for small-scale projects that require little competition. These IQCs are very important for funding the day-to-day operations of many contractors. Many agencies, especially in the Department of Defense, are often flush with monies they find difficult to spend. Savvy contractors who understand budgets and funding mechanism are able to thrive by helping agency personnel spend their money!

Hiring Structure

It is extremely important to understand this procurement process if you are interested in working for international consulting and contracting firms. The process creates a job market situation which is very fluid, unstable, and unpredictable. A typical consulting firm structure consists of a core staff, associates, and consultants.

Many firms keep a small **core staff** which is employed full-time to respond to RFPs and manage a lean organizational infrastructure. As contracts are won, they hire two types of additional personnel – often on a consulting basis – for implementing the contract. **Associates** normally work closely with the core staff on several projects; these individuals are relatively loyal to the firm and are given a disproportionate amount of contract work as contractors or subcontractors. **Consultants** are less closely linked to the firm; they have specific skills not found among the core staff or associates, and they tend to freelance with several such firms. Therefore, many positions with these firms are short-term positions tied to specific contracts, ranging from one month to one or more years. Most contracts are for one year, with options to renew contracts up to two to three years before resubmitting them for open competition.

Given this structure, you must consider whether you want a full-time organization position or a contract-specific position as either an associate or consultant. An organization position may be more stable and predictable, but not necessarily so. For example, most contracting and consulting firms are small organizations employing fewer than 50 individuals. Many specialize in a particular government function or public policy area and work primarily with one or two government agencies. A few firms straddle the public and private sectors by doing contract work for both government and business. Many international consulting firms, for example, only work in the fields of health care, population planning, rural development, or military hardware and software. Others specialize in educational development and human resource management. Given the highly competitive nature of their work, many of these firms find they must quickly staff up and staff down depending on which contracts they receive. If they receive a large contract, they may need to more than double or triple their staff overnight. If they lose a large contract, everyone except the president may go off the payroll and, instead, work on a daily consulting basis. For many small firms, contracting work is a feast-or-famine business.

On the other hand, large firms with several large contracts – especially defense contractors – will maintain a relatively large permanent staff. They normally can afford to do this, because their overhead and profits are greater on larger contracts.

Contractors and Consultants in Foreign Aid

Several contractors and consulting firms are organized to acquire contracts with federal agencies and international organizations. These include huge firms such as PricewaterhouseCoopers, which does contract work with both public and private institutions and maintains an international staff of 70,000 in over 100 countries; medium-sized firms with staffs of 10 to 50 individuals; and one- or two-person firms which primarily rely on short-term contracts with a single agency or office. These firms provide every conceivable service from constructing roads and dams to dispensing food and condoms in developing countries.

The contracting and consulting business is widespread throughout the international arena. However, its exact dimensions are difficult to measure since much of the work of contractors and consultants is not visible to the public. Government agencies may have responsibility for administering foreign aid programs, but much of what they take credit for is done by contractors. Many agencies primarily obligate funds which are, in turn, dispensed to contractors and consultants who actually get the work done. The agency, in turn, primarily becomes involved in dispensing funds, monitoring contractors, and evaluating contract performance.

The World Bank, United Nations, and several federal agencies are the major funding sources for these contracting and consulting firms. Federal agencies most frequently using international contractors are the U.S. Agency for International Development, Department of Agriculture, Department of State, Department of Defense, the Central Intelligence Agency, and the Department of Homeland Security.

Take, for example, the U.S. Agency for International Development. This is a good case for getting a sense of how the government procurement process operates in the international arena and how it affects the operation of contractors and consultants as well as several nonprofit or nongovernmental (NGOs) organizations discussed in the next section. USAID is one of the largest dispensers of government contracts to large, small, and minority consulting firms. Since USAID is primarily organized to obligate funds for development projects in Third and Fourth World countries, numerous consulting firms in the United States and abroad are recipients of USAID funding. The contracts deal with every conceivable type of service and project, from rebuilding Iraq's educational system to improving agricultural production and entrepreneurial capabilities in many parts of Africa. USAID, for example, classifies contractors according to a variety of activity categories:

- Accounting and Financial Management
- Agriculture
- Architecture and Engineering
- Auditing
- Development Information/Evaluation
- Development Management
- Disaster Assistance

- Education
- Energy
- Environmental/Natural Resources
- Foreign Language Instruction
- Health (Planning and Delivery)
- Housing and Urban Development
- Macroeconomic Analysis
- Management Assistance/Skills
- Management Consulting Services
- Nutrition and Multisectoral Development
- Printing Services
- Procurement Services
- Records Management
- Rural/Regional Income Generation

A USAID contracting officer is assigned to each category. This individual issues solicitations, negotiates, and regularly communicates with the firms doing work under USAID contracts.

USAID does business with over 2,000 contractors in the United States and abroad. While many job opportunities are available with U.S. firms, additional opportunities are available with firms located in Third World countries which receive "Host Country Contracts." As part of USAID's emphasis on decentralization, capacity building, and private sector initiatives, more and more USAID contracts are earmarked for consulting firms in Third World countries. Since many of these firms lack basic capabilities to develop proposals and implement projects, some will hire experienced Americans to help them get and manage USAID contracts. The contracting officer attached to each USAID mission should have a list of local consulting firms and will usually make the list available upon request.

Personal Services Contracts

If you are interested in doing independent consulting, your best strategy will be to network with government employees who are responsible for contracting out services. In many cases, agencies prefer giving certain work to individuals rather than incurring the overhead costs involved with contracting out to an established firm. In addition, agencies can avoid lengthy competitive procedures and maintain closer control when they contract directly with individuals for amounts less than $10,000 or use a special category of contracts – the Personal Services Contract (PSC) – for larger amounts. Many individuals have been able to create consulting jobs for themselves by proposing to agency personnel new projects requiring their expertise.

You should be aware of this category of contracts frequently used in international consulting: Personal Services Contracts. These contracts are convenient ways for an agency to acquire specific expertise as well as additional personnel without disturbing personnel ceilings or increasing the agency payroll. Individuals are hired on one- to three-year contracts to perform specific services within the agency. Normally these positions are announced in the *Federal Business Opportunities*. Like many other international employers, USAID often requests a Curriculum Vitae (CV) rather than a resume. The curriculum vitae will place heavy emphasis on educational background, publications, and professional activities. A one- to two-page resume normally associated with job hunting in the United States would be inappropriate for such a position, although we recommend attaching a summary resume to such a curriculum vitae.

While agencies are required to announce their intent to conclude a Personal Services Contract, often the positions are "wired" for individuals who already have worked for the agency – especially a former employee who has retired or started a consulting business – or who helped develop a project for the agency and thus created his or her own full-time consulting position with the agency.

Useful Resources

Several useful information sources are available for locating opportunities with various contracting and consulting firms. The single most comprehensive source of names, addresses, phone numbers, and annotated descriptions of firms is found in *The Consultants and Consulting Organizations Directory* (Gale Group/Thomson Learning). Most libraries have current editions of this three-volume directory. It lists over 3,000 consulting firms according to the following categories:

1. Agriculture, Forestry, and Landscaping
2. Architecture and Interior Design

3. Arts and Entertainment
4. Business and Finance
5. Data Processing, Telecommunications, and Information Services
6. Education and Personal Development
7. Engineering, Science, and Technology
8. Environment
9. Health, Medicine, and Safety
10. Human Resources
11. Management
12. Manufacturing/Industrial/Transportation Operations
13. Marketing and Sales
14. Social Issues and Concerns

Since these volumes include all types of consulting firms, regardless of their public or private orientation as well as domestic or international operations, you will need to read through the various annotated descriptions to find which firms are primarily involved in international contract work. Although this is the best directory of such firms, keep in mind it does not include all contracting and consulting firms – only those willing to reveal information on their operations to the Gale Group/Thomson Learning. Many firms do not want to publicize their operations through this or other public information resource directories. Consequently, you will have to locate these firms through other resources and efforts.

One of the most useful resources for identifying international contracting and consulting firms doing business with the federal government is the *Federal Business Opportunities* (www.fedbizopps.gov), an online listing of current procurement opportunities that exceed $25,000. This site identifies which firms received contracts for what amounts. A good job search strategy is to continuously monitor who receives contracts and contact the firm when you see an award made in your area of expertise or interest. But you must do this immediately upon seeing the announcement since there is a lag time between the award of a contract and its announcement in the *FBO.*

We suggest this *FBO* job search strategy because typically firms operate in the following manner: The firm submits a proposal complete with a management structure, job descriptions, and resumes. But once they receive the award, the proposed staff changes due to the unavailability of some individuals proposed. At this time, the contractor must find new personnel and get them approved for the contract. In other words, the contractor now has a personnel problem or vacancy which must be filled immediately. If your qualifications and timing are right, you may find a job very quickly with such a firm. At the same time, you will make an important contact which could lead to having your resume included in other proposals. Most contractors are happy to receive resumes since they are continuously in need of personnel to propose for, as well as staff, new projects. As noted earlier, many contractors maintain in-house resume or talent banks which they refer to when dealing with their personnel needs. "Staffing-up" is always a problem employers prefer to solve before it becomes a major project implementation issue with clients.

You should also monitor the section of the *FBO* dealing with impending contracts. Once you become familiar with various specialty areas within the consulting business, you can nearly predict which firms will submit proposals for which projects. Knowing this, you can call a firm and mention your interest and availability in being included in their proposal. They may even offer you a short-term contract to help write the proposal should you have such interests and skills. In some cases, individuals manage to get included in two or more proposals for the same contract, thus better ensuring they will get the work once the contract is awarded. Some firms have no problems with your inclusion in competitors' proposals while others frown on such opportunism. But in the contracting game, where competition is keen, the basic goal is to get the contract and cash flowing.

Another source of information on contractors is the contracts procurement, or acquisitions, office in each agency. Some agencies, such as the U.S. Agency for International Development, provide lists of firms doing contract work with them. In fact, you can go the "Development Links" section of the USAID website for a partial list of contractors that do business with USAID:

www.usaid.gov/about/resources

Others are less organized and willing to provide such information. Also, ask the officials **which** contractors are doing **what** and **whom** you might contact. Sometimes these individuals are very open with such information and will make several useful suggestions. On the other hand, agency officials may guard this information as private and confidential, even though it is public information. In this instance, you may consider formally requesting the information through the Freedom of Information Act.

You will find that some firms largely specialize in one function in a single agency whereas other firms do contract work in one or many functional areas with several agencies. For example, if you are interested in working for a firm in the field of energy or environmental protection, you should contact the Contracts Office at the Department of Energy or Environmental Protection Agency for a list of contractors. Once you have this information, you will know whom to contact. The firms working with these agencies also may be doing similar work in other agencies and in private industry. Call the firms and let them know you are interested in working for them. Try to set an appointment for an interview. Make sure you get your resume in their database. Indeed, many firms refer to this database when they need personnel for new projects. While they may not have a vacancy at the time you contact them, they very well may submit a proposal which results in a position for you.

Many international contracting and consulting firms periodically recruit on the Internet as well as place employment ads in either the classified or business sections of major newspapers, especially the Sunday editions of *The Washington Post* and *The New York Times*. You should monitor these sections of the newspaper. However, don't expect to get a job by responding to these ads. Many firms periodically place such ads in order to increase the number of resumes for their files. Sometimes they are in the process of bidding on a project, so they advertise for resumes to put in a particular proposal. If you manage to get your resume in the proposal and the firm wins the contract, you have a job. But more often than not, such ads are "fishing expeditions" with no particular vacancy available at the time of the ad. They want to build their stock of resumes for certain skill areas in the event they need to quickly respond to an RFP.

Professional Positions

Most international contracting and consulting firms hire individuals with strong analytical, communication, and technical skills along with language and area skills and extensive international work experience. Given the nature of consulting work, consultants are hired as problem-solvers. They must quickly analyze situations, devise plans of action, and often implement projects. Such activities require a great deal of analytical skill and the ability to communicate to clients both orally and in writing. Projects continuously require paper flows – work plans, monthly reports, memos, evaluations, studies – between the consultants and clients. If you are both a good and fast writer, stress these facts to potential employers. They especially need smart, quick-thinking, fast writers.

While most firms hire general support staff positions for word-processors, receptionists, secretaries, and accountants, most continuously seek technical specialists. Defense contractors and construction firms hire a disproportionate number of engineers, systems analysts, and computer specialists. Rural development firms hire a disproportionate number of agronomists and agricultural marketing specialists. Research firms hire policy analysts with skills unique to specific programs and agencies. Other firms need specialists in a variety of areas. If you survey the *Federal Business Opportunities* notices, you will quickly get a sense of which technical specialties are in demand.

It is much easier to break into an international contracting and consulting firm if you have previous government experience in a specialty area involving contractors. Your special knowledge and contacts with agency personnel will make you very marketable among firms working in your area. Indeed, much of the revolving door with government involves employees leaving an agency and working for the same contractor they previously worked with from within the agency. These individuals become key contact people and informants for the firm. Furthermore, since agency personnel usually think they are "unique" – believing outsiders can't possibly understand their problems, situations, and needs – they prefer working with one of their own who can speak their agency "language."

Educational qualifications also are important with international contracting and consulting firms. They prefer individuals with MAs and PhDs because government places heavy emphasis on educational qualifications of contractors' personnel when awarding contracts. After all, agency personnel working with contracts tend to be well educated – many have MAs and PhDs. When it comes to educational background, they prefer working with consultants who are at least their equal or have higher educations. As the very minimum, a BA degree is expected, but an MA or PhD is much preferred. As noted earlier, this is in line with the general emphasis within the international job market on educational qualifications. Education has a much different meaning in terms of "qualifications" in other cultures. The American egalitarian emphasis on "job performance skills" is not widely embraced throughout the world.

But how do you break into the international contracting and consulting game if you don't have experience, technical skills, or advanced degrees? If you have strong analytical, writing, and technology skills, along with basic foreign language and area skills as well as some international experience, you should be able to land a position through sheer persistence. These firms continuously need such skills. Often they find their technical personnel with government experience cannot write. Therefore, they need staffers who can write and edit. If you get into a firm based on your analytical and writing skills, you may be able to quickly pick up the technical aspects of the work and in time be able to work directly with clients on projects. In the meantime, you will probably stay in the background providing support for technical personnel.

This is a very basic and typical pattern of how individuals break into the government consulting business and become specialists in a short time even though they lack experience as a government employee. In the long run, the best skill to have is an ability to work with agency personnel who are suspicious of outsiders and who feel their agency is unique. They respond best to firms they feel recognize their uniqueness, respond to their problems, and can be trusted. Responsiveness and trust are perhaps the most important elements in developing and maintaining a good contractor-client relationship. On-the-job experience in interacting with clients is the basic requirement for becoming an effective consultant. Education and previous government experience will not be enough.

Key Contractors

Several thousand contractors do international work in both the public and private sectors. Representing a broad spectrum of products and services, from architecture, engineering, and construction to health care, accounting, and management, the following firms are especially noted for doing work with government and international agencies abroad. While many of them also do a great deal of business in the private sector, they are especially noted for their public sector presence, especially their work with USAID, the United Nations, and the World Bank. For more information on these firms, visit their websites. Many of these firms post job vacancies and outline employment procedures on their home pages.

- ABB Lummus Global   www.abb.com/lummus
- Abt Associates, Inc.   www.abtassoc.com
- Advanced Systems Development   www.asd-inc.com
- American Institutes for Research   www.air.org
- ARD, Inc.   www.ardinc.com
- Arkel International, Ltd.   www.arkel.com
- Bechtel Group, Inc.   www.bechtel.com
- R.W. Beck, Inc.   www.rwbeck.com
- Louis Berger Group, Inc.   www.louisberger.com
- Black and Veatch   www.bv.com
- Booz Allen Hamilton   www.bah.com
- John T. Boyd Company   www.jtboyd.com
- Boyle Engineering Corp.   www.boyleengineering.com
- Buchart-Horn, Inc.   www.bh-ba.com
- Burns and Roe Enterprises   www.roe.com
- CACI International. Inc.   www.caci.com
- Camp Dresser & McKee, Inc.   www.cdm.com
- Carter & Burgess, Inc.   www.c-b.com
- CBI Industries, Inc.   www.chicagobridge.com
- Checchi and Company
  Consulting, Inc.   www.checchiconsulting.com
- Chemonics International   www.chemonics.com
- Conservation International   www.conservation.org
- Creative Associates
  International, Inc.   www.caii-dc.com
- Development Alternatives, Inc.   www.dai.com
- Development Associates, Inc.   www.devassoc.com
- Dillingham Construction Corp.   www.dillingham
  construction.com
- DMJM + Harris, Inc.   www.dmjmharris.com
- DPRA, Inc.   www.dpra.com
- Earth Satellite Corporation   www.earthsat.com
- EarthTech   www.earthtech.com
- Engineering-Science, Inc.   www.parsons.com
- Fluor Corporation   www.fluor.com
- Foster Wheeler International
  Corporation   www.fwc.com
- The Futures Group International   www.tfgi.com

- Gannett Fleming   www.gannettfleming.com
- Heery International, Inc.   www.heery.com
- Hellmuth, Obata & Kassabaum   www.hok.com
- International Resources Group   www.irgltd.com
- John Snow, Inc.   www.jsi.com
- Labat-Anderson, Inc.   www.labat.com
- LTS Corporation.   www.ltscorporation.com
- Mathtech, Inc.   www.mathtechinc.com
- Metcalf & Eddy International   www.m-e.com
- Montgomery Watson Harza   www.mwhglobal.com
- Morrison-Maierle/CSSA, Inc.   www.m-m.net
- Multi Consult Milano   www.multiconsult.com
- Nathan Associates   www.nathanassoc.com
- Navigant Consulting, Inc.   www.rmiinc.com
- PADCO, Inc.   www.padcoinc.com
- Parsons Brinckerhoff
  International   www.pbworld.com
- Parsons Corporation   www.parsons.com
- Pragma Corporation   www.pragmacorp.com
- Raytheon Engineering &
  Construction   www.raytheon.com
- Sheladia Associates, Inc.   www.sheladia.com
- Washington Group International   www.wgint.com
- Wilbur Smith Associates, Inc.   www.wilbursmith.com
- SRI International   www.sri.com
- STV Group   www.stvinc.com
- University Research Corporation   www.urc-chs.com
- Washington Consulting Group   www.washcg.com
- Wimberly Allison Tong & Goo   www.watg.com

Defense Contractors

The U.S. Department of Defense spends billions of dollars each year on contractors and consultants. Many of their contracts are with firms involved with weapons systems and operations abroad. The nine largest defense contractors include:

- Boeing-MacDonnell Douglas
- General Dynamics
- General Electric
- General Motors
- Grumman
- Lockheed
- Martin Marietta
- Raytheon
- United Technologies

Few people are knowledgeable about smaller contractors that do work with various military-, intelligence-, and security-related agencies of the government. Many of these companies specialize in such critical technology areas as chemical and biological systems, electronics, guidance and navigation control, information warfare, marine systems, nuclear systems, sensors and lasers, signature control, space systems, and weapons effects and countermeasures. We identify hundreds of military contractors and their websites in Chapter 13 of our companion military transition book, *Military Transition to Civilian Success* (Impact Publications, 2006).

Business Consulting Firms

The major international consulting firms, which primarily work in the private sector but also do some government and nonprofit work, include the following companies. Many of these highly competitive firms, such as the Boston Consulting Group, are known for their cutting-edge international work and are famous for being some of the best companies to work for in terms of salaries, benefits, advancement opportunities, and corporate cultures. BCG's website (www.bcg.com) offers useful information on the company as well as the job search in general:

- **Arthur D. Little Inc.**   www.adlittle.com
- **Bain and Company**   www.bain.com
- **BearingPoint Consulting**   www.bearingpoint.com
- **Booz Allen Hamilton**   www.bah.com
- **Boston Consulting Group**   www.bcg.com
- **CGI/American Management Systems**   www.cgiams.com
- **Deloitte and Touche**   www.deloitte.com
- **Ernst & Young**   www.ey.com
- **Hay Group, Inc.**   www.haygroup.com
- **Hewitt Associates**   www.hewitt.com
- **Hill & Knowlton**   www.hillandknowlton.com

- KPMG   www.kpmg.com
- McKinsey and Co. Inc.   www.mckinsey.com
- PricewaterhouseCoopers   www.pwcglobal.com

Nonprofit and Volunteer Opportunities

Numerous nonprofit and volunteer organizations offer excellent opportunities to break into, as well as pursue long-term careers, in the international job market. Similar to many contracting and consulting firms, nonprofit and volunteer organizations operating in the international arena are disproportionately involved in social and economic development efforts in Third and Fourth World countries.

International nonprofits are modern-day missionaries who are less motivated by an evangelical zeal to save souls than by a commitment to humanity – help the very poor move into the mainstream of development. They feed the hungry, care for women and children, promote improved health care standards, provide needed medical assistance and education, improve sanitation, evacuate and resettle refugees, respond to natural and man-made disasters, develop rural water and sanitation systems, promote family planning and prenatal care, develop rural lending institutions and cooperatives, assist in marketing crops, and promote community development efforts. They are the major catalysts for change in much of the developing world. They rely heavily on funding from government agencies, especially USAID, and foundations as well as from their own fund-raising efforts.

International nonprofit organizations appeal to a certain type of person who has a missionary zeal to improve the conditions of poor people throughout the world. They tend to be dedicated to certain human values and committed to helping others. Working conditions for employees of these organizations can be difficult, and pay is often low. But these organizations generate a sense of personal satisfaction that cannot always be matched by working for businesses, government, or private contracting firms.

While many of these groups are funded by individual and corporate contributions, most also receive contracts and grants from government agencies and foundations. Many nonprofits, such as CARE and Save the Children Foundation which are heavily funded through USAID, function as the humanitarian assistance arm of the U.S. government. Some of the more enterprising child survival groups, such as Foster Parents Plan, Children International, Childreach, and Christian Children's Fund, also operate individual "sponsorship" programs for generating income. You may frequently see on television their highly effective ads which use a variety of major media personalities to solicit for sponsors who pay anywhere from $12 to $25 a month to "sponsor" a child.

NGOs and PVOs are increasingly playing a major role in developing countries. Funding agencies view these groups as most capable of making a difference in developing countries. Their extensive field staffs, commitment to change, and adaptability make them favorite candidates for funding by government agencies and foundations. They continue to expand their operations in Third and Fourth World countries. Consequently, many of these organizations may experience significant growth during the coming decade.

If you are interested in pursuing a cause or making a difference in the lives of others, you should seriously consider working for a nonprofit organization. While most of these organizations pay medium to low salaries, they do provide unique and extremely rewarding opportunities to get involved in development that are largely absent in other types of organizations except, perhaps, the U.S. Peace Corps and specialized agencies of the United Nations.

The following international nonprofit organizations are some of the major players in international relief and development efforts. Many are huge organizations with staffs in excess of 1,000 and with annual budgets exceeding $300 million. Some organizations may have 90 percent of their staffs assigned to field operations abroad whereas others may have less than 50 percent stationed abroad. Many of these organizations also operate large volunteer programs. You will probably recognize many of the names, such as the Red Cross, that was involved in the South and Southeast Asian tsunami relief efforts in 2004-2005, and the Melinda and Bill Gates Foundation that is involved in developing innovative health and learning solutions for the global community, with special emphasis on HIV/AIDS in Africa.

The Organizations

International groups known as nonprofit organizations are frequently referred to as Nongovernmental Organizations (NGOs) or Private Voluntary Organizations (PVOs). Most of these organizations are primarily oriented toward promoting a particular international issue or cause. In contrast to more than 100,000 nonprofit organizations operating within the United States, international nonprofits are fewer in number and operate almost solely in the international arena. They span a broad spectrum of issues and causes:

- foreign affairs
- education
- housing
- energy
- economic development
- population planning
- food
- social welfare

- relief
- community development
- human rights
- religion
- rural development
- children and youth
- water resources
- health

Examples of different types of nonprofit organizations and their diverse missions abound throughout the international arena. Most of these organizations cluster around important health, agricultural, social welfare, and disaster issues that are inadequately dealt with in most poor countries: medical services, population planning, agricultural productivity, community development, employment generation, refugee resettlement, and natural disaster relief. Nonprofit organizations such as the International Voluntary Service, Catholic Relief Service, and CARE provide similar development services as the U.S. Peace Corps. The Population Council's involvement in family planning and health issues affects all other development issues in Third World countries. The World Affairs Councils function to increase the awareness of Americans concerning international issues. The Council for International Exchange of Scholars (Fulbright-Hays) and Meridian House International focus on promoting educational and cultural exchanges.

The major nonprofit international organizations which hire international specialists for headquarter and field locations and have full-time staffs of at least 20 and an annual budget exceeding $5 million include:

- **ACCIÓN International**   www.accion.org
- **Adventist Development &**
  Relief Organization   www.adra.org
- **Africare**   www.africare.org

- Agricultural Cooperative
  Development International   www.acdivoca.org
- American Friends Service
  Committee   www.afsc.org
- Catholic Medical Mission Board   www.cmmb.org
- Catholic Relief Services   www.crs.org
- Christian Children's Fund, Inc.   www.christianchildrens
  fund.org
- Church World Service   www.churchworldservice.org
- Cooperative for American Relief
  Everywhere, Inc. (CARE)   www.care.org
- Direct Relief International   www.directrelief.org
- EnterpriseWorks/VITA   www.enterpriseworks.org
- Food for the Hungry   www.fh.org
- Foster Parents Plan International   www.fosterparentsplan.ca
- Heifer Project International   www.heifer.org
- Holt International Children's
  Services   www.holtintl.org
- Institute of Cultural Affairs   www.icaworld.org
- Interchurch Medical Assistance   www.interchurch.org
- International Executive Service
  Corps   www.iesc.org
- International Eye Foundation   www.iefusa.org
- International Planned
  Parenthood Federation   www.ippf.org
- International Rescue Committee   www.theirc.org
- Lutheran World Relief   www.lwr.org
- MAP International   www.map.org
- Mennonite Economic
  Development Associates, Inc.   www.meda.org
- PACT   www.pactworld.org
- Pathfinder International   www.pathfind.org
- Project Hope   www.projecthope.org
- Population Council   www.popcouncil.org
- Population Reference Bureau   www.prb.org
- Salvation Army   www.salvationarmyusa.org
- Save the Children   www.savethechildren.org

- **United Methodist Committee
  on Relief** www.methodistrelief.org
- **World Concern** www.worldconcern.org
- **World Relief** www.wr.org
- **World Vision International** www.wvi.org

Many of these nonprofit organizations, including religious-affiliated organizations, are major recipients of USAID contracts. They work closely with the USAID bureaucracy as well as many private contracting firms and universities that are also major recipients of USAID funding. As such, they play an important role in the peripheral network of organizations involved in U.S. foreign policy efforts. However, many other nonprofits are not linked to the government in this manner. Organizations such as Oxfam America, a noted self-help development and disaster relief organization operating in Africa, Asia, Latin America, and the Caribbean, the Pearl S. Buck Foundation that works with Amerasian children, and numerous religious organizations doing development-related missionary work abroad have their own funding sources.

Most of these nonprofit organizations are headquartered in the United States – primarily Washington, DC, New York City, and a few other East Coast cities – but have field operations in many countries throughout Latin America, Africa, and Asia. Most of the job opportunities will be in the field and thus require individuals with certain technical and linguistic skills along with some international experience.

Voluntourism and Legacy Travel

Volunteer work and alternative travel have been around for a long time. Often associated with young, inexperienced, and liberal people with few resources – stereotypical backpackers in search of alternative travel experiences – today such volunteer work and travel appeal to much older, experienced, conservative, and affluent travelers who are seeking greater purpose in their lives.

Indeed, a new twist to international nonprofit organizations are tour groups and foundations that focus on voluntourism and what we call "legacy travel." These organizations sponsor two- to six-week purpose-driven trips to assist people in developing countries. These are working vacations with a nonprofit emphasis. Upscale travelers may pay $5,000 to $10,000 for a four-week tour that involves working in an orphanage, building homes, teaching children, mentoring, helping refugees, rescuing animals, preserving the environment, or joining an archaeological or restoration tour for three weeks and then enjoying sightseeing, shopping, great restaurants, and five-star resorts and spas during the final week. Individuals participating in such tours derive an enormous amount of satisfaction by "doing good" when traveling abroad. Many of them also make financial contributions for sustaining their development efforts. For U.S. residents, a large percentage of this travel also is tax deductible.

Other groups participate in legacy travel. Such travel is designed for people who want to leave a legacy behind without actually getting their hands dirty by doing physical labor. Disproportionately wealthy, these people travel to places where they have a wonderful time meeting local people, learning about local needs, getting involved in projects with a purpose, and deciding to make financial contributions, such as providing building, equipment, and program support to schools, orphanages, or hospitals. Their financial commitments may be substantial and long-term, especially if they decide to "sponsor" programs and facilities.

We see voluntourism and legacy travel as growing phenomena with both nonprofit organizations and tour groups. The demographics and economics favor growth in these areas. In fact, voluntourism and legacy travel respond to growing trends among retirees who want to:

- travel
- be engaged
- meet new people with other walks of life
- learn more about other countries and cultures
- have a purpose and do good
- leave a legacy behind

Indeed, some nonprofit organizations have begun to organize such tours as part of their revenue-generating plans.

If you love to both travel and do good works, you should seriously consider getting involved in this increasingly popular form of tourism and travel. For more information on voluntourism and legacy travel, consult several of the following resources with an eye toward getting involved on the business end of this type of travel:

Volunteer Vacations: Short-Term Adventures That Will Benefit You and Others, Bill McMillon, Anne Geissinger, and Doug Cuttchines (Chicago Review Press, 2006)

How to Live Your Dream of Volunteering Overseas, Joseph Collins, Stefano DeZerega, and Zahara Heckscher (Penguin, 2001)

The Backdoor Guide to Short-Term Job Adventures, Michael Landes (Ten Speed Press, 2005)

Vacation Work's International Directory of Voluntary Work, Louise Whetter (Vacation Work/Peterson's, 2000)

Green Volunteers: The World Guide to Voluntary Work in Nature, Fabio Ausenda and Erin McLoskey (Universe Books, 2003)

World Volunteers: The World Guide to Humanitarian and Development Volunteering, Fabio Ausenda and Erin McLoskey (Universe Books, 2003)

Alternative Travel Guide, Ron Mader and Bill Nolting, eds. (Transitions Abroad, 2003)

The following websites also will introduce you to the new world of voluntourism:

- Global Community Service Foundation — www.globalvoluntourism.org
- VolunTourism — www.voluntourism.org
- Voluntourism.com — www.voluntourism.com
- Sustainable Travel International — www.sustainabletravelinternational.org
- World Volunteer Web — www.worldvolunteerweb.org
- TransitionsAbroad — www.transitionsabroad.com
- GoNOMAD — www.gonomad.com
- GlobeAware — www.globeaware.org
- ResponsibleTravel.com — www.responsibletravel.com

- Explorations in Travel   www.volunteertravel.com
- Global Volunteers   www.globalvolunteers.org
- International Volunteer
  Programs Association (IVPA)   www.volunteerinternational.org

Nonprofits on the Internet

Gateway Sites

Several websites function as gateway sites to the nonprofit sector. Two sites, www.idealist.org and www.guidestar.org, are incredibly comprehensive gateway sites to the nonprofit sector, both international and domestic. Indeed, they may be the only two sites you need for connecting with the nonprofit sector. These sites also link to hundreds of nonprofits:

- **Action Without Borders**   www.idealist.org
- **Charity Village**   www.charityvillage.com
- **Council on Foundations**   www.cof.org
- **Foundation Center**   www.fdncenter.org
- **GuideStar**   www.guidestar.org
- **Independent Sector**   www.independentsector.org
- **Internet Nonprofit Center**   www.nonprofits.org
- **Volunteer Match**   www.volunteermatch.org

The following websites function as online job boards for nonprofits. They include hundreds of job vacancy announcements.

- Community Career Center   www.nonprofitjobs.org
- Jobs In Nonprofit   www.jobsinnonprofit.com
- Nonprofit Jobs   www.nonprofit-jobs.org
- National Council of
  Nonprofit Associations   www.ncna.org

Guides to Nonprofit Employers

The following websites provide direct access to numerous international nonprofit organizations. Many of these websites include job announcements.

- AIESEC   www.aiesec.org
- Global Health Council   www.globalhealth.org
- IAESTE   www.iaeste.org
- InterAction   www.interaction.org
- Intercristo   www.intercristo.com
- International Service Agencies   www.charity.org
- PACT   www.pactworld.com
- Volunteers for Peace   www.vfp.org

Major International Nonprofit Employers

The following nonprofit organizations have international operations in several countries around the world. They regularly hire individuals for both U.S.-based and field positions. Nonprofits followed with an asterisk (*) were selected by *Worth* magazine in December 2001 as among 100 best charities because of their ability to work with other groups, stay focused on their missions, and get things done through local leaders. Many of these organizations are very exciting international employers:

- Academy for Educational
  Development   www.aed.org
- ACCION International*   www.accion.org
- Adventist Development and
  Relief Agency International   www.adra.org
- Africare, Inc.   www.africare.org
- Agricultural Co-op
  Development International   www.acdivoca.org
- Air Serv International   www.airserv.org
- American Friends
  Service Committee   www.afsc.org
- American Jewish Joint
  Distribution Committee   www.ajc.org
- American Red Cross
  International Services   www.redcross.org/services/intl
- American Refugee Committee*   www.archq.org
- AmeriCares Foundation   www.americares.org
- Amnesty International USA   www.amnesty-usa.org
- Ashoka*   www.ashoka.org

- Asia Foundation — www.asiafoundation.org
- Battelle Memorial Institute — www.battelle.org
- Bread for the World — www.bread.org
- Brother's Brother Foundation — www.brothersbrother.org
- CARE* — www.care.org
- Catholic Relief Services — www.catholicrelief.org
- Centre for Development and Population Activities — www.cedpa.org
- Childreach — www.childreach.org
- Christian Children's Fund — www.christianchildrensfund.org
- Church World Service — www.churchworldservice.org
- Compassion International — www.ci.org
- Conservation International* — www.conservation.org
- Direct Relief International* — www.directrelief.org
- Doctors Without Borders* — www.dwb.org
- Educational Development Center, Inc. — www.edc.org
- EnterpriseWorks/VITA — www.enterpriseworks.org
- Esperanca, Inc. — www.esperanca.org
- Family Health International — www.fhi.org
- FINCA* — www.villagebanking.org
- Food for the Hungry, Inc. — www.fh.org
- Freedom From Hunger* — www.freedomfromhunger.org
- Global Health Council — www.globalhealth.org
- Goodwill Industries* — www.goodwill.org
- Greenpeace — www.greenpeaceusa.org
- Habitat for Humanity* — www.habitat.org
- Heifer International* — www.heifer.org
- Helen Keller International — www.hki.org
- The Hunger Project — www.thp.org
- Institute of International Education — www.iie.org
- InterExchange — www.interexchange.org
- International Catholic Migration Commission — www.icmc.net
- International Center for Research on Women* — www.icrw.org

- International Development
  Enterprises — www.ideorg.org
- International Executive
  Service Corps — www.iesc.org
- International Eye Foundation — www.iefusa.org
- International Medical Corps* — www.imc-la.org
- International Rescue
  Committee — www.theirc.org
- LASPAU – Academic and
  Professional Programs for
  the Americas — www.laspau.harvard.edu
- Laubach Literacy
  International — www.laubach.org
- Lutheran Immigration
  and Refugee Service — www.lirs.org
- Lutheran World Relief — www.lwr.org
- MAP International — www.map.org
- Mennonite Central Committee — www.mcc.org
- Mercy Corps International* — www.mercycorps.org
- National Wildlife Federation* — www.nwf.org
- Nature Conservancy* — www.nature.org
- OIC (Opportunities Industrial
  Centers) International — www.oicinternational.org
- Operation USA* — www.opusa.org
- Opportunity International — www.opportunity.org
- Oxfam America* — www.oxfamamerica.org
- PACT (Private Agencies
  Collaborating Together)* — www.pactworld.org
- Partners of the Americas — www.partners.net
- Pathfinder International — www.pathfind.org
- People to People Health
  Foundation (Project HOPE) — www.projecthope.org
- Physicians for Human Rights* — www.phrusa.org
- PLAN International — www.plan-international.org
- Planned Parenthood
  Federation — www.plannedparenthood.org
- Population Action
  International — www.populationaction.org

- Population Council   www.popcouncil.org
- Population Reference Bureau   www.prb.org
- Population Services
  International   www.psi.org
- Program for Appropriate
  Technology in Health   www.path.org
- Project Concern
  International   www.projectconcern.org
- Refugees International*   www.refugeesinternational.
  org
- Research Triangle Institute   www.rti.org
- Salvation Army World
  Service Office   www.salvationarmy.org
- Save the Children Foundation   www.savethechildren.org
- Sierra Club   www.sierraclub.org
- Special Olympics*   www.specialolympics.org
- Technoserve*   www.tns.org
- U.S. Catholic Conference
  Office of Migration and
  Refugee Services   www.nccbuscc.org/mrs
- U.S. Fund for UNICEF*   www.unicefusa.org
- Unitarian Universalist
  Service Committee   www.uusc.org
- Volunteers in Overseas
  Cooperative Assistance   www.acdivoca.org
- Winrock International
  Institute for Agricultural
  Development   www.winrock.org
- World Concern   www.worldconcern.org
- World Council of Credit
  Unions   www.woccu.org
- World Education   www.worlded.org
- World Relief Corporation   www.worldrelief.org
- World Resources Institute*   www.wri.org
- World Vision Relief and
  Development, Inc.   www.worldvision.org
- World Wildlife Fund*   www.worldwildlife.org
- Worldteach   www.worldteach.org

- Worldwatch Institute   www.worldwatch.org
- Y.M.C.A.   www.ymca.net
- Y.W.C.A.   www.ywca.org
- Zero Population Growth   www.zpg.org

Education, Research, and Associations

The following nonprofit education, research, and professional and trade organizations variously function as think tanks, lobbying groups, and training organizations. Most do a great deal of international work:

- American Enterprise Institute   www.aei.org
- Brookings Institution   www.brook.edu
- CATO Institute   www.cato.org
- Center for Strategic and
  International Studies (CSIS)   www.csis.org
- Chamber of Commerce   www.uschamber.org
- Consultative Group on
  International Food Policy
  Research Institute   www.cgiar.org
- Council for International
  Exchange of Scholars   www.cies.org
- Council of the Americas   www.counciloftheamericas.org
- Council on Foreign Relations   www.cfr.org
- Council on International
  Educational Exchange (CIEE)   www.ciee.org
- Earthwatch Institute   www.earthwatch.org
- Foreign Policy Association   www.fpa.org
- Freedom House   www.freedomhouse.org
- Heritage Foundation   www.heritage.org
- Hoover Institute on War,
  Revolution, and Peace   www.hoover.org
- Hudson Institute   www.hudson.org
- Human Rights Watch   www.hrw.org
- International Center   www.internationalcenter.com
- International Schools Services www.iss.edu

- Meridian International Center   www.meridian.org
- NAFSA/Association of
  International Educators   www.nafsa.org
- Near East Foundation   www.neareast.org
- RAND Corporation   www.rand.org
- Rodale Institute   www.rodaleinstitute.org
- U.S.-China Business Council   www.uschina.org
- United States Olympic
  Committee   www.olympic-usa.org
- Urban Institute   www.urban.org
- World Learning   www.worldlearning.org
- Youth for Understanding
  International Exchange   www.yfu.org

Volunteer Opportunities

You will also find numerous volunteer groups operating in Third World countries. Many of these groups, such as **Amigos de las Americas** (5618 Star Lane, Houston, TX 77057, Tel. 800-231-7796, www.amigoslink.org) and **Volunteers for Peace** (1034 Tiffany Road, Belmont, VT 05730, Tel. 802-259-2759, www.vfp.org), offer students and others opportunities to work on development projects in Third World countries. Many groups require you to pay for your own transportation, food, and housing – which are often minimal – but they do provide excellent opportunities to participate in international development projects without having to join the U.S. Peace Corps or some other type of organization. If you lack international experience and want to "test the waters" to see if this type of international lifestyle is for you, consider joining a volunteer group for three to six months that would put you in a work situation abroad. You will acquire valuable experience and learn a great deal about the Third World and the network of government agencies, nonprofit organizations, and contracting firms operating abroad – as well as yourself. Several websites provide information on international volunteer opportunities:

- **Amnesty Volunteers**   www.amnesty-volunteer.org
- **Cross-Cultural Solutions**   www.crossculturalsolutions.org
- **Explorations in Travel**   www.volunteertravel.com

- Global Volunteers   www.globalvolunteers.org
- Green Volunteers   www.greenvolunteers.org
- Idealist   www.idealist.org
- International Partnership
  for Service Learning   www.volunteeringabroad.org
- International Volunteer   www.volunteerinternational.
  Programs Association   org
- Peace Work   www.peacework.org
- SCI International Volunteer
  Service   www.sci-ivs.org
- United Nations Volunteers   www.unv.org
- Volunteer International   www.volunteerinternational.
  Projects   com
- Volunteers for Peace   www.vfp.org
- Volunteers in Technical
  Assistance   www.vita.org
- World Volunteer Web   www.worldvolunteerweb.org

Useful Resources

When conducting research on international nonprofit organizations, you should examine several directories and websites that identify who's who in the international nonprofit arena. Start with these print directories:

- *Encyclopedia of Associations: International Organizations*
- *Encyclopedia of Associations: National Organizations*
- *Yearbook of International Organizations*

These publications are found in the reference section of most major libraries. Many of the NGOs, such as InterAction (www.interaction.org), also have numerous linkages to other NGOs and PVOs. If you follow these linkages, you will come into contact with numerous nonprofit organizations that operate in the international arena.

Several books on international jobs and careers identify and discuss numerous nonprofit organizations offering job opportunities:

- *Careers in International Affairs*
- *The Global Citizen*

- *International Careers*
- *International Job Finder*
- *International Jobs*
- *Jobs and Careers With Nonprofit Organizations*
- *The Nonprofit's Job Finder*

The following directory focuses specifically on nonprofit international organizations:

Member Profiles: Published by InterAction, 1717 Massachusetts Avenue, NW, Suite 701, Washington, DC 20036, Tel. 202-667-8227. Profiles over 160 private humanitarian agencies that are members of the American Council for Voluntary International Action, one of the largest and most active groups of nonprofit organizations involved in all forms of development assistance, from health care and refugee aid to child care, environment management, human rights, disaster relief, and community development. Includes a searchable CD-ROM. $81.00. It also publishes *Global Work: InterAction's Guide to Volunteer, Internship, and Fellowship Opportunities*, which sells for $18.00. For online order information, visit the "Publications" section on www.interaction.org.

If you are interested in international volunteer opportunities, including internships, you will find numerous useful directories and books to assist you in locating organizations whose missions most meet your interests and needs:

- *Alternative Travel Directory*
- *Alternatives to the Peace Corps*
- *The Directory of International Internships*
- *Directory of Overseas Summer Jobs*
- *Directory of Volunteer Opportunities*
- *The Directory of Work and Study in Developing Countries*
- *Global Work*
- *How to Live Your Dream of Volunteering Overseas*
- *The International Directory of Voluntary Work*
- *The International Directory of Youth Internships*
- *International Internships and Volunteer Programs*
- *International Workcamp Directory*
- *Invest Yourself: The Catalogue of Volunteer Opportunities*

- *Jobs Abroad: Over 3,000 Vacancies of Interest to Christians*
- *Response: Directory of Volunteer Opportunities*
- *U.S. Voluntary Organizations and World Affairs*
- *Volunteer! The Comprehensive Guide to Voluntary Service in the U.S. and Abroad*
- *Volunteer Vacations*
- *Volunteer Work*
- *Work Abroad*
- *Work, Study, Travel Abroad*
- *Work Your Way Around the World*
- *Working Holidays*
- *World Volunteers: The World Guide to Humanitarian and Development Volunteering*

If you are a **Returned Peace Corps Volunteer** (RPCV), you are in good luck. The Peace Corps takes care of its own, which now consists of 175,000 former Volunteers and 7,810 current Volunteers and trainees. You will want to use the job services available through the Returned Volunteer Services office: Peace Corps, 1111 20th Street, NW, Washington, DC 20526, Tel. 202-692-1430 or Fax 202-692-1431, or visit the RPCV section on the agency's website:

www.peacecorps.com/rpcv

It may well be worth your time and effort to visit this office. After all, Washington, DC is located in the heart of hundreds of organizations offering international job opportunities for those interested in pursuing jobs and careers with nonprofit organizations as well as with consulting firms and educational organizations relevant to the Peace Corps experience. Better still, many of these organizations are staffed by individuals who are part of the growing "old boy/girl network" of ex-Peace Corps Volunteers who look favorably toward individuals with Peace Corps experience. At the same time, many nonprofit organizations, consulting firms, and educational organizations automatically contact this office when they have impending vacancies. Please do not contact this office unless you are a returned Volunteer. This already over-worked office can only provide information and services to its former Volunteers and staff members – both long-term and recently separated. If you left the Peace

Corps 20 years ago, you can still use this service. It has an excellent library of international resources as well as numerous job listings relevant to its Volunteers. It also publishes twice a month a job listing bulletin called *Hotline*, which includes employment and educational opportunities for returned Peace Corps Volunteers. Anyone can access this publication online by going to this section of the Peace Corps website:

www.peacecorps.gov/index.cfm?shell=resources.former.hotline

In March 2006, the paper version of the *Hotline* will be replaced with a e-newsletter. Former volunteers should contact the RPCV office to get on the e-mail list.

You also may want to join the National Peace Corps Association (1900 L Street, NW, Suite 205, Washington, DC 20036-5002, Tel. 202-293-7728, www.rpcv.org), a network of 16,000 former volunteers with 140 affiliated alumni groups – a good organization through which to conduct an active networking campaign. Annual membership costs $50.

Job Search Strategies

Use the same strategies for landing a job with an international nonprofit organization as you would for any other nonprofit organization – respond to job vacancies (usually found on an organization's website) with an outstanding resume and cover letter, but work the "hidden job market" by researching organizations, making inside contacts through networking, and following up. **The international job arena is a highly networked community**: whom you know and your ubiquitous "connections" will serve you well in finding a job with an international nonprofit. You should do a great deal of networking, informational interviewing, and moving your face, name, and resume among key people associated with these organizations at both the staff and board levels. Success in landing such a job will take time, tenacity, and a positive attitude. Your best locations for literally "hitting the streets" and "pounding the pavement" for international nonprofit organizations will be Washington, DC and New York City.

Indeed, many international nonprofit organizations are headquartered in these two cities, but many of them maintain substantial field operations in developing countries. While most nonprofits hire through headquarters, many also hire directly in the field. If you are already in the field and neither have the time nor money to travel to Washington or New York City to conduct an intensive job search, make sure you develop contacts with field representatives in your area. Nonprofit organizations tend to be very field oriented, and thus many useful job contacts can be made at the field level. Your research on each organization will determine how, where, and with whom to best target your job search within each organization.

9

✈

The Exciting World of Business Travel

S TROLL THROUGH MOST ANY major airport and you'll see who really does the greatest amount of on-the-job traveling – business people – especially those in sales and marketing. While flying, they work on their computers and hand-held devices. As your plane empties, several fellow briefcase-laden passengers begin activating their cell phones to confirm appointments with clients or check their offices for messages. Then it's into a taxi, rental car, or shuttle bus and on to a hotel and meetings.

This business travel ritual is repeated thousands of times each hour in airports throughout the world. If you love selling and marketing products in distant locations, it's a ritual you may want to join.

Business Travel

Business travel appeals to many people, especially those who enjoy going first-class. Depending on your company, you may regularly fly business or first-class, stay in five-star hotels, dine in fine restaurants, enjoy top entertainment and sports activities, and meet interesting and exciting people. This type of work can become addictive, as it enables you to participate in a first-class lifestyle.

However, business travel is not for everyone, especially for many married individuals with families, or those who travel in less than first-class style. It's also burdensome for many business people who must constantly waste time in long airport security lines and suffer the abuses of airlines. If you are always on the road, you may become somewhat jaded to this travel lifestyle. Indeed, many businesspeople who must travel a great deal in their work discover the joys of travel decline the more they travel. Many now prefer limiting their travels to only a few days each month or a few weeks each year.

Nonetheless, if you want to travel a great deal and get paid for it at the same time, consider finding a job or pursuing a mobile career in business. Your best options are jobs in sales and marketing. A job in international business may give you opportunities to frequently travel and live abroad.

Management

Top management in corporations – corporate chairpersons, presidents, and vice presidents – frequently travel as part of their corporate responsibilities. Some use the corporate jet rather than fly commercial. They inspect plant and field operations, meet key clients, negotiate contracts, and attend major meetings. They usually travel in style – first-class all the way, from hotels and restaurants to 18-hole golf courses. Getting one of these jobs, of course, requires advancing to the top of a corporate hierarchy.

Many other lower level management and support personnel also travel a great deal. Chief operating officers, chief financial officers, and corporate lawyers travel to field sites, meet with corporate clients, and attend annual meetings. Again, acquiring these jobs requires advancement within a corporate hierarchy. You first must get a job with the company and then advance accordingly within the organization.

Sales

If you want a job involving travel, try sales with a medium- to large-sized company. Companies that have regional, national, or international sales territories offer the best on-the-job travel opportunities. Before long you will probably be on the road regularly, visiting numerous cities and towns where you will market your company's products, revisit old clients, prospect for new leads, and cultivate new clients.

Marketing at Trade Shows

If your interests lie in marketing, you should consider representing company products at trade shows. Individuals participating in these shows travel a great deal. Conveying a first-class image of their companies, they often stay in fine hotels and dine in good restaurants.

Thousands of trade shows are held each year throughout the United States and abroad. Most last from three to seven days. In the United States they tend to be held in major cities, such as New York, Washington, DC, Chicago, San Francisco, Los Angeles, New Orleans, and Miami, which have large conference and convention facilities.

International Business

Businesses employ the largest number of individuals in the international arena. Indeed, as the global economy continues to expand and nations become more economically interdependent, so too does international trade and the role of international businesses.

> *Don't expect to find many entry-level international business positions except in sales.*

Opportunities in international business cover a wide range of organizations and jobs. They include jobs with such traditional organizations as banks, oil and chemical companies, manufacturers, importers, and exporters. Positions involve everything from political risk analysis and force protection/security to sourcing for new products and management, sales, and marketing positions.

Breaking In

While businesses may employ many people internationally, don't expect to find many entry-level international business positions except in sales.

In contrast to other types of organizations – government and nonprofit – which may hire individuals for entry-level international positions, businesses generally promote employees to positions that involve international operations only **after** several years of progressive experience within the organization.

Breaking into international business often requires extensive experience within particular industries – more so than the knowledge of foreign languages, area studies, or international experience. Most large corporations, for example, assign employees to foreign operations as one step in a promotion hierarchy that requires key personnel to have foreign experience prior to advancing to other positions within the company. Many well established companies have few overseas assignments because they have already developed talented local staffs that have the requisite skills to function locally.

An ideal company providing international travel opportunities would be one just starting to develop overseas operations. During their initial stage of developing new markets and establishing local bases of operations, they normally send employees abroad. As more and more companies expand their operations abroad or broaden the scope of operations into new countries, numerous opportunities should be available for working abroad. Many of the positions will involve marketing, sales, security, consulting, finance, and sourcing for new parts and products. Consequently, your best opportunities in international business may be with small companies just starting to enter the international arena or expanding into new locations. Many large corporations with established operations abroad will be closed to individuals seeking entry-level international positions.

Many small international companies look for individuals with management and marketing skills who also enjoy working abroad. Many of these positions may be in international sales and involve working from a home base in New York, London, Rome, Singapore, Hong Kong, or Tokyo. Breaking into these firms requires having the right "connections" to people who make the hiring decisions. It involves networking within the international business community. One of the best ways to get such connections is to know people who already work in the international business community. You might, for example, attend a semester abroad program in Europe, Asia, or Latin America that involves studying the local international business community. Alternatively, you might acquire an internship with an international business that puts you in the heart of the international business community where you develop numerous contacts with individuals in many different businesses. These people may later become your ticket to gaining entry to many international businesses.

Several of the organizations and programs outlined in the educational section of Chapter 6 should help you in making connections to the international business community. You should also consider taking international business-related courses in college as well as such bread-and-butter business courses as accounting, finance, and marketing along with one or two foreign languages. If you are a business major, you should consider participating in an international business internship or other international work-related business experience. Two of the best such programs are:

Association Internationale des Etudiants en Sciences Economiques et Commerciales (AIESEC-U.S.): Public Relations Director, AIESEC-U.S., Inc., 127 W. 26th Street, New York, NY 10001, Tel. 212-757-4062, Fax 212-757-3774. Website: www.aiesec.org. Claims to be the world's largest student organization consisting of a network of 50,000 members in more than 83 countries and territories at more than 800 universities. AIESEC facilitates the exchange of thousands of students and recent graduates each year who work as trainees (interns) or volunteers with a variety of organizations, from nonprofits and government organizations to multinational and small businesses. It includes a global network of 11,000 organizations.

Association for International Practical Training (AIPT): Park View Boulevard, 10400 Little Patuxent Parkway, Suite 250, Columbia, MD 21044, Tel. 410-997-2200, Fax 410-992-3824, e-mail: aipt@aipt.org. Website: www.aipt.org. Arranges global training and cultural exchange experiences for U.S. and international students with businesses around the world. Serves as the U.S. affiliate of the International Association for the Exchange of Students for Technical Experience (IAESTE), a network of more than 70 countries that coordinates on-the-job training for university students in the fields of engineering, computer science, mathematics, natural and physical sciences, architecture, and agricultural science.

In the case of AIESEC, you will need to be involved in a local chapter in order to participate in this student-operated program. Check first to see if your college or university has a chapter. If not, visit AIESEC's website for contact information on local chapters as well as how to establish a chapter.

Several companies, such as Chase Manhattan Bank, Salomon Brothers, IBM, Monsanto, United Technologies, General Electric, and Allied-Signal, have established summer internship programs in a variety of business areas. You will have to contact these companies directly for application information. For information on these and other international internship opportunities, see our resources in Chapter 7.

You might also consider creating your own internship by contacting companies directly and selling them on the idea of letting you work for them as an unpaid or low-paid intern. This form of volunteerism within the business community may be well received by some small companies that will welcome getting an offer they can't refuse!

Not all international business opportunities are with U.S.-based multi-national corporations or small businesses. Indeed, many high-tech and supply chain firms in India hire hundreds of American interns each year. Don't neglect foreign-based businesses that may be interested in American management and marketing skills – two major American business strengths that are highly sought in many countries. Many foreign companies interested in breaking into the American, European, or Asian markets or managing their existing supply chain relationships may be interested in your technical and international business skills or your general management and marketing expertise. Again, you learn about these companies through the process of networking within particular countries and selling your skills to potential foreign employers.

Know Your Business

Numerous types of businesses offer a large variety of international job and career opportunities:

- Information technology
- Commercial and investment banking
- Marketing
- Management
- Finance
- Accounting
- Consulting

- News media and broadcasting
- Entertainment (motion pictures, videos, games)
- Telecommunications
- Architectural and engineering services
- Construction
- Transportation
- Aerospace
- Shipping
- Insurance
- Publishing and printing
- Retailing and trading
- Sourcing for parts/products
- Mining
- Natural resource production (mining, petroleum, natural gas)
- Manufacturing product lines (food, beverages, chemicals, paper, wood products, fiber, pharmaceuticals, computers, electronics, cosmetics, sporting goods, toys, musical instruments, industrial and farm equipment, apparel, appliances, tobacco, plastics, rubber, motor vehicles, military hardware)

Corporate United States plays a major role in world trade. Thousands of American businesses operate abroad and thousands more will be entering the international arena in the coming decade. Indeed, of the 500 largest world traders, 157 – or 31.4 percent of the total – are U.S. corporations; Japan follows next with 150 companies. Collectively, European countries have the largest number of companies in the top 500 – 161. The U.S. barely remains dominant at present, with seven of the 20 largest world traders being U.S. corporations.

Other large international companies included in the top 500 are leaders in aerospace, steel, beverage, photo, paper, computer, construction, machinery, health care, textile, energy, and building materials industries. Some of the major international businesses include the following:

Company	Major Products/Services
Allied Signal	aerospace, chemical, oil, gas
Amerada Hess	petroleum exploration/production
American Cyanimid	pharmaceuticals, chemicals
American Home Products	prescription drugs/home products

AT&T	communications
Avon Products	cosmetics
Bell & Howell	business equipment
BellSouth	communication
Black & Decker	electrical tools, machines, appliances
Boeing	aircraft and aerospace manufacturer
Borg-Warner	automotive parts, chemicals
Carnation	food manufacturer
Caterpillar Tractor	earth-moving equipment
Chevron	oil
Coca-Cola	beverage manufacturer
CPC International	food manufacturer
Dell Computers	computers
Dow Chemical	chemical manufacturer
DuPont	chemicals
Eastman Kodak	photographic supplies and equipment
Eli Lilly	pharmaceuticals and cosmetics
Emerson Electric	electronics manufacturer
Exxon	oil
Firestone Tire & Rubber	tire producer
Ford Motor	auto manufacturer
General Dynamics	aerospace, chemical, oil, gas
General Motors	auto manufacturer
Goodyear Tire & Rubber	tire manufacturer
Grace Offshore	oil well work-over/completion
Grumman International	aircraft and aerospace
Hewlett-Packard	computers and electronics
Honeywell	computers and automated systems
IBM	computers, electronics
ITT	communications, hotels, electronics
Lockheed Martin	aircraft and aerospace
Minnesota Mining & Manuf.	3M product line
Monsanto	chemicals
Motorola	electronics manufacturer
Ogilvy Group	advertising
Pepsi-Cola International	beverage manufacturer
Pfizer International	pharmaceuticals and health care
Philip Morris	tobacco and beverages

Phillips Petroleum	oil producer
Raytheon	high-tech electronics producer
RCA Corporation	communications/electronics producer
Revlon	cosmetics
R.J. Reynolds Tobacco	tobacco products
Rockwell International	aviation and electronics
Sperry	computers/data processing equip.
Texaco	oil producer
Texas Instruments	computers and electronics
TRW	electronics and equipment producer
Union Carbide	chemical and plastics manufacturer
Unisys	technology consulting/services
Weyerhaeuser	wood producer
Xerox	computers, data processing

Some of the major banks and financial companies operating in the United States and with extensive international operations include:

American Express	Goldman Sachs
Bank of New York	Manufacturers Hanover Trust
Bank of Tokyo-Mitsubishi	Merrill Lynch
Bank of America	Morgan Stanley
Barclays	Paine Webber
Chemical Bank	Prudential Bache Securities
Citicorp	Salomon Brothers
Dai-Inchi Kangyo Bank	Smith Barney
Deutsche Bank	Sumitomo Mitsui Banking Corp.
Fidelity Group	Tokai Bank
Fuji Bank	

All of these multinational companies offer numerous international job and career opportunities at home and abroad regardless of one's nationality.

America's Most Admired Employers

Fortune Magazine's annual survey of America's most admired companies (March 6, 2006) includes many firms that offer international and travel opportunities. You may want to check out the websites of these firms (use the popular www.google.com or www.yahoo.com search engines to find the URLs):

FINANCIAL INDUSTRY

1. **Securities**
   1. Merrill Lynch
   2. Lehman Brothers Holdings
   3. Bear Stearns
   4. Goldman Sachs Group
   5. Franklin Resources
   6. A.G. Edwards

2. **Megabanks**
   1. Wells Fargo
   2. Bank of America
   3. Citigroup
   4. Wachovia

3. **Superregional Banks**
   1. Bank of New York
   2. M&T Bank Corp.
   3. State Street
   4. BB&T
   5. PNC Financial Services Group

4. **Financial Data Services**
   1. Dun & Bradstreet
   2. First Data
   3. DST Systems

5. **Mortgage Services**
   1. Gold West Financial
   2. Countrywide Financial
   3. Washington Mutual
   4. Stewart Information Services
   5. LandAmerica Financial Group

6. **Insurance: Life and Health**
   1. Northwestern Mutual
   2. New York Life
   3. AFLAC
   4. Massachusetts Mutual Life
   5. TIAA-CREF

7. **Insurance: Property, Casualty**
   1. Berkshire Hathaway
   2. Chubb
   3. Allstate
   4. Progressive
   5. Hartford Financial Services
   6. State Farm Insurance

CONSUMER PRODUCTS

8. **Food Production**
   1. Bunge
   2. Pilgrim's Pride
   3. Smithfield Foods
   4. Corn Products International
   5. Tyson Foods

9. **Beverages**
   1. Anheuser-Busch
   2. Pepsi Bottling Group
   3. PepsiAmericas
   4. Coca-Cola

10. **Consumer Food Products**
    1. Nestlé
    2. PepsiCo
    3. General Mills
    4. Kellogg
    5. Unilever

11. **Apparel**
    1. Nike
    2. Liz Claiborne
    3. VF
    4. Polo Ralph Lauren
    5. Timberland

12. **Household & Personal Products**
    1. Procter & Gamble
    2. Estée Lauder
    3. Colgate-Palmolive

4. Avon Products
5. Kimberly-Clark

13. Tobacco
1. Altria Group
2. R.J. Reynolds Tobacco

CONTRACTED SERVICES

14. Diversified Outsourcing
1. Aramark
2. Convergys
3. Iron Mountain
4. Cintas
5. ServiceMaster

15. Temporary Help
1. Manpower
2. Robert Half International
3. MPS Group

16. Health Care: Insurance
1. UnitedHealth Group
2. Aetna
3. WellPoint
4. PacifiCare Health Systems
5. WellChoice

17. Health Care: Facilities
1. Health Management Assoc.
2. Manor Care
3. HCA
4. Triad Hospitals
5. DaVita

SHELTER

18. Furniture
1. Herman Miller
2. HNI
3. Leggett & Platt

19. Homebuilders
1. KB Home
2. Pulte Homes
3. Centex
4. Toll Brothers
5. Lennar
6. Ryland Group

20. Real Estate
1. Simon Property Group
2. Boston Properties
3. Vornado Realty Trust
4. Host Marriott

21. Home Equipment, Furnishings
1. Fortune Brands
2. Newell Rubbermaid
3. Masco

22. Engineering, Construction
1. Jacobs Engineering Group
2. Peter Kiewit Sons
3. CH2M Hill
4. Fluor
5. Granite Construction

23. Building Materials, Glass
1. USG
2. Vulcan Materials
3. Martin Marietta Materials
4. Owens Corning

STORES AND DISTRIBUTORS

24. Wholesalers: Electronic, Office
1. CDW
2. Arrow Electronics
3. Graybar Electric
4. Tech Data
5. Ingram Micro

25. Wholesalers: Diversified
1. True Value
2. Airgas
3. Hughes Supply
4. W.W. Grainger
5. Fisher Scientific International

26. Wholesales: Food, Grocery
1. Sysco
2. CHS
3. Supervalu
4. United Natural Foods
5. Performance Food Group

27. Wholesalers: Health Care
1. Henry Schein

2. Cardinal Health
3. McKesson
4. Patterson

28. General Merchandisers
1. Nordstrom
2. Target
3. Wal-Mart Stores
4. J.C. Penney
5. Federated Department Stores

29. Specialty Retailers
1. Home Depot
2. Best Buy
3. Costco Wholesale
4. Lowe's
5. Limited Brands
6. Staples

30. Food and Drug Stores
1. Walgreen
2. Publix Super Market
3. Safeway
4. Kroger
5. CVS

31. Food Services
1. Starbucks
2. McDonald's
3. Brinker International
4. CBRL Group
5. Yum Brands

NATURAL RESOURCES

32. Mining, Crude-Oil Production
1. Apache
2. Peabody Energy
3. Anadarko Petroleum
4. Occidental Petroleum
5. Devon Energy

33. Metals
1. Worthington Industries
2. Alcoa
3. Nucor
4. Alcan
5. Phelps Dodge

34. Pharmaceuticals
1. Johnson & Johnson
2. Genentech
3. Amgen
4. Eli Lilly
5. Abbott Laboratories

35. Packaging, Containers
1. Sealed Air
2. Pactiv
3. Ball
4. Silgan Holdings
5. Bemis

36. Chemicals
1. DuPont
2. BASF
3. Dow Chemical
4. PPG Industries
5. Bayer

37. Forest and Paper Products
1. International Paper
2. Weyerhaeuser
3. Georgia-Pacific
4. Plum Creek Timber
5. MeadWestvaco

COMPUTERS AND
& COMMUNICATIONS

38. Computers
1. IBM
2. Apple Computer
3. Xerox
4. Hewlett-Packard
5. Pitney Bowes

39. Internet Services, Retailing
1. Google
2. eBay
3. Yahoo
4. IAC/InterActiveCorp

40. Computer Peripherals
1. EMC
2. Seagate Technology
3. Lexmark International

41. Computer Software
 1. Intuit
 2. Adobe Systems
 3. SAP
 4. Microsoft
 5. Electronic Arts

42. Telecommunications
 1. AT&T Inc.
 2. Sprint Nextel
 3. Verizon Communications
 4. Comcast
 5. BellSouth

43. Network Communications
 1. Qualcomm
 2. Cisco Systems
 3. Motorola
 4. Corning
 5. Scientific-Atlanta

44. Information Tech. Services
 1. Accenture
 2. Perot Systems
 3. Electronic Data Systems
 4. Science Applications Intl.

POWER

45. Petroleum Refining
 1. Exxon Mobil
 2. BP
 3. Chevron
 4. ConocoPhillips
 5. Royal Dutch Shell

46. Electric and Gas Utilities
 1. Exelon
 2. FPL Group
 3. Southern
 4. Dominion Resources
 5. Entergy

47. Energy
 1. WPS Resources
 2. Oneok
 3. Duke Energy
 4. TXU
 5. Williams

48. Oil and Gas Equipment, Svcs.
 1. FMC Technologies
 2. Schlumberger
 3. Smith International
 4. BJ Services
 5. Baker Hughes

49. Pipelines
 1. Kinder Morgan Energy Partners
 2. Enterprise Products Partners
 3. Enbridge Energy Partners
 4. Plains All American Pipeline

MEDIA AND ENTERTAINMENT

50. Media and Entertainment
 1. Walt Disney
 2. Univision Communications
 3. Time Warner
 4. CBS
 5. News Corp.

51. Publishing
 1. Washington Post
 2. E.W. Scripps
 3. New York Times
 4. Tribune
 5. McGraw-Hill
 6. Gannett

52. Hotels, Casinos, Resorts
 1. Marriott International
 2. Hilton Hotels
 3. Harrah's Entertainment
 4. MGM Mirage

PRECISION

53. Semiconductors
 1. Texas Instruments
 2. Applied Materials
 3. Intel
 4. Advanced Micro Devices
 5. Analog Devices

54. Electronics
 1. General Electric
 2. Siemens
 3. Emerson Electric

4. Royal Philips Electronics
5. Sony

55. Precision Equipment
1. Medtronic
2. St. Jude Medical
3. Stryker
4. Becton Dickinson
5. Zimmer Holdings

THINGS THAT MOVE

56. Airlines
1. Continental Airlines
2. Southwest Airlines
3. AMR
4. Alaska Air Group
5. ExpressJet Holdings

57. Motor Vehicle Parts
1. Johnson Controls
2. Lear
3. ArvinMeritor
4. Brigestone
5. Goodyear Tire & Rubber

58. Industrial and Farm Equipment
1. Illinois Tool Works
2. Deere
3. Caterpillar
4. ITT Industries
5. Black & Decker
6. Ingersoll-Rand

59. Transportation, Logistics
1. Expeditor Intl. of Washington
2. C.H. Robinson Worldwide
3. Sirva

4. CNF
5. Alexander & Baldwin

60. Railroads
1. Union Pacific
2. Norfolk Southern

61. Delivery
1. United Parcel Service
2. FedEx
3. Brinks

62. Aerospace and Defense
1. United Technologies
2. Lockheed Martin
3. Northrop Grumman
4. General Dynamics
5. Boeing

63. Trucking
1. YRC Worldwide
2. J.B. Hunt Transport Services
3. Landstar System
4. Werner Enterprises
5. Arkansas Best

64. Automotive Retailing, Services
1. CarMax
2. United Auto Group
3. AutoNation
4. Lithia Motors

65. Motor Vehicles
1. Toyota Motor
2. BMW
3. Honda Motor
4. Nissan Motor
5. DaimlerChrysler

Useful Resources

For a more complete listing, including U.S. firms operating in specific countries, consult the following business websites which function as excellent gateway sites, online databases, and research tools:

- CEO Express   www.ceoexpress.com
- Hoover's Online   www.hoovers.com

- D&B's Million Dollar Databases — www.dnbmdd.com/mddi
- BizTech Network — www.brint.com
- AllBusiness — www.allbusiness.com
- BizWeb — www.bizweb.com
- Business.com — www.business.com
- America's CareerInfoNet — www.acinet.org
- Newspapers USA — www.newspapers.com
- Annual Reports — www.annualreportservice.com
- Chambers of Commerce — www.chamberofcommerce.com
- Daily Stocks — www.dailystocks.com
- The Corporate Library — www.thecorporatelibrary.com
- Forbes 500 — www.forbes.com/lists
- Fortune 500 — http://money.cnn.com/magazines/fortune
- Harris InfoSource — www.harrisinfo.com
- Inc. 500 — www.inc.com/inc500
- Moodys — www.moodys.com
- NASDAQ — www.nasdaq.com
- Standard & Poors — www.standardandpoors.com
- Thomas Regional and Thomas Register — www.thomasnet.com
- Internetnews.com — www.internetnews.com/bus-news/

Also, examine the following print directories:

- *American Register of Exporters and Importers*
- *Bernard Klein's Guide to American Directories*
- *Directory of American Firms Operating in Foreign Countries*
- *Directory of Foreign Firms Operating in the U.S.*
- *Directory of U.S. Firms Operating in Latin America*
- *Dun and Bradstreet Exporter's Encyclopedia*
- *Dun and Bradstreet's Middle Market Directory*
- *Dun and Bradstreet's Million Dollar Directory*
- *Encyclopedia of Business Information Sources*
- *Geography Index*
- *The International Corporate 1,000*

- *Jane's Major Companies of Europe*
- *Major Companies of Europe*
- *The Multinational Marketing and Employment Directory*
- *Poor's Register of Corporations, Directors, and Executives*
- *Principal International Business*
- *Standard Directory of Advertisers*
- *The Standard Periodical Directory*
- *Standard and Poor's Industrial Index*
- *Standard Rate & Data Business Publications Directory*
- *Thomas' Register of American Manufacturers*
- *World Business Directory*

In addition, many of the contracting and consulting firms identified in Chapter 8 could be incorporated with those found in this chapter. Large firms, such as the M.W. Kellogg Company, Ralph M. Parson Company, Metcalf & Eddy International, and Lummus Crest, operate throughout the world in developing and implementing major engineering and construction projects, especially roads, bridges, dams, airports, tunnels, sewerage systems, nuclear power facilities, petrochemical factories, and pharmaceutical plants. Chapter 8 also lists numerous businesses involved in providing financial and technical assistance services to developing countries in the areas of accounting, agricultural development, health care, education, and energy. Major firms such as Ernst & Young and PricewaterhouseCoopers are identified there too. You may also want to get a copy of the current annual edition of *The Business Phone Book USA*, which includes the names, addresses, phone and fax numbers, and websites of thousands of businesses involved in the international arena.

10

✈

Short- and Long-Term Travel-Work Adventures

I N THIS FINAL CHAPTER we briefly examine several additional job and career opportunities for travel lovers. These range from such major employers as the military and merchant marine to short-term and long-term employment and travel-work adventures abroad, including self-employment and entrepreneurship. We reveal numerous online and offline resources to assist you in conducting an effective international job search.

Working Around the World

Have you ever thought of just taking off to travel or to work your way around the world? Few people have the free time and financial independence to roam the globe in such a carefree manner. Many young people – especially college students using their summer vacations or taking a semester off to travel abroad – and retirees decide to engage in this type of travel. They're not really interested in the work end of the travel/work equation. What they really want is to enjoy a particular travel style that also enables them to live abroad for short periods of time and experience other cultures by working closely with the locals. Working while traveling helps finance their travel addiction.

Roaming the globe and working at the same time poses numerous challenges. Indeed, we regularly receive inquiries from many young people and their parents on how to both travel and work abroad. Most of these people are primarily interested in finding short-term minimum wage jobs – earn just enough to help meet ongoing travel expenses. They do not expect this type of work will lead to long-term jobs or careers abroad. Their primary goal is to make a lengthy trip abroad more financially feasible as well as have an opportunity to meet people from different cultures. Many will seek volunteer opportunities that give them room and board in exchange for their labor. Several resources listed in Chapter 8 on volunteering (pages 259-262) should prove useful to these individuals.

Restrictions

Finding jobs abroad can be difficult even under the best of circumstances. Most countries have very restrictive work-permit requirements. Except for the European Union (EU) countries, where employment in member countries is relatively open (no work permits required for EU citizens), and some Eastern European countries, most countries protect local labor by placing restrictions similar to the following on foreign workers:

1. **Foreigners are forbidden to acquire jobs that compete with local labor and skills.** When applying for a work permit and resident visa, employers must provide evidence that the job in question cannot be filled by a local worker with similar skills.

2. **Work permits and resident visas are temporary and thus must be renewed periodically** through a Ministry, Department, Bureau, or Office of Labor – every 6, 12, or 24 months. The bureaucracy normally takes its time in processing such applications. You will witness a great deal of bureaucratic inertia in the process of acting on your application – an indication that granting work permits to foreigners is not a top priority government function! For information on work permit requirements, visit www.goinglobal.com and www.workpermit.com.

3. **Foreigners must pay local taxes and special resident visa fees.** They may be restricted in taking local currency out of the country. Leaving the country even for a short holiday may require tax clearances – including a large cash deposit – and special permission so you can re-enter without invalidating your work permit and resident visa.

4. **Work permit and resident visa requirements may restrict the number of times foreigners can exit and re-enter a country.** In some countries the work permit and resident visas become invalid upon leaving the country. Consequently, the whole application process must be once again initiated upon entering the country.

While many of these restrictions seem illogical and the bureaucratic process can be slow, they are designed with one purpose in mind – discourage foreign workers. Not surprisingly, countries increasingly emphasize "locals only" employment/ immigration policies due to a combination of nationalism and high unemployment rates.

However, as numerous young people discover each year as they travel

> *You can bypass many work permit rules by finding jobs in the "gray market" of each country.*

and work abroad, you can bypass many work permit rules by finding jobs in the "gray market" of each country. If you only plan to work one or two months, and you can find an employer willing to hire you, chances are you will be able to find and complete your employment before the local authorities catch up with you and your employer.

Short-Term Employment

Short-term, minimum-wage jobs abroad are most abundant in the travel and hospitality industry, agriculture, natural resources, and foreign language instruction. These include such jobs as:

- waiter/waitress
- cook and kitchen helper
- hotel/resort worker

- bartender
- courier
- tour guide
- camp worker
- salesperson
- factory worker
- childcare worker
- ski instructor
- miner
- oil rigger
- fruit and vegetable farmer/picker
- construction worker
- fisherman and fish processor
- English teacher

Five of the best sources providing contact information for acquiring short-term jobs and volunteer experiences abroad are:

The Back Door Guide to Short-Term Job Adventures, 4th Edition, Michael Landes (Ten Speed Press, 2005)

The BIG Guide to Living and Working Overseas, 4th Edition, Jean-Marc Hackey (Intercultural Systems/Systèms Interculturels, Inc., 2005). Also available as an online subscription edition: www.workingoverseas.com.

Summer Jobs Abroad, David Woodworth and Ian Collier, Editors (Vacation Work, annual)

Volunteer Vacations: Short-Term Adventures That Will Benefit You and Others, Bill McMillon, Anne Geissinger, and Doug Cuttchines (Chicago Review Press, 2006)

Work Your Way Around the World, Susan Griffith (Vacation Work, annual)

Each of these books provides descriptions of potential employers as well as names, addresses, and telephone numbers for contacting them.

Vacation Work also publishes several other unique guides to short-term jobs abroad:

The Au Pair and Nanny's Guide to Working Abroad, Susan Griffith and Sharon Legg

The Good Cook's Guide to Working Abroad, Katherine Parry

Summer Jobs Britain, Emily Hatchwell

Working in Ski Resorts, Victoria Pybus

Working With Animals: The UK, Europe, and Worldwide, Victoria Pybus

Transitions Abroad Publishing produces two books focusing on work, travel, and study abroad resources. Many of the opportunities featured in these books are short-term:

Alternative Travel Directory: The Complete Guide to Work, Study, Travel Overseas, 7th Edition, Clayton Hubbs, Editor (Transitions Abroad Publishing, 2002)

Work Abroad: The Complete Guide to Finding a Job Overseas, 4th Edition, Clayton Hubbs, Susan Griffin, and William Nolting, Editors (Transitions Abroad Publishing, 2002)

In addition to publishing *Overseas Summer Jobs* and *Work Your Way Around the World,* Vacation Work publishes several other useful books for individuals interested in short-term work abroad:

Directory of Jobs and Careers Abroad
International Directory of Voluntary Work
Kibbutz Volunteer
Live and Work in Australia and New Zealand
Live and Work in Belgium, The Netherlands & Luxembourg
Live and Work in France
Live and Work in Germany

Live and Work in Italy
Live and Work in Japan
Live and Work in Russia and Eastern Europe
Live and Work in Scandinavia
Live and Work in Spain and Portugal
Teaching English Abroad
The Teenager's Vacation Guide to Work, Study & Adventure

You should also review current and back issues of *Transitions Abroad,* which includes numerous informative articles about working abroad; many are written by students who recently completed a summer or semester abroad. The special *"Educational Travel Directory"* issue published each year in June is worth examining. This issue provides an invaluable bibliography of travel and work abroad resources. For subscription information (one year, six issues, for $28), contact:

Transitions Abroad
Box 3000
Denville, NJ 07834
Tel. 866-760-5340
E-mail: info@TransitionsAbroad.com
www.TransitionsAbroad.com

You may want to consider enrolling in an educational program that takes you abroad in lieu of finding short-term, minimum wage employment that can be more trouble than it is worth. For information on hundreds of such programs, some very inexpensive, examine *Transitions Abroad,* especially the June resource directory. Several of the publications listed in Chapter 6 should be helpful in locating relevant programs.

Students and others interested in studying abroad should examine the following annual guides published by Peterson's:

Study Abroad
Summer Study Abroad

Also, be sure to check out the many websites for student internships and study abroad programs, which we identified in Chapter 6 (pages 195-201). **Study Abroad Links** (www.studyabroadlinks.com) functions as one of the most comprehensive gateway sites to the world of study abroad programs.

If you are determined to travel the globe without any particular job or career in mind, you should be able to find employment along the way in a variety of different fields. However, expect to find relatively low level jobs which do not pay a great deal. Rejected by locals as inferior jobs, many of these jobs tend to go to immigrants and other foreign workers who will work hard for low wages. A good guide to this type of work is Susan Griffith's annual *Work Your Way Around the World*.

Needless to say, this type of employment is not for everyone. But many people find such travel-work to be one of the most interesting and exciting experiences of a lifetime. They meet new people, experience different cultures, and participate in unique lifestyles they would never have encountered had they traveled as ordinary tourists or students. Such adventures can have unexpected consequences – motivate one to pursue more permanent employment, perhaps even a career, involving travel abroad.

Long-Term Employment

In addition to the many resources we identified in Chapters 5-9 on long-term public and private sector international employment, be sure to check out the many international job search and relocation resources available through Going Global. Available both online (www.goinglobal.com) and offline (*Going Global Career Guide*), this unique employment database covers 23 high-interest countries, from Australia to the United Kingdom. Offering more than 10,000 job resources on these countries, it includes everything from employment trends, job fairs, and work permits to taxes, cost of living, resume writing, recruiters, and cultural advice. Individual country volumes can be previewed online as well as purchased as e-books from www.goinglobal.com. The materials can be acquired offline as a massive 800-page directory to all 23 countries (see the "Career Resources" section at the end of this book or visit the international section of Impact's CareerStore – www.impactpublications.com). Also, be sure to review Jean-Marc Mackey's *The BIG Guide to Living and Working Overseas* (page 284) and his related website: www.workingoverseas.com.

Several other websites provide useful job search information on international jobs. We especially recommend the following gateway sites:

- Escape Artist   www.escapeartist.com
- AIRS   www.airsdirectory.com/
                           jobboards
- The Riley Guide   www.rileyguide.com/
                           internat.html
- 4International Careers
  and Jobs   www.4icj.com
- About.com   http://jobsearch.about.com/cs/
                           internationaljobs1

Several other websites offer international job listings and online resources for conducting an effective global job search. The largest international employment website with hundreds of job listings and useful career advice is operated by Monster.com:

- Monster Work Abroad   http://workabroad.monster.com

Other international job websites worth exploring include the following:

- Overseas Jobs   www.overseasjobs.com
- PlanetRecruit   www.planetrecruit.com
- JobPilot   www.jobpilot.net
- Top Jobs   www.topjobs.co.uk
- Jobs Abroad   www.jobsabroad.com
- Jobs Bazaar   www.jobsbazaar.com
- International Jobs Center www.internationaljobs.org
- Expatica Jobs   www.expatica.com/jobs/
- Expat Exchange   www.expatexchange.com

Other useful expatriate websites worth surveying include:

- AAFSW Foreign Service
  Lifelines   www.aafsw.org
- American Citizens Abroad www.aca.ch
- Association of Americans
  Resident Overseas   www.aaro.org
- Australians Abroad   www.coolabah.com
- British Expat   www.britishexpat.com

- British Expats   www.british-expats.com
- Canadian Foreign Service
  Community Association   www.fsca-acse.org
- Canadians Abroad   www.geocities.com/canadians_
  Resource Guide   abroad
- Foreigner in America   www.foreignerinamerica.com
- French Expatriates   www.expatries-france.com
- Expat Expert   www.expatexpert.com
- Expat Focus   www.expatfocus.com
- Expat Grapevine   www.expatgrapevine.com
- Expatica   www.expatica.com
- Expatriates.com   www.expatriates.com
- Federation of American
  Women's Clubs Overseas   www.fawco.org
- Global Outpost Services   www.outpostexpat.nl
- Going-There   www.going-there.com
- Living Abroad   www.livingabroad.com
- Network for Living Abroad   www.liveabroad.com
- People Going Global   www.peoplegoingglobal.com

You will also find dozens of region-, country-, and city-specific expatriate websites. For example,

- AllPraha.com   www.allpraha.com
- Americans in Greece   www.geocities.com/Athens/7243
- Americans in Prague   www.americansinprague.com
- Americans in the UK   www.americanexpats.co.uk
- Asian Expats   www.asiaxpat.com
- Belgium Expats   www.xpats.com
- British Expats   www.britishexpats.com
- British-Expats   www.british-expats.com
- Expat Hong Kong   www.expathongkong.com
- Expat Shanghai   www.expatsh.com
- ExpatAccess (Europe)   www.expataccess.com
- Expatriates.com   www.expatriates.com
- Expatriates-online.com   www.expatriates-online.com
- Expats in Australia   www.expatsinaustralia.com
- Expats in Brazil   www.expat.com.br

- Expats in Brussels — www.expatsinbrussels.com
- Expats in China — www.expatsinchina.com
- Expats in Denmark — www.foreignhelp.dk
- Expats in Indonesia — www.expat.or.id
- Expats in Italy — www.expatsinitaly.com
- Expats in Pusan — www.pusanweb.com
- Expats in Singapore — www.expatsingapore.com
  www.aasingapore.com
- Expats in Sweden — www.expatsinsweden.com
- Expats in Thailand — www.thailandtips.com
  www.ethailand.com
- Expats in Turkey — www.ykcguide.com
- ExpatVillage (Argentina) — www.expatvillage.com
- Gringoes.com (Brazil) — www.gringoes.com
- Japan in Your Palm — www.japaninyourpalm.com
- Living in Indonesia — www.expat.or.id
- Passport2Manila — www.passport2manila.com
- Shanghai Expats — www.shanghaiexpat.com
- Singapore Expats — www.singaporeexpats.com
- Spain Expat — www.spainexpat.com
- Virtual Netherlands — www.xpat.nl
- Virtual Vienna — www.virtualvienna.net

For a comprehensive listing of over 100 expatriate sites, visit the expatriate linkage sections on EscapeArtist.com:

www.escapeartist.com/expatriate/expatriate1.htm
www.escapeartist.com/expatriate/expatriate2.htm

Merchant Marine

Always wanted to hop on a freighter and travel the Seven Seas? Perhaps the Merchant Marine is for you. While you may not become the captain of the ship, you might become a cook, oiler, deckhand, engineer, mate, or deck officer. You'll be responsible for moving valuable cargo from one port to another.

Water transport workers operate and maintain deep sea merchant ships, tugboats, towboats, ferries, dredges, research vessels, and other waterborne craft on the oceans and the Great Lakes, in harbors, on rivers and canals, and on other waterways. A typical deep sea merchant ship has a captain, three deck officers or mates, a chief engineer and three assistant engineers, plus six or more seamen and oilers. Merchant mariners also have an electrician, machinery mechanics, and a radio officer.

The life of a merchant mariner involves long periods at sea as well as on shore. If you have a family, expect to be gone more than you will be at home. A typical sailor may go to sea for 30 to 90 days and then take 30 to 60 days off before returning for the next journey. Many people enjoy this lifestyle. However, many others quit working the ships after only a few years. This lifestyle appeals to only certain types of individuals.

While many potential merchant mariners may think they will have an opportunity to visit numerous ports, the truth is that few sailors have much time to really visit their ports of call. Typically a ship waits its turn to unload cargo and then proceeds to its next destination. While in port, crew members may spend a few hours on shore – not enough time to really visit the local sites, meet new people, or encounter a new culture.

It's still possible to break into the Merchant Marine with little training or experience, especially if you are willing to start at the very bottom as an ordinary seaman who normally works on deck or in the engineering department. Advancement to the next level – able seaman – requires passing an examination.

If you apply for an engineering or deck officer position, you must be licensed. You acquire this license by graduating from the U.S. Merchant Marine Academy, which is located in Kings Point, New York, or by completing a program offered by one of the six state merchant marine academies. Advancement to officer positions within the Merchant Marine requires a great deal of experience at sea as well as the ability to pass several examinations. An unlicensed seaman needs to be a U.S. citizen and receive a U.S. Public Health Service medical certificate.

Competition for jobs in the Merchant Marine will be keen in the decade ahead as the number of jobs continues to decline in response to a declining U.S. shipping industry. Unions are accepting fewer new members, and Merchant Marine academies are facing difficult times placing their graduates. The average annual salary for full-time merchant mariners is just under $40,000. Captains and harbor pilots average nearly $80,000 a year.

For information on merchant marine careers, training, and licensing requirements, contact the following organizations:

- **Maritime Administration**   www.marad.dot.gov
- **U.S. Coast Guard**   www.uscg.mil
- **U.S. Merchant Marine
  Academy**   www.usmma.edu

The Military

If you are looking for a job that involves travel and you don't mind a great deal of structure and regimentation in your life, the military may be the right place for you. Most Armed Services personnel routinely relocate to new bases every three to five years. Many assignments will place you abroad in either Europe or Asia. And many jobs within the military involve frequent travel between headquarters and bases as well as between bases and different training and meeting sites.

Given growing U.S. military involvement in conflicts around the world as well as heightened homeland security concerns, the U.S. Army and U.S. Marines have increased their recruitment efforts since 2002. The Armed Services continue to hire nearly 300,000 individuals each year. Indeed, as the nation's single largest employer, the Armed Forces employ nearly 1.5 million active duty personnel in just about every conceivable position. Nearly 500,000 are stationed outside the U.S.

Operating bases which, in effect, function as self-contained communities, the services hire doctors, dentists, medical support personnel, engineers, lawyers, paralegals, accountants, procurement officers, teachers, administrative support personnel, electronic equipment operators and repair personnel, food handlers, transportation and traffic managers, supply managers, corrections specialists, police, firefighters, and truck drivers in addition to infantry, demolition, weapons, aircraft, artillery, combat, and rocket specialists.

The general trend is to hire more highly educated and skilled individuals in the Armed Forces. Consequently, entrance requirements into all services are likely to become more restrictive and selective in the decade ahead. For more information on careers with the military, including the examination process, see *America's Top Military Careers* (JIST Publishing), *The Complete Idiot's Guide to Careers in the U.S. Military* (Alpha), *Guide to Joining the Military* (Arco), *How to*

Prepare for the ASVAB (Barron's Educational Series), and *ASVAB for Dummies* (John Wiley & Sons). For information on joining the military, contact your local recruitment office or visit these websites:

- U.S. Air Force Jobs   www.airforce.com
- U.S. Army Jobs   www.goarmy.com
- U.S. Coast Guard Jobs   www.gocoastguard.com
- U.S. Marine Jobs   www.marines.com
- U.S. Navy Jobs   www.navyjobs.com

Become an Independent Entrepreneur

The world is a big place with lots of exciting jobs for people who love to travel. The jobs we've outlined in this book should give you a sampling of what others who enjoy traveling do for a living, especially those who love working and living abroad. If you are entrepreneurial and really value your independence, you should consider working as a consultant or free-lancer. Better still, start a business that enables you to travel to places you love to visit. It could be a travel business, import/export business, consulting firm, or freelance travel writer or photographer. Most important of all, find something you really love to do and do it in exciting places.

If you are interested in starting your own business, we strongly recommend visiting various sections of the Small Business Administration's website, especially the useful section on determining whether or not you are best suited for the entrepreneurial life:

www.sba.gov/starting_business/startup/areyouready.html

You also should visit this section of their website, which includes a listing of several free online courses on starting a business:

www.sba.gov/training/courses.html

One of the most popular and useful such courses recommended by the Small Business Administration is entitled "Entrepreneurship: Starting and Managing Your Business" and presented by MyOwnBusiness.org:

www.myownbusiness.org/course_sba.html

Available in 13 sessions, it's offered as both a free or enhanced fee-based ($85.00) course. Whatever you do, make sure you take this course.

You also may want to consult Paul and Sarah Edwards's *Finding Your Perfect Work* (Putnam) and Doug Gray's *Have You Got What It Takes? The Entrepreneur's Complete Self-Assessment Guide* (Self-Counseling Press). These books provide useful exercises for assessing your suitability to becoming an entrepreneur. For a good overview of the many decisions you must make in establishing a small business, see Bernard Kamaroff's *Small-Time Operator* (Bell Springs Publishing). This book provides you with all the basic information you need for starting your own business, including ledger sheets for setting up your books. Several other books provide similar how-to advice for the neophyte entrepreneur:

- *The 2-Second Commute*
- *101 Small Business Ideas for Under $5,000*
- *199 Great Home Businesses You Can Start (and Succeed In) for Under $1,000*
- *The $100,000+ Entrepreneur*
- *Adams Streetwise™ Small Business Start-Up*
- *Business Plans Kit for Dummies (with CD-ROM)*
- *How to Buy, Sell, and Profit On eBay*
- *How to Start, Run, and Stay in Business*
- *Home-Based Business for Dummies*
- *Kick Start Your Dream Business*
- *McGraw-Hill Guide to Starting Your Own Business*
- *Six-Week Start-Up*
- *Small Business Kit for Dummies*
- *Small Business Marketing for Dummies*
- *The Small Business Start-Up Kit*
- *Start Your Own Business*
- *The Successful Business Plan*
- *What Business Should I Start?*
- *What No One Ever Tells You About Starting Your Own Business*

Several websites also can provide assistance in starting a business:

- **Small Business Administration**   www.sba.gov/starting_business
- **Startup Journal**   www.startupjournal.com

- BizMove.com   http://bizmove.com
- Business Know-How   http://businessknowhow.com
- AllBusiness   www.allbusiness.com

The federal government will help you with several publications available through the Small Business Administration (SBA). Check out the "Library" section of the SBA website, which includes over 200 free publications, including e-books, as well as numerous resource links related to starting a business:

www.sba.gov/lib/library.html

The Internal Revenue Service (www.irs.gov/businesses/small/article/0,,id=99336,00.html) offers a great deal of tax and accounting information to start-up businesses. The U.S. Chamber of Commerce (www.uschamber.com) as well as its local chapters offer useful information. Other good online resources to help you start a business include:

- American Express   http://home.americanexpress.com/home/open.shtml?referrer=ushome&section=globalnav
- Business Owner's Toolkit http://toolkit.cch.com
- CEO Business Express   www.ceoexpress.com/default.asp
- Entrepreneur.com   www.entrepreneur.com
- Kauffman eVenturing   www.eventuring.org
- eWeb   http://eweb.slu.edu
- Home Biz Tools   http://homebiztools.com
- Inc.com   www.inc.com/guides/start_biz
- Quicken Small Business   www.quicken.com/small_business
- SCORE   www.score.org
- State Resource Centers   www.itssimple.biz/resource_center
- Yahoo Small Business   http://smallbusiness.yahoo.com

More and more people are declaring independence from the conventional work world by starting their own businesses. The thrill of independence, coupled with a work/lifestyle that involves travel, may be your perfect job. Hire yourself to do what you really love to do. In so doing, you may turn your love of travel into an exciting business in which work and play become one and the same!

Index

The Authors

FOR MORE THAN TWO DECADES Ron and Caryl Krannich have pursued a passion – assisting hundreds of thousands of individuals, from students, the unemployed, and ex-offenders to military personnel, international job seekers, and CEOs, in making critical job and career transitions. Focusing on key job search skills, career changes, and employment fields, their impressive body of work has helped shape career thinking and behavior both in the United States and abroad. Their sound advice has changed numerous lives, including their own!

Ron and Caryl are two of America's leading career and travel writers who have authored more than 80 books. A former Peace Corps Volunteer and Fulbright Scholar, Ron received his Ph.D. in Political Science from Northern Illinois University. Caryl received her Ph.D. in Speech Communication from Penn State University. Together they operate Development Concepts Incorporated, a training, consulting, and publishing firm in Virginia. Caryl also is president and Ron is vice-president of a distance learning institution, USA-Global Institutes of Education.

The Krannichs are both former university professors, high school teachers, management trainers, and consultants. As trainers and consultants, they have completed numerous projects on management, career development, local government, population planning, and rural development in the United States and abroad. Their career books focus on key job search skills, military and civilian career transitions, government and international careers, travel jobs, and nonprofit organizations and include such classics as *High Impact Resumes and Letters*, *Interview for Success*, and *Change Your Job, Change Your Life*.

Their books represent one of today's most comprehensive collections of career writing. With over 3 million copies in print, their publications are widely available in bookstores, libraries, and career centers. No strangers to the world of Internet employment and travel, they have written *America's Top Internet Job Sites*, *Haldane's Best Employment Websites for Professionals*, *The Directory of Websites for International Jobs*, and *Travel Planning on the Internet* and published several Internet recruitment and job search books. Ron served as the first Work Abroad Advisor to Monster.com. Ron and Caryl also have developed several career-related websites: www.impactpublications.com, www.winningthejob.com, www.exoffenderreentry.com, and www.veterans world.com. Many of their career tips appear on such major websites as www.monster.com, www.careerbuilder.com, www.campuscareercenter. com, and www.employmentguide.com.

Ron and Caryl live a double life with travel being their best kept *"do what you love"* career secret. Authors of more than 20 travel-shopping guidebooks on various destinations around the world, they continue to pursue their international and travel interests through their innovative *Treasures and Pleasures of . . . Best of the Best* travel-shopping series and related websites: www.ishoparoundtheworld.com and www.travel-smarter.com. When not found at their home and business in Virginia, they are probably somewhere in Europe, Asia, Africa, the Middle East, the South Pacific, the Caribbean, or the Americas following their other passion – researching and writing about quality antiques, arts, crafts, jewelry, hotels, restaurants, and sightseeing as well as adhering to the career advice they give to others: *"Pursue a passion that enables you to do what you really love to do."* Their passion is best represented on www.ishoparound theworld.com.

As both career and travel experts, the Krannichs' work is frequently featured in major newspapers, magazines, and newsletters as well as on radio, television, and the Internet. Available for interviews, consultation, and presentations, they can be contacted as follows:

Ron and Caryl Krannich
krannich@impactpublications.com

Career and Travel Resources

THE FOLLOWING CAREER RESOURCES are available from Impact Publications. Books by the authors are highlighted in **bold**. Full descriptions of each title can be found on Impact Publication's website: www.impactpublications.com. Complete the following form or list the titles, include postage, enclose payment, and send your order to:

IMPACT PUBLICATIONS
9104 Manassas Drive, Suite N
Manassas Park, VA 20111-5211 USA
1-800-361-1055 (orders only)
Tel. 703-361-7300 or Fax 703-335-9486
E-mail address: query@impactpublications.com
Quick & easy online ordering: www.impactpublications.com

Orders from individuals must be prepaid by check, moneyorder, Visa, MasterCard, or American Express. We accept telephone and fax orders.

Qty.	TITLES	Price	TOTAL
Featured Title			
____	Jobs for Travel Lovers	$19.95	____
International and Travel Jobs			
____	American Foreign Service Officer Exam	19.95	____
____	Au Pair and Nanny's Guide	17.95	____
____	Back Door Guide to Short-Term Job Adventures	21.95	____
____	**Best Resumes & CVs for International Jobs**	24.95	____

____	The BIG Guide to Living and Working Overseas	49.95 ____
____	Careers in International Affairs	24.95 ____
____	Careers in International Business	14.95 ____
____	Careers in Travel, Tourism, and Hospitality	17.95 ____
____	Career Opportunities in Travel and Tourism	18.95 ____
____	**Complete Guide to International Jobs and Careers**	24.95 ____
____	Cool Careers for Girls in Travel and Hospitality	13.95 ____
____	Directory of Jobs and Careers Abroad	19.95 ____
____	**Directory of Websites for International Jobs**	19.95 ____
____	Flight Attendant Job Finder and Career Guide	16.95 ____
____	Global Citizen	16.95 ____
____	Global Resume and CV Guide	17.95 ____
____	Going Global Career Guide	195.00 ____
____	How to Get a Job in Europe	22.95 ____
____	How to Get a Job on a Cruise Line	16.95 ____
____	International Jobs	19.95 ____
____	International Job Finder	19.95 ____
____	Jobs in Russia and the Newly Independent States	15.95 ____
____	Kennedy's Directory of International Recruiters	149.95 ____
____	Living, Studying, and Working in France	17.00 ____
____	Living, Studying, and Working in Italy	17.00 ____
____	So, You Want to Join the Peace Corps	12.95 ____
____	Summer Jobs Abroad	17.95 ____
____	Teaching English Abroad	19.95 ____
____	Teaching English Overseas	19.95 ____
____	Vault Guide to International Careers	19.95 ____
____	Volunteer Vacations	19.95 ____
____	Work Abroad	15.95 ____
____	Work Worldwide	14.95 ____
____	Work Your Way Around the World	19.95 ____
____	Working Abroad	17.95 ____

Government and Nonprofit Jobs

____	Book of U.S. Government Jobs	21.95 ____
____	**Complete Guide to Public Employment**	19.95 ____
____	**Directory of Federal Jobs and Employers**	21.95 ____
____	Federal Applications That Get Results	23.95 ____
____	Federal Jobs in Law Enforcement	14.95 ____
____	FBI Careers	18.95 ____
____	Ten Steps to a Federal Job	39.95 ____

Study Abroad, Internships, Volunteering

____	Alternative Travel Directory	19.95 ____
____	Financial Aid for Research & Creative Activities Abroad	45.00 ____
____	Financial Aid for Study & Travel Abroad	39.50 ____
____	How to Live Your Dream of Volunteering Overseas	17.00 ____
____	International Directory of Volunteer Work	15.95 ____
____	Internships (annual)	26.95 ____
____	Study Abroad	29.95 ____
____	Summer Study Abroad	29.95 ____

___ Volunteer Vacations	17.95	___
___ Worldwide College Scholarship Directory	23.99	___
___ Worldwide Graduate Scholarship Directory	26.99	___

Customs, Culture, and Etiquette

___ Art of Coming Home	21.95	___
___ Art of Crossing Cultures	17.95	___
___ Breaking Through Culture Shock	18.95	___
___ Do's and Taboos Around the World	15.95	___
___ Do's and Taboos of Humor Around the World	15.95	___
___ Do's and Taboos of Using English Around the World	14.95	
___ Gestures: Do's and Taboos of Body Language Around the World	16.95	___
___ Global Etiquette Guide to Africa and the Middle East	17.95	___
___ Global Etiquette Guide to Asia	17.95	___
___ Global Etiquette Guide to Europe	17.95	___
___ Global Etiquette Guide to Mexico and Latin America	17.95	___
___ Global Smarts	27.95	___
___ Kiss, Bow, or Shake Hands	19.95	___
___ Mind Your Manners	24.95	___
___ Multicultural Manners	16.95	___
___ Survival Kit for Overseas Living	16.95	___
___ The Ugly American	13.95	___

Resumes, Letters, and Portfolios

___ 101 Best Cover Letters	11.95	___
___ 101 Best Resumes	10.95	___
___ 101 More Best Resumes	11.95	___
___ 101 Great Tips for a Dynamite Resume	13.95	___
___ 175 Best Cover Letters	14.95	___
___ **201 Dynamite Job Search Letters**	19.95	___
___ 201 Killer Cover Letters	16.95	___
___ Adams Resume Almanac, with Disk	19.95	___
___ Best Career Transition Resumes for $100,000+ Jobs	24.95	___
___ Best Cover Letters for $100,000+ Jobs	24.95	___
___ Best KeyWords for Resumes, Cover Letters, & Interviews	17.95	___
___ **Best Resumes and CVs for International Jobs**	24.95	___
___ Best Resumes for $75,000+ Executive Jobs	16.95	___
___ Best Resumes for $100,000+ Jobs	24.95	___
___ Best Resumes for People Without a Four-Year Degree	16.95	___
___ Cover Letters for Dummies	16.99	___
___ Cover Letters That Knock 'Em Dead	10.95	___
___ e-Resumes	16.95	___
___ Electronic Resumes and Online Networking	13.99	___
___ Everything Cover Letter Book	12.95	___
___ Everything Resume Book	12.95	___
___ Executive Job Search for $100,000 to $1 Million+ Jobs	24.95	___
___ Expert Resumes for Computer and Web Jobs	16.95	___
___ Federal Resume Guidebook	21.95	___
___ Gallery of Best Cover Letters	18.95	___

___	Gallery of Best Resumes	18.95	___
___	Gallery of Best Resumes for 2-Year Degree Graduates	18.95	___
___	Global Resume and CV Guide	17.95	___
___	**Haldane's Best Cover Letters for Professionals**	15.95	___
___	**Haldane's Best Resumes for Professionals**	15.95	___
___	**High Impact Resumes and Letters**	19.95	___
___	**Military Resumes and Cover Letters**	21.95	___
___	**Nail the Cover Letter!**	17.95	___
___	**Nail the Resume!**	17.95	___
___	Power Resumes	12.95	___
___	Proven Resumes	19.95	___
___	Resume Catalog	15.95	___
___	Resume Shortcuts	14.95	___
___	Resumes for Dummies	16.99	___
___	Resumes for the Health Care Professional	14.95	___
___	Resumes That Knock 'Em Dead	12.95	___
___	Sales and Marketing Resumes for $100,000 Careers	19.95	___
___	**The Savvy Resume Writer**	12.95	___

Testing and Assessment

___	Career Tests	12.95	___
___	Discover What You're Best At	14.00	___
___	Do What You Are	18.95	___
___	Finding Your Perfect Work	16.95	___
___	Gifts Differing	16.95	___
___	I Could Do Anything If Only I Knew What It Was	16.00	___
___	I Don't Know What I Want, But I Know It's Not This	14.00	___
___	**I Want to Do Something Else, But I'm Not Sure**		
	What It Is	15.95	___
___	I'm Not Crazy, I'm Just Not You	16.95	___
___	Making Vocational Choices	29.95	___
___	Now, Discover Your Strengths	30.00	___
___	Pathfinder	14.00	___
___	Please Understand Me II	15.95	___
___	What Should I Do With My Life?	14.95	___
___	What Type Am I?	14.95	___
___	What's Your Type of Career?	17.95	___
___	Who Moved My Cheese?	19.95	___

Attitude and Motivation

___	100 Ways to Motivate Yourself	18.99	___
___	Attitude Is Everything	14.95	___
___	Change Your Attitude	15.99	___
___	Reinventing Yourself	18.99	___

Inspiration and Empowerment

___	Create Your Own Future	16.95	___
___	Do What You Love, the Money Will Follow	13.95	___
___	Dream It, Do It	16.95	___

____ Goals!	14.95	____
____ Luck Is No Accident	15.95	____
____ Seven Habits of Highly Effective People	15.00	____

Career Exploration and Job Strategies

____ 25 Jobs That Have It All	12.95	____
____ 50 Cutting Edge Jobs	15.95	____
____ 95 Mistakes Job Seekers Make and How to Avoid Them	13.95	____
____ 100 Great Jobs and How to Get Them	17.95	____
____ 101 Ways to Recession-Proof Your Career	14.95	____
____ Alternative Careers in Secret Operations	19.95	____
____ America's Top 100 Jobs for People Without a Four-Year Degree	19.95	____
____ America's Top Jobs for People Re-Entering the Workforce	19.95	____
____ Best Jobs for the 21st Century	19.95	____
____ Career Change	14.95	____
____ Change Your Job, Change Your Life	21.95	____
____ Cool Careers for Dummies	19.95	____
____ High-Tech Careers for Low-Tech People	14.95	____
____ Job Hunting Guide: Transitioning From College to Career	14.95	____
____ Job Hunting Tips for People With Hot and Not-So-Hot Backgrounds	19.95	____
____ Knock 'Em Dead	12.95	____
____ Me, Myself, and I	17.95	____
____ No One Will Hire Me!	13.95	____
____ Quit Your Job and Grow Some Hair	14.95	____
____ Rites of Passage at $100,000 to $1 Million+	29.95	____
____ What Color Is Your Parachute?	17.95	____

Directories

____ American Salaries and Wages Survey	230.00	____
____ Directory of Executive Recruiters	49.95	____
____ Encyclopedia of Associations	680.00	____
____ Enhanced Occupational Outlook Handbook	39.95	____
____ Headquarters USA	212.00	____
____ Job Hunter's Sourcebook	160.00	____
____ Moving and Relocation Directory	235.00	____
____ Occupational Outlook Handbook	17.95	____
____ O*NET Directory of Occupational Titles	39.95	____
____ Professional Careers Sourcebook	150.00	____
____ Scholarships, Fellowships, and Loans	240.00	____

Internet Job Search

____ 100 Top Internet Job Sites	12.95	____
____ America's Top Internet Job Sites	19.95	____
____ Career Exploration On the Internet	24.95	____
____ Directory of Websites for International Jobs	19.95	____

____ e-Resumes 11.95 ____
____ Electronic Resumes and Online Networking 13.99 ____
____ Everything Online Job Search Book 12.95 ____
____ Guide to Internet Job Searching 14.95 ____
____ Haldane's Best Employment Websites for Professionals 15.95 ____
____ Job-Hunting On the Internet 11.95 ____

Dress, Image, and Etiquette

____ Dressing Smart for Men 16.95 ____
____ Dressing Smart for Women 16.95 ____
____ Dressing Smart in the New Millennium 15.95 ____
____ New Professional Image 14.95 ____
____ Power Etiquette 14.95 ____

Networking

____ A Foot in the Door 14.95 ____
____ How to Work a Room 14.00 ____
____ Masters of Networking 16.95 ____
____ The Savvy Networker 13.95 ____

Interviews

____ 101 Dynamite Questions to Ask At Your Job Interview 13.95 ____
____ Haldane's Best Answers to Tough
Interview Questions 15.95 ____
____ Interview for Success 15.95 ____
____ Job Interview Tips for People With Not-So-Hot
Backgrounds 14.95 ____
____ Job Interviews for Dummies 16.99 ____
____ Nail the Job Interview! 13.95 ____
____ The Savvy Interviewer 10.95 ____
____ Sweaty Palms 13.95 ____

Salary Negotiations

____ Dynamite Salary Negotiations 15.95 ____
____ Get a Raise in 7 Days 14.95 ____
____ Haldane's Best Salary Tips for Professionals 15.95 ____
____ Salary Negotiation Tips for Professionals 16.95 ____

Unique Travel Guides and Companions

____ 100 Things to Do Before You Die 15.95 ____
____ 1,000 Places to See Before You Die 18.95 ____
____ Air Travel Tales From the Flight Crew 14.95 ____
____ Come Back Alive 14.95 ____
____ Fly Cheap! 14.95 ____
____ Plane Insanity 13.95 ____
____ The Plane Truth 14.95 ____
____ Travel Planning on the Internet 19.95 ____

___	Traveling Woman: Great Tips for Safe & Healthy Trips	14.95	___
___	Treasures and Pleasures of Bermuda	16.95	___
___	Treasures and Pleasures of Mexico	19.95	___
___	Treasures and Pleasures of Paris	18.95	___
___	Treasures and Pleasures of Singapore	18.95	___
___	Treasures and Pleasures of South America	23.95	___
___	Treasures and Pleasures of Southern Africa	19.95	___
___	Treasures and Pleasures of Thailand and Myanmar	21.95	___
___	World's Most Dangerous Places	22.95	___
___	You Can Travel Free	15.95	___

SUBTOTAL   ___

Virginia residents add 5% sales tax   ___

POSTAGE/HANDLING ($5 for first
product and 8% of SUBTOTAL) $5.00

8% of SUBTOTAL -------------------------------------- ___

TOTAL ENCLOSED ----------------------- ___

SHIP TO:

NAME _____

ADDRESS _____

_____

_____

PAYMENT METHOD:

❑ I enclose check/moneyorder for $ _____ made payable to
IMPACT PUBLICATIONS.

❑ Please charge $ _____ to my credit card:
  ❑ Visa   ❑ MasterCard   ❑ American Express   ❑ Discover

  Card # _____ Expiration date: ____/____

  Signature _____

Keep in Touch . . .
On the Web!